American
Portrait
Prints

Proceedings of a Conference held at the National Portrait Gallery in May 1979

THE AUTHORS ELLEN MILES
Associate Curator, National Portrait Gallery

GORDON M. MARSHALL
Assistant Librarian, Library Company of Philadelphia

WENDY WICK REAVES
Curator of Prints, National Portrait Gallery

KATHARINE MARTINEZ
Chief Librarian, Cooper-Hewitt Museum Library, Smithsonian Institution

DAVID TATHAM
Professor of Art History, Syracuse University

WILLIAM F. STAPP
Curator of Photographs, National Portrait Gallery

DARYL R. RUBENSTEIN
Author and Lecturer

ALAN FERN
Director, National Portrait Gallery

American Portrait Prints

Proceedings of

the Tenth Annual

American Print Conference

Edited by
Wendy Wick Reaves

Published for the
National Portrait Gallery
Smithsonian Institution

University Press of Virginia
Charlottesville

This publication is made possible in part by a
generous grant from the Barra Foundation, Inc.

THE UNIVERSITY PRESS OF VIRGINIA
Copyright © 1984 by the Smithsonian Institution

First published 1984

Library of Congress Cataloging in Publication Data

American Print Conference (10th : 1979 : National Portrait
  Gallery)
  American portrait prints

  Includes index.
  1. Portrait prints—United States—Congresses.
I. Reaves, Wendy Wick, 1950-   . II. National Portrait
Gallery (United States) III. Title.
NE260.A43 1979 769'.42'0973   83-3534
ISBN 0-8139-0981-3

Printed in the United States of America

Contents

Foreword

When the National Portrait Gallery first began to collect American portrait prints in earnest about a decade ago, our principal objective was to add the likenesses of significant individuals not otherwise represented in the permanent collection of the Gallery. It soon became clear, however, that this area of our holdings would be more meaningful if we were to acquire as many different prints as possible of all important persons. We now regularly devote an area of the Gallery to the display of American portrait prints from the eighteenth century to the present, and certain examples provide the likenesses of their subjects throughout the permanent installation of selections from our collections in other media. Portrait prints also figure significantly in our temporary exhibitions.

In the process of building our holdings of American portrait prints, our enthusiasm has been quickened by the unexpected artistic merit of a number of practitioners in the field, especially that of several nineteenth-century lithographers such as Charles Fenderich, Francis D'Avignon, Albert Newsam, Charles Crehen, and Leopold Grozelier. At the same time, we sense a growing interest on the part of our public in the portrait prints of this and other periods exhibited in our galleries.

We were, therefore, particularly pleased to be able to host the Tenth American Print Conference devoted to the subject of American portrait prints. We are grateful to the participants in that Conference and are privileged to offer this publication of their papers to a wider audience, which we trust will share both our appreciation of their efforts and our anticipation of the treasures that are yet to be unearthed in the field of American portrait prints.

Marvin Sadik, *Former Director*
National Portrait Gallery
Smithsonian Institution

Preface

H istorical prints," a misleading but commonly used term for eighteenth- and nineteenth-century graphic Americana, includes a wide variety of material ranging from separately published engravings or lithographs to book and magazine illustrations, almanac covers, sheet-music titles, broadsides, advertisements, and posters. These images from the past have only recently attracted scholarly attention as important documents of American culture. The neglect is understandable, for pictorial material of this type is generally a commercial art, a popular art, and frequently a derivative art—precisely the elements that most curators of fine prints would be likely to spurn. Although the originality, refinement, and rarity we expect from a work of art is sometimes missing, these images are important illustrations of American life.

Through the publications of the annual American Print Conference, the neglect is beginning to be redressed. The Conference held at the National Portrait Gallery in May 1979 was the tenth meeting of the group, so this volume joins a growing body of literature. Pictorial Americana, falling as it does between academic fields, is being studied in these reports by authors with different points of view. Academic historians of American civilization, history, or art, curators of museums or historical societies, librarians, specialized collectors—all discuss the material with a variety of perspectives and scholarly techniques. The mixture introduces a rich cross-fertilization of ideas and approaches.

This volume addresses the subject of portrait prints produced in America from the late eighteenth to the late nineteenth century, with a glimpse into the twentieth. In one sense it is a narrow concentration and excludes a great variety of images, sometimes more colorful (even when printed in black and white) and engaging than portraiture. But it allows us to focus on the changes that appeared in printmaking techniques, aesthetics, and marketing as each new generation approached the same subject. The general attitude toward portraiture on the part of both the artist and the buying public changed dramatically. For example, the innovations of the physiognotrace, the daguerreotype, and the photograph had a major effect on the portrait artists Saint-Mémin, Newsam, and D'Avignon. And the early-nineteenth-century public's desire for an accurate likeness evolved into an interest in more interpretive portraiture during the etching revival, where character was probed and artistic effect explored. The essays in this work relate the histories of individual artists or publishing ventures; taken together, they reflect these major changes in portraiture and suggest more subtle ones. It is largely because portrait prints were commercial, popular in the sense of being widely distributed, and often derivative that they are such valuable documents.

The commercial spirit that motivated nineteenth-century printmaking is one underlying theme of this book. Competition was fierce in the picture industry. Ingenuity, adaptability, and promotion counted as much as artistic talent. In their struggles to outdo each other, artists undertook ambitious projects to publish portraits in series or in multivolume books, and many of them failed. The ones who succeeded resorted to quicker and cheaper printmaking techniques, mass marketing, or extravagant promotional claims. Saint-Mémin's laborious engraving process gave way to Johnston's stipple technique, which in turn was eclipsed by the faster and easier method of lithography used by Johnston, Newsam, and D'Avignon. When Sartain revived the mezzotint process, he used steel plates rather than the softer copper and was able to mass-produce illustrations by the thousands. Delaplaine's first step in publishing his multivolume illustrated biographies was to issue elaborate proposals to lure subscribers. The commercial impulse that motivated these artists and entrepreneurs speaks eloquently about the era in which each one lived and worked.

The result was the creation of a popular art. As the century progressed, portraits were published not just for a local community but for shipment throughout the country. Privately commissioned portrait prints gave way to the well-marketed images of famous personalities published in editions of a hundred thousand. Biographers and art historians must calculate the influence that such a large circulation implies. The nineteenth-century campaign manager must have been elated as lithographs of his candidate, no matter how crudely drawn, were published in town after town. Recently one of the many chromolithographs of George Washington after Gilbert Stuart's famous painting turned up in an old miner's cabin out in Idaho, one more indication that this image of our nation's first President was known to almost all Americans.

These portraits were generally reproductions of paintings or photographs, and because of their derivative nature they document a vast quantity of lost original portraits and buried facts about the artists. A painter's or photographer's reputation could be made or broken by the ability of the printmaker, and nineteenth-century artists were extremely conscious of this fact. The concern that a print do justice to the original portrait appears throughout the essays. "Engraving is not a copy," John Neagle wrote, "but a translation from color to black and white, and in order to make it successful, the engraver should enter into the spirit and feeling of the painter." Henry Inman moved to Philadelphia partially because he liked the way the "young prodigy" Albert Newsam copied his paintings as lithographs.

While gaining validity as historic documents, these pictures must not be overlooked as legitimate works of art. Considered as such in their own time, they were bought by serious collectors in addition to the average souvenir hunter. As unknown prints and printmakers are brought to light, we begin to realize that the graphic arts cannot be separated from the fine arts in our history, as they frequently have been. Many of our most famous nineteenth-century artists had their earliest training or periodic employment in printmaking. In recognizing the achievement and studying the works of a great painter, we should not forget his illustrations for a giftbook annual, his lithographic music sheet, his drawing for *Harper's Weekly*. And those printmakers who remained in the graphic arts should not be neglected as artists. Who can deny that D'Avignon was one of our brilliant nineteenth-century draftsmen? Although he used daguerreotypes as the source for his portraits, he translated them with exquisite sensitivity into a new medium. Who can forget, once introduced to them, Johnston's lively little portraits of actors and actresses, drawn from life, in character, as they expounded and cavorted on stage? Or the sumptuous textures of Sartain's mezzotints, adding their own romantic flourish to the Sully or Neagle portraits they interpret? There is a valid artistic heritage beneath that commercial spirit—and skill, originality, and imagination. It is hoped that this volume will introduce some new names and some new faces that will delight us and inform us about our forgotten past.

A conference report is really two different projects—the conference and the report. The Tenth American Print Conference never would have taken place without the initial inspiration of Sinclair Hitchings of the Boston Public Library or the complete support and continual guidance of our former Director, Marvin Sadik. A great many people on the staff of the National Portrait Gallery helped to plan the details of the Conference. I hope that they already know how appreciative I am for their contribution of time, effort, and ideas. Special thanks go to the real organizer of the event, my assistant Maureen O'Brien Herbert, who was cheerfully efficient, responsible, and tireless throughout.

The greatest credit for the Report goes, of course, to the authors themselves, who worked very hard in researching and presenting their lectures and went to great effort to revise the papers for publication. Beyond the scholarly contribution of each individual—which speaks for itself—I am especially grateful for every author's patience, cooperation, and extra work during the editing process. My only deeply felt regret is that one of them, Daryl Rubenstein, never saw the final product.

Also critical for the production of the book were the extensive efforts of Frances Wein, Publications Officer at the National Portrait Gallery; Barbara Bither, Curatorial Assistant; and, especially, Ann Shumard and Eloise Harvey, who took a remarkably good-natured and conscientious approach to an enormous typing job.

Finally, it was through the generosity of the Barra Foundation that the good ideas and hard work of all these people have found a permanent form in *American Portrait Prints*.

Wendy Wick Reaves
Curator of Prints
National Portrait Gallery

American
Portrait
Prints

Saint-Mémin, Valdenuit, Lemet

Federal Profiles

ELLEN MILES

The profile portrait drawings and engravings made by Charles Balthazar Julien Févret de Saint-Mémin while he was in the United States between 1793 and 1814 are well known. When one of the largest collections of his engravings (fig. 1), once owned by the artist himself, was given to the National Portrait Gallery in 1974 by Mr. and Mrs. Paul Mellon, extensive research was begun on the artist, the style of his portraiture, and the identity of his subjects.[1]

1 The Saint-Mémin engravings given to the National Portrait Gallery form one of the two largest collections of the artist's work. The second is at the Corcoran Gallery of Art. These and several smaller collections were compiled from duplicates kept by the artist and taken to Dijon, France, when he returned there in 1814. The engravings now at the National Portrait Gallery were acquired shortly after the artist's death in 1852 by Elias Dexter, the New York publisher, who used them to compile his large volume, *The St.-Mémin Collection of Portraits: Consisting of Seven Hundred and Sixty Medallion Portraits, Principally of Distinguished Americans* ... (New York, 1862). Purchased from Dexter's estate by Edward G. Kennedy of New York in 1897, they were then sold to Hampton L. Carson, who exhibited them at the Grolier Club in 1899. At the Carson sale in 1904, the collection went to Philadelphia publisher William Campbell. A subsequent owner, before its purchase in 1954 by Paul Mellon, was William Pearson Jenks of Philadelphia.

In the National Portrait Gallery's collection, each portrait has been trimmed to the edge of the circle and then glued, with other engravings, to one of sixteen folio sheets. Most engravings were then identified and dated. This was done before they were published by Dexter in 1862. The writing is not the artist's.

1

Sheet 9 (detail), Saint-Mémin Collection. (*National Portrait Gallery, Smithsonian Institution*)

Research on the Saint-Mémin collection led to a decision to write a complete catalogue of the artist's work in the United States, since the 761 engravings at the National Portrait Gallery represented about 85 percent of this material. The cataloguing process is almost finished. In addition to providing identifications and dates for the portraits themselves, this catalogue, when published, will permit Saint-Mémin's American work to be viewed chronologically for the first time. Second, the catalogue will make it possible to relate his work to that of his contemporaries. While the picture of Saint-Mémin which emerges is not radically different from the one we already had—that of a diligent and capable, but not unusually creative portrait draftsman—it is possible to see how his chance arrival in the United States and his need to follow an income-producing profession have left us a visual "Who's Who" of several major East Coast cities in the period between 1796 and 1810.

The scope of this essay is more limited. Its focus is on the physiognotrace method of portraiture, a description of its use in France, and its impact in the United States. The discussion is based on Saint-Mémin's career and the tangential work of two other émigré artists, Thomas Bluget de Valdenuit and Louis Lemet. It is now possible to place Saint-Mémin's portraiture within this broader context and thus to better evaluate and define his style.

Saint-Mémin's career as a portrait artist was a matter of chance. He was born in Dijon, France, in 1770, a member of the Burgundian nobility.[2] He was sent to Paris in 1784, where he was enrolled in the French military academy (l'Ecole Militaire). On graduating, he joined the Gardes-Françaises, the household guard of Louis XVI. When this guard was disbanded at the beginning of the French Revolution in 1789, he returned to Dijon, where he may have studied at the drawing academy founded by François Devosge, a well-known neoclassical French painter. According to early biographers, he also showed interest in various mechanical inventions and in mathematics.

The following summer, 1790, Saint-Mémin left France for Switzerland. He was soon joined by his parents and sisters, since by this time the new republican government of France had abolished the nobility and confiscated its estates. In March 1793, after serving briefly with the army of Louis Joseph de Bourbon, Prince of Condé, Saint-Mémin journeyed with his father and Pierre Mourgeon, their valet, across the Atlantic to claim the sugarcane estates in Santo Domingo that belonged to his mother, the daughter of the solicitor general of the council of Port-au-Prince. During the European leg of the journey, Saint-Mémin and his father visited universities, libraries, and public and private art collections. Arriving first in Canada, Saint-Mémin made two watercolor drawings of

2 The major sources of Saint-Mémin's biography are Philippe Guignard, *Notice Historique sur la Vie et les Travaux de M. Févret de Saint-Mémin* (Dijon, 1853); published in English as the preface of Dexter, *The St.-Mémin Collection of Portraits;* Fillmore Norfleet, *Saint-Mémin in Virginia* (Richmond, 1942); Musée de Dijon, Palais des Etats de Bourgogne, *Charles-Balthazar-Julien Févret de Saint-Mémin,* introduction by Pierre Quarré (Dijon, 1965); and Madeleine Herard, "Contribution à l'Etude de l'Emigration de Charles-Balthazar-Julien Févret de Saint-Mémin aux Etats-Unis de 1793 à 1814," *Mémoires de l'Académie des Sciences, Arts, et Belles-Lettres de Dijon* 117 (1963–65):129–76.

the port of Halifax (now at the Public Archives of Canada, Ottawa) and two portraits of Indian children, now unlocated but noted by his father in a journal kept on the voyage.[3] The men then traveled to New York, arriving in October 1793.

There they stayed. Continuing to Santo Domingo was impossible because of the rebellion there of the French slaves who had worked the sugarcane plantations, and it was not until 1802 that Saint-Mémin's father was able to go to Cap Français. Finding themselves both stateless and estateless, the men settled in New York. Saint-Mémin, needing a means of employment, turned to drawing and engraving. By 1794 they had allied themselves with the powerful Livingston family, and John Livingston introduced Saint-Mémin to books in the public library that explained the techniques of engraving. From Livingston's house, near the East River, Saint-Mémin made his first American drawing, *View of the City and Harbour of New York, Taken from Mount Pitt, the Seat of John R. Livingston, Esqre.*[4] Between 1794 and 1796 he seems to have found little employment as an engraver. He did engrave, in 1795, a *Plan of Tivoli Laid Out into Town Lots,* depicting the new Hudson River town developed by another French émigré, Peter de la Bigarre, on land acquired from the Livingston family. The following year, his *Plan of the Siege of Savannah* was published in the *Monthly Military Repository;* and he also made etchings of two views of New York, one after his drawing from Mount Pitt and another entitled *View of the City of New York Taken from Long Island.* His name first appeared in a New York City directory in 1796, at 11 Fair Street, but no occupation is given.[5]

---

3   Pierre Quarré, "Le Voyage de Bénigne-Charles Févret de Saint-Mémin et de Son Fils de Fribourg à New York en 1793," *Mémoires de l'Académie des Sciences, Arts, et Belles-Lettres de Dijon* 121 (1970–72):159–81. The journal is at the Newberry Library, Chicago.

4   Saint-Mémin's nonportrait engravings are catalogued in David McNeely Stauffer, *American Engravers upon Copper and Steel* (New York, 1907), 1:231–32, 2:453; I. N. Phelps Stokes, *The Iconography of Manhattan Island, 1498–1909* (New York, 1915–28), 1:437–41; and I. N. Phelps Stokes and Daniel C. Haskell, *American Historical Prints . . .* (New York, 1932), pp. 67, 72. See also Helen Wilkinson Reynolds, "Peter de Labigarre and the Founding of Tivoli," *Dutchess County Historical Society Yearbook* 14 (1929):45–60; and Norfleet, pp. 12–13.

5   John Low, *The New-York Directory and Register for 1796* (New York, 1796).

At about this time, Saint-Mémin began his partnership with Thomas Bluget de Valdenuit, another former French military officer. Born in Les Riceys (Aube) in 1763, Valdenuit first met Saint-Mémin in New York thirty years later, having arrived there from Guadeloupe.[6] The two are said to have visited Niagara Falls, where they each made a drawing, both now unlocated. By 1795 Valdenuit was in Baltimore, in touch with a French artist known only by his last name, Bouché. The two men advertised plans to open a drawing school.[7] Bouché, who had lived in Maryland for several years, continued to operate the school; but Valdenuit returned to New York by 1796, the date of his first portraits made in partnership with Saint-Mémin.

It appears, from the drawings themselves as well as from biographical evidence, that Valdenuit directly influenced Saint-Mémin's future portrait career by introducing him to the method of making likenesses by physiognotrace. Philip Guignard, Saint-Mémin's earliest biographer and his old friend, wrote in 1853 that "a witness of his first success, one of his compatriots of the old garde-du-corps, suggested to him the idea of drawing portraits in profile, and of engraving them. This style, invented by Chrétien in 1786, had been very popular in Paris, but was almost unknown in America."[8] Although the wording of Guignard's subsequent statements implies that this "witness" was not Valdenuit, later writers on physiognotrace portraiture, particularly René Hennequin, believed that it was in fact Valdenuit who suggested making the profile portraits.[9]

There is good evidence that the later writers were right. In the first

6 The most complete biography of Valdenuit (1763–1846) is in René Hennequin, "Le Physionotrace aux Etats-Unis (1793–1814): Mm. de Saint-Mémin et de Valdenuit, Compatriotes de Quenedey," *Un "Photographe" de l'Epoque de la Revolution et l'Empire: Edme Quenedey des Riceys (Aube), Portraitiste au Physionotrace* (Troyes, France, 1926–27), 2:78–85.

7 George C. Groce and David H. Wallace, *The New-York Historical Society's Dictionary of Artists in America, 1564–1860* (New Haven, 1957), p. 643, entry for "Valdenuit."

8 Guignard, p. 9.

9 Hennequin, *Un "Photographe" de l'Epoque*, 2:78–79. See also Howard C. Rice, Jr., "An Album of Saint-Mémin Portraits," *Princeton University Library Chronicle* 13, no. 1, (Autumn 1951): 24–25.

place, Valdenuit worked with Bouché in Baltimore at a time when Bouché was making small profile portrait drawings set in circles.[10] Rembrandt Peale, also in Baltimore at the time, imitated this style in some of his early efforts at portrait drawing in 1799 and 1800.[11] Second, and more important, Valdenuit had firsthand knowledge of the work of the two artists in Paris, Gilles-Louis Chrétien and Edme Quenedey, who had started the craze for physiognotrace portraits in the 1780s. For their own records, Chrétien and Quenedey kept a notebook of sitters, marking each portrait engraving with an identifying cipher and recording in the notebook opposite the cipher the sitter's name, payments, and other information.[12] From this source we know that Valdenuit, who became Saint-Mémin's partner in New York in 1796, had been drawn by the physiognotrace method himself in Paris in 1788.[13]

The physiognotrace had been invented by Gilles-Louis Chrétien in 1786, when he was court musician at Versailles.[14] After working with it for two years, he brought the device to Paris in 1788, where he became partners with Edme Quenedey, whose drawing of the physiognotrace they used (fig. 2) documents its dimensions and working method. The machine was the size of an easel, about five feet high.[15] It stood on three legs, and in the center, on a flat vertical surface, it held a large piece of paper, about

10 Examples of Bouché portraits include *Unidentified Man (?George Mason IV),* Gunston Hall, signed and dated 1794; *Unidentified Man,* Maryland Historical Society, signed and dated 1794; and *Robert Gilmor II,* inscribed 1798, recorded in the J. Hall Pleasants files, Maryland Historical Society.

11 *Four Generations of Commissions: The Peale Collection of the Maryland Historical Society* (Baltimore, 1975), pp. 71–73.

12 René Hennequin, *Avant les Photographies: Les Portraits au Physionotrace* (Troyes, 1932), pp. 1–3, 283–300. The original notebook is now in the Institut d'Histoire et de Géographie de la Ville de Paris.

13 Ibid., p. 112, no. 569, illustrated.

14 Hennequin, *Un "Photographe" de l'Epoque,* 1:14.

15 Mary Martin, "The Physionotrace in France and America," *Connoisseur* 74 (1926): 144–48, 151–52, illustrated p. 145; Hennequin, *Avant les Photographies,* p. 3, illustrated; Howard C. Rice, Jr., "Saint-Mémin's Portrait of Jefferson," *Princeton University Library Chronicle* 20 (1959):182–92, illustrated.

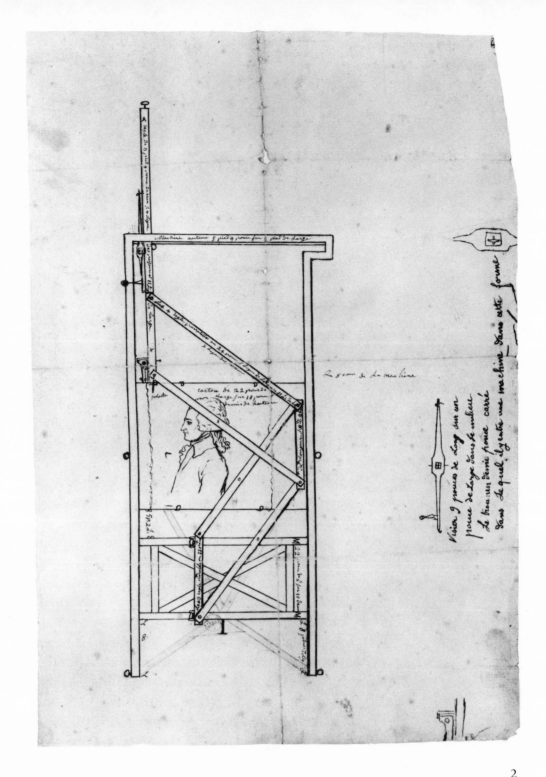

Physiognotrace invented by Gilles-Louis Chrétien. Ink drawing, circa 1788,
by Edme Queneday. (*Department of Prints, Bibliothèque Nationale, Paris*)

twenty inches high. Attached to the crossbars at the bottom of the stand
was one end of a movable device called a pantograph, whose rodlike
sections extended upward across the sheet of paper. Attached to the top of
the pantograph was a rod with a small eyepiece in the center (top left

8

3

Joel Barlow, 1754-1812. Engraving, circa 1793, by Gilles-Louis Crétien after Jean-Simon Fournier, 5.9 cm. (diameter). (*National Portrait Gallery, Smithsonian Institution*)

5

Caleb Swan, d. 1809. Engraving, 1799, by Saint-Mémin, 5.6 cm. (diameter). (*Corcoran Gallery of Art*)

corner of fig. 2). As the operator stood and looked through the eyepiece at the sitter, he moved the vertical rod to follow the sitter's profile, and a pencil at the lower end of the rod traced the profile on the paper.

Quenedey described the physiognotrace process in two letters in the *Journal de Paris* in 1788, noting that in a six-minute sitting a life-size portrait was drawn.[16] Then, if the sitter wished, a reduced image would be made and engraved, and four days after the sitting, twelve engravings of the portrait would be ready. Examples of the physiognotrace portrait engravings made in Paris include that of the American poet Joel Barlow (fig. 3) made in about 1793 by Chrétien and Fournier. The National Portrait Gallery's drawing of Caleb Swan (fig. 4) is an example of Saint-Mémin's results with the physiognotrace. Here, it is possible to see the pencil outline made by the machine on the paper. After the general areas of the portrait were blocked out, the artist would complete the drawing in chalk. The next stage of the process, if the sitter so desired, was to reduce the portrait in order to make an engraving. A small drawing on translucent paper which appears to be part of the reduction process is owned by the Chicago Art Institute (although it may instead be a tracing of the engraving).[17] The portrait engraving of Caleb Swan (fig. 5) when printed was in

16 Hennequin, *Un "Photographe" de l'Epoque,* 1:16–18.

17 The drawing is illustrated in André Chamson, "Physionotrace Profiles," *Antiques* 9 (1926): 147, when it was in the collection of Elinor Merrell. It can be identified with Quenedey and Chrétien's engraved portrait of Jacques Guillaume LeGrand, made in Paris in 1788–89, and marked with the cipher E9. See Hennequin, *Avant les Photographies*, p. 73, no. 341.

Caleb Swan, d. 1809. Chalk drawing, 1799, by Saint-Mémin, 54.6 × 38.4
cm. (paper). (*National Portrait Gallery, Smithsonian Institution*)

reverse of the original drawing. This engraving, from the Corcoran Gallery, has not been trimmed to the edge of the image and therefore retains the plate inscription that Saint-Mémin put on many of his engravings giving his name and the city where the portrait was made.[18]

Further evidence that the physiognotrace was introduced by Valdenuit to Saint-Mémin comes from the portraits that he and Saint-Mémin made in New York during their partnership, which lasted less than a year. Their advertisement in the *New York Daily Advertiser* of February 3, 1797, shows that they were doing the same type of portraiture as that described by Quenedey in Paris nearly ten years earlier. It read:

> *Physiognotrace. Likenesses Engraved. The subscribers beg leave to inform their Friends and the Public in general, that they take and engrave Portraits on an improved plan of the celebrated Physiognotrace of Paris, and in a style never introduced before in this country. From the expedition with which the work is done, and the moderation of the terms, they presume to hope that they will give satisfaction to those, who, protectors of the Arts, will please to encourage them with their commands. An exhibition of their performance may be seen at Messrs. Jno. J. Stapples and Sons, No. 169 Pearl Street, or by applying at their lodgings, No. 11 Fair Street. St. Memin & Valdenuit.[19]*

The earliest prints of the partnership, five in all, bore the inscription: "Drawn by Valdenuit & Engraved by St. Memin No. 11 Fair St. N. York."[20] Two drawings survive from this group, one of which is signed by Valdenuit. It is dated "1796," the earliest date to appear on any of these drawings. The second form of inscription, found on sixteen prints, reads: "St. Memin & Valdenuit, No. 11 Fair Street, N. York."[21] Of these, five original drawings still exist, and three of them have Valdenuit's signature.

18 The collection of 833 Saint-Mémin engravings at the Corcoran Gallery of Art was purchased by William Wilson Corcoran from the London dealer Henry Stevens in 1874 or 1875. Stevens had acquired the collection from Saint-Mémin's heirs in France after the artist's death in 1852.

19 Rita S. Gottesman, *The Arts and Crafts in New York, 1777–1799* . . . (New York, 1954), pp. 43–44, no. 104.

20 Corcoran Gallery of Art, Saint-Mémin collection, fol. 1.

21 Ibid., fols. 1–2.

The rest of the prints from the partnership were inscribed both with names and "No. 27 Pine St. N. York" as an address.[22] The fact that Saint-Mémin and Valdenuit engraved only twenty-one portraits at Fair Street indicates that their partnership was still young when they moved. During the remaining months of their joint venture, the artists were listed in Longworth's *American Almanack* for 1797 as "Valdenuit & St. Memin, physiognotracists, 27 Pine Street." Twenty engravings were made during this period. Of the six surviving chalk drawings from this group, four are signed by Valdenuit.

In September 1797 Valdenuit returned to France, after the death of his uncle. Of his drawings, about twenty signed examples survive. In addition to the prints made with Saint-Mémin, he had also engraved two portraits after paintings by Grimaldi—probably William de Grimaldi, an English miniaturist.[23] Saint-Mémin continued on his own in New York, offering profile drawings and prints. Approximately seventy-eight engravings bear his name alone in the inscription with the same "No. 27 Pine St." address.[24]

The inscriptions on the engravings indicate a close working relationship between Valdenuit and Saint-Mémin in 1796 and 1797. Comparison of their portrait drawings supports this interreliance and suggests that Saint-Mémin's earliest drawing style imitated Valdenuit's. Only after his partner left did Saint-Mémin gradually achieve the greater tonal range and related de-emphasis of line that is characteristic of his work. To see Saint-Mémin's early imitation of Valdenuit and the gradual evolution of his own personal style, it is best to begin with a comparison between two firmly documented drawings, Saint-Mémin's *Caleb Swan,* made in Philadelphia in 1799 (see fig. 4) and Valdenuit's *George Clinton,* signed and dated "Valdenuit 1797" (fig. 6). Their similarities include size and technique. Both drawings measure about twenty by fifteen inches, and both were made with black chalk, using white chalk highlights. Both drawings

22   Ibid., fols. 2–3, 52–53.

23   One engraving (a modern restrike) is owned by the Metropolitan Museum of Art, New York, erroneously identified as of Elizabeth dePeyster Peale; the second is listed in Mantle Fielding, *American Engravers upon Copper and Steel* 3 (New York, 1917):290, no. 1727.

24   Corcoran collection, fols. 3–8, 50–51, 55.

6

George Clinton, 1739-1812. Chalk drawing, 1797, by Thomas Bluget de Valdenuit, 49.8 × 35.5 cm. (paper). (*Oneida Historical Society, Utica, N.Y.*)

Daniel Kemper, 1749-1847. Chalk drawing, 1798, by Saint-Mémin, 54.6 × 41.9 cm. (paper). (*United States Army War College, Carlisle, Pa.*)

are also composed primarily of lines, to which shading has been added. However, while Saint-Mémin's *Caleb Swan* shows strong contrasts of light and dark and a firmly drawn, bold line, Valdenuit's *George Clinton* shows a more delicate line, lightly handled. The shading in Valdenuit's portrait is made with a light wash, having a gray rather than black tonality.

This comparison is of portraits made two years apart. However, if we look at an earlier Saint-Mémin portrait, of Daniel Kemper, signed and dated 1798 (fig. 7) and done in New York, we see that Saint-Mémin's style was even then heavier in touch than Valdenuit's. However, the *Kemper* drawing does come closer than the *Swan* to the delicacy of Valdenuit's style. A third comparison, of Valdenuit's *Clinton* with Saint-Mémin's signed portrait of Samuel Sitgreaves (fig. 8), also made in 1798, shows the same difference in style. It can be said, then, that Valdenuit's portraits are delicately drawn, the lines are fine, the washes gray in tone. In contrast, Saint-Mémin's drawings are more boldly executed, with darker lines and greater contrasts in the washed areas of the portrait.

Of the fifty-six drawings from the New York period, twenty are signed by Valdenuit and three by Saint-Mémin. The remaining unsigned drawings are difficult to attribute. Many of these were engraved; but the different inscriptions do not accurately identify the artist. For example, nine engravings identifying Saint-Mémin as the artist were taken from drawings signed by Valdenuit. However, five of the New York drawings exist in duplicate. Because of these, it is now possible to further identify the separate styles of Saint-Mémin and Valdenuit. The sitters in these portraits are Daniel Kemper, Samuel Sitgreaves, Governor and Mrs. Clinton, and Lady Mary Johnson. (There are, in fact, four drawings of Lady Johnson.) The reason for these duplicates is unknown, and they occur rarely after this period. Perhaps they were offered to family members of the important early patrons.

Of these pairs, the illustrated Saint-Mémin drawing of Daniel Kemper is a duplicate of a signed Valdenuit portrait of Kemper at the State Historical Society of Wisconsin, and a comparison bears out the conclusions presented already about the differences in the two artists' styles. In the second pair—the two drawings of Samuel Sitgreaves— each is closer in character to the other; both may be by Saint-Mémin.

In the Clinton portraits, the difference is most clear. The portrait of Governor Clinton by Valdenuit (see fig. 6) is accompanied by an unsigned

8

Samuel Sitgreaves, 1764-1824. Chalk drawing, 1798, by Saint-Mémin,
54.9 × 39 cm. (paper). (*Washington Cathedral*)

Cornelia Tappen Clinton, 1744-1800. Chalk drawing, 1797, by Thomas
Bluget de Valdenuit, 49.8 × 35.5 cm. (paper). (*Munson-Williams-Proctor
Institute, Utica, N.Y.*)

10

Cornelia Tappen Clinton, 1744-1800. Chalk drawing, 1797, by Saint-Mémin, 54.3 × 36.8 cm. (paper). (*Metropolitan Museum of Art, Purchase, 1940 Anonymous Gift*)

drawing of his wife, Cornelia Tappen Clinton (fig. 9). The two are a pair, in size, tonality, and technique. A duplicate pair of Clinton drawings, both unsigned (figs. 10 and 11), appears more firmly drawn. On the basis of style, particularly as seen in the draftsmanship and shading that is similar to his previous work, this duplicate pair can now be attributed to Saint-Mémin. The prints of the two portraits were made by Saint-Mémin, with inscriptions that do not mention Valdenuit. This engraving process took place at the time, or after, the duplicates were made, as shown by close comparison of the drawings with the prints. The engraving of Governor Clinton was made from the drawing at the Metropolitan, now attributed to Saint-Mémin, while the engraving of Mrs. Clinton was made from the drawing at Utica, attributed to Valdenuit. All four drawings were examined at the National Portrait Gallery conservation laboratory in 1978, along with the signed Saint-Mémin drawings of Daniel Kemper and Samuel Sitgreaves. The two Clinton drawings that served as the sources for the engravings were found to have slight nonpigment indentations over the surface, lines which correspond to the main compositional elements. These are probably related to the engraving process and are the nonpencil lines made by the pantograph, or copying machine.

The fifth set of duplicates from New York is the group of portraits of Lady Mary Johnson, wife of Sir John Johnson, a prominent New York loyalist who moved to Canada after the Revolution. There are two versions of this portrait, but four actual drawings. The first version (fig. 12), showing only a few curls on top of the headdress, is the source for the engraved plate; the second version (fig. 13) is a later replica. In style, all four drawings appear to be entirely the work of Valdenuit, although the engraving is inscribed "St. Memin No. 27 Pine St. N. York."

In summary, it appears to have been Valdenuit who introduced the physiognotrace method of making portraits, and his lightly drawn style dominated the year of their partnership. There is little or no stylistic difference between many of the unsigned drawings and those signed by Valdenuit. It is possible that some of these were done by Saint-Mémin, in which case his early style was virtually a duplication of Valdenuit's. Nevertheless, drawings that can be documented as Saint-Mémin's show a slightly more boldly drawn image, with greater tonal variation from dark to light.

Having produced about 130 portraits (some with Valdenuit) in the first two years of his new profession, Saint-Mémin moved in November

11

George Clinton, 1739-1812. Chalk drawing, circa 1797, by Saint-Mémin,
54.3 × 36.8 cm. (paper). (*Metropolitan Museum of Art, Purchase, 1940*
Anonymous Gift)

Lady Mary Johnson, 1753-1815. Chalk drawing, 1797, by Thomas Bluget de Valdenuit, 52.7 × 39.1 cm. (paper). (*Joel and Murray Woldman, Alexandria, Va.*)

13

Lady Mary Johnson, 1753-1815. Chalk drawing, 1797, by Thomas Bluget de Valdenuit, 47.6 × 33.5 cm. (paper). (*McCord Museum, Montreal*)

1798 to Burlington, New Jersey, near Philadelphia.[25] By this time he and his father had been joined by Mme de Saint-Mémin and one of the artist's sisters, Adélaïde. In Burlington the ladies opened a school for girls which was attended by a number of young Philadelphians. On January 8, 1799, Saint-Mémin placed his first Philadelphia advertisement in the *Aurora and General Advertiser*. It began with the same offer made in New York: "The subscriber begs leave to inform the public that he takes and engraves portraits on an improved plan of the celebrated physiognotrace of Paris and in a style never introduced in this country." He added that "a great number of portraits of distinguished persons, who honoured the artist with their patronage at New York, may be seen at S. Chaudron's No. 12, South Third Street, or at the subscriber's No. 32 South Third Street. He delivers with the original portrait, the plate engraved, and twelve copies of the same."

Saint-Mémin worked in Philadelphia until the spring of 1803, producing portraits at about the same rate as in New York, that is, about sixty a year. His advertisements in Philadelphia suggest that he shared a shop with Simon Chaudron, the French émigré silversmith. Many of his subjects were French refugees like himself, members of the Masonic lodge called L'Amenité Lodge. Along with local sitters, he attracted senators, congressmen, and other members of the federal government. Sometime in the spring of 1803 Saint-Mémin apparently decided that business was slow and moved to Baltimore, where he advertised in the *Federal Gazette* from April 29 to May 27.

In November 1803, in the Philadelphia *Aurora*, there appeared a new advertisement, much like Saint-Mémin's, which read: "Physiognotrace Likeness Engraved. The subscriber has the honor to inform the public, that he continues taking likenesses at his usual place, No. 1, South Third Street, near the corner of Market Street, where a number of portraits may be seen. Ladies and gentlemen may have their likenesses taken as large as life, with a certain number of small engravings, or the large likeness only, on the most moderate terms. For further particulars apply at the above place, L. Lementt [*sic*]." The same address had also appeared in an earlier unsigned physiognotrace advertisement placed in several January 1803 issues of the *Aurora* which began, "The physiognotrace is removed from No. 12, South Third Street, to No. 1, same street." This notice may have

25   Norfleet, p. 20.

been the first Philadelphia advertisement for Louis Lemet, the third artist to be considered in this chapter, rather than the last for Saint-Mémin. Judging from the style of Lemet's work, from the phrase "continues taking likenesses at his usual place" used in the following November, and from his claim, made in New York City in 1805, that he had been the "late partner of Mr. St. Memin," it appears that Lemet worked with Saint-Mémin for a brief period in Philadelphia. In his later New York advertisements, Lemet states that he was returning there after an absence of six years, which would put his earlier departure at about the same time as Saint-Mémin's. One wonders if Lemet could have been Saint-Mémin's partner in New York after Valdenuit had left.

None of Saint-Mémin's engravings or advertisements mention Lemet. Lemet's drawings, however, are so close to Saint-Mémin's that they have until now been taken as his work. A portrait of Charles Graff, of Philadelphia (fig. 14), for example, was attributed until recently to Saint-Mémin. It can now be reattributed to Lemet on the basis of an engraving at the Maryland Historical Society (fig. 15) catalogued as "Unidentified Man" and inscribed "Drawn & engr. by L. Le Met Philad." Close examination of details shows the two portraits to be the same image, one in reverse of the other, as was usual.

The confusion of Lemet's and Saint-Mémin's work is not surprising. When we compare *Charles Graff* with Saint-Mémin's now-familiar *Caleb Swan,* we see an overall similarity in their composition and in their contrasts of light and dark. The tinted paper is the same, and the drawing of Graff is in what is often considered a Saint-Mémin frame. When we compare details, we see that some shading techniques, such as that around the nostril and eyelid, are identical. Other details, however, are quite different. Lemet, for example, uses a shorthand arc for the eyebrow, stuck over the eye like a rainbow, whereas Saint-Mémin's eyebrow, as is typical of his style, relates to the bone structure of the forehead and eye socket. Like Valdenuit, Lemet seems more linear and less tonal than Saint-Mémin. He also seems a little lazier, omitting the shading along the bridge of the nose.

Other Lemet portraits can also be identified, using the few known engravings—about twelve—that have been located (Maryland Historical Society; Historical Society of Pennsylvania). One of these is a drawing of Timothy Palmer (fig. 16). The sitter, a bridge designer and engineer, was

14
Charles Graff, 1779-1846. Chalk drawing, 1803-5, by Louis Lemet, 48.3 ×
35.5 cm. (sight measurement). (*Mrs. Edmund H. Cabeen, Wayne, Pa.*)

15
Charles Graff, 1779-1846. Engraving, 1803-5, by Louis Lemet, 5.5 cm. (diameter). (*Maryland Historical Society*)

in Philadelphia in 1804 to supervise the building of a bridge over the Schuylkill River. The engraving (fig. 17) is inscribed as the work of Lemet. (A later strike, from the late nineteenth century, has been published as a portrait of Benjamin Rush and bears a facsimile of Rush's signature.[26] However, comparison of this with other likenesses of Rush shows that Rush had a longer head than Palmer.) In the drawing of Palmer, Lemet used a quicker shading stroke than in his portrait of Graff. A third Lemet drawing (recently acquired by the American Philosophical Society), *Colonel Joseph Shippen*, corresponds to an identified Lemet engraving owned by a descendant.

Having advertised in Philadelphia through the end of 1804, Lemet returned to New York "after an absence of six years from this city" and offered "his services . . . in his professional line. The terms are always the same, that is $25 for a large likeness, $12 for small engravings, including the copper plate, for Gentlemen, and $35 for Ladies, and $38 for large likenesses, without the engraving."[27] By the fall of 1805 Lemet was offering the same type of portrait in Albany,[28] where his trade card was

26 Robert Erwin Jones, "Portraits of Benjamin Rush, M.D., by His Contemporaries," *Antiques* 108 (July 1975): 102, illustrated fig. 12.

27 *New-York Commercial Advertiser*, March 15, 1805, quoted by Norfleet, p. 25.

28 Stauffer, *American Engravers*, 1:160–61.

Timothy Palmer, 1751-1821. Chalk drawing, 1803-5, by Louis Lemet, 50 × 38 cm. (approximate). (*Historical Society of Old Newbury, Newburyport, Mass.*)

17
Timothy Palmer, 1751-1821. Engraving, 1803-5, by Louis Lemet, 5.5 cm. diameter. (*Historical Society of Pennsylvania, Philadelphia*)

engraved by Gideon Fairman (fig. 18). A number of portraits of upstate New Yorkers which have been attributed to Saint-Mémin may instead be the work of Lemet, who remained in Albany until the late 1820s before returning to New York City, where he died in 1832.

18
Louis Lemet's trade card. Engraving, 1805-10, by Gideon Fairman, 6.1 × 8.4 cm. (paper). (*Historical Society of Pennsylvania, Philadelphia*)

In 1803 Saint-Mémin began to follow the pattern of working in a city for several months and then moving on or returning to Burlington, New Jersey, where his mother and sister lived and where he apparently engraved many of the plates. Thus, in the years 1803 to 1807 he worked in Baltimore, Washington, and Alexandria, Virginia. In Washington, by then the federal capital, Saint-Mémin drew portraits of William Thornton, Thomas Jefferson, and others, including a group of Indians who had accompanied Lewis and Clark to Washington after the Louisiana territory expedition.[29] The total number of portraits made between 1796 and 1810 numbers about nine hundred, almost fifty times as many as are known by Valdenuit or Lemet.

Later in his life, in a letter to his friend M. Sauvegeot about his years in the United States, Saint-Mémin wrote: "For my ability in the drawing phase of art I make no claims, since I made use of an instrument in order to obtain the most essential features, and since, if there is any merit in the delicacy and studied exactness of the likeness, the draughtsman owes his ability, so entirely independent of his efforts, to providence; the possessor enjoys this faculty without having any right to be vain about it." Instead, Saint-Mémin saw as his great accomplishment "that of having overcome the greatest difficulties before reaching the goal. . . . The creation of my little engravings is so much my work that I was obliged to be at the same time draughtsman and engraver, builder of pantograph, physiognotrace and small-sized press, manufacturer of *roulettes* and other instruments necessary to engraving, brayer of my ink, and, furthermore, my own printer."[30]

Apparently Saint-Mémin had mixed feelings about his work in the United States. Nevertheless, he was clearly proud of it, and in this same letter to Sauvegeot, to whom the artist gave a group of his American portrait engravings, Saint-Mémin noted that "I took care to mark [the portraits] with dates and names of the individuals in order that the result of my labor would have more interest." After returning to France in 1814, he turned his artistic talents to administration, becoming the director of the Dijon Museum, and to the preservation of works of art by others. Saint-Mémin's career in the United States, however, the result of chance and misfortune, has left us a lively profile of federal society.

29 Norfleet, pp. 29–37.

30 Quoted, ibid., pp. 63–65.

The Golden Age of Illustrated Biographies

Three Case Studies

GORDON
M.
MARSHALL

The pseudonymous "Fag" announced it first in his humorous piece in the February 1815 *Port Folio:* The biographical age had begun. By 1830 the trickle satirized by "Fag" had become a flood. That year the *New York Mirror* reported that "the eagerness with which every species of biography is read in the present day has led to the adoption of this phrase—biography mania." In the first fifty years of the nineteenth century, more historical biographies were published than any other literary form except the novel. One historian, Jared Sparks, ran a literature factory and earned a handsome living from heroic biography. He was not alone in this cottage industry. Biography (and its allied disciplines of history and travel reportage) was the first literary form to be successfully established on a professional and profitable basis.[1]

The War of 1812, ending on the triumphal note of Andrew Jackson's victory at New Orleans, had infected many with protoromantic patriotism. Artists and authors were poised to march to a new tune; "Americanize" was to be their watchword. It was a time for heroes and hero-worship. The reading public turned from the romantic novel of the late eighteenth century to the true-to-life adventure biography. Testing the market in 1828 with his *Life and Voyages of Christopher Columbus*, Washington Irving

1 "Fag," "A New Plan for Writing Lives," *Port Folio,* 3d ser., 5, no. 2 (Feb. 1815):195–97; "An Author's Evenings—Biography," ibid., 4th ser., 3, no. 1 (Jan. 1817): 29–32, refers to the "rage for biography"; *New York Mirror* 7 (May 15, 1830): 359; "Art. I—American Biography," *American Quarterly Review* 1, no. 1 (March 1827): 1–38; and William Charvat, *Literary Publishing in America, 1790–1850* (Philadelphia, 1959), pp. 73–74.

earned twenty-five thousand dollars and continued writing essentially biographical or historical works for the rest of his career. Biography and history were at the top of the American best-seller list, pushed aside only by the historical fiction of Cooper, Scott, and Dickens.[2]

Although biographies of individuals were the most popular, collected biographies were a staple from the beginning. The thirst for self-improvement, combined with a rising nationalism, made the public eager to have thirty heroes for the price of one. Countless single-volume biographical dictionaries, with their drab exteriors, prosaic text, and barely recognizable illustrations, crowd the shelves of our research libraries.[3]

But, as is often the case when art and commerce intersect, the best of the illustrated collected biographies were not the most financially successful. Although considered the pinnacle of the bookmakers' art by contemporary critics, Joseph Delaplaine's *Repository of the Lives and Portraits of Distinguished Americans* (1816-18), John and Joseph M. Sanderson's *Biography of the Signers to the Declaration of Independence* (1819–27), and James B. Longacre and James Herring's *National Portrait Gallery of Distinguished Americans* (1833-39) are little known today. Histories of publishing in this period barely mention their names. Occasionally a historian will cite Sanderson's series in a list of previous biographers of his subject, and art historians sporadically will make use of the engravings from all three. But rarely are they considered as their creators intended—as complete entities. None of the current works on the history of fine printing and the book as an art object discuss any of these works.[4]

2 Charvat, *Literary Publishing*, pp. 75–76.

3 *Monthly Anthology* (1810), cited in Frank Luther Mott, A *History of American Magazines, 1741–1850* (Cambridge, Mass., 1966) pp. 420–21; Edward H. O'Neill, *Biography by Americans, 1658–1936: A Subject Bibliography* (Philadelphia, 1939), lists 142 titles of collected biographies published before 1860, and preliminary research indicates that there were many more.

4 The lone exception to this neglect was the international bibliophile Raphäel Esmerian, who selected the morocco quarto embossed plaque binding of Longacre and Herring's *National Portrait Gallery* as one of four nineteenth-century American books worthy of inclusion in his prestigious binding collection. See *Bibliothèque Raphäel Esmerian: Quatrième Partie Livres Illustrés du XIXe Siècle*, 5 vols. in 6 parts (Paris, n.d.), 4:11–12, item no. 2.

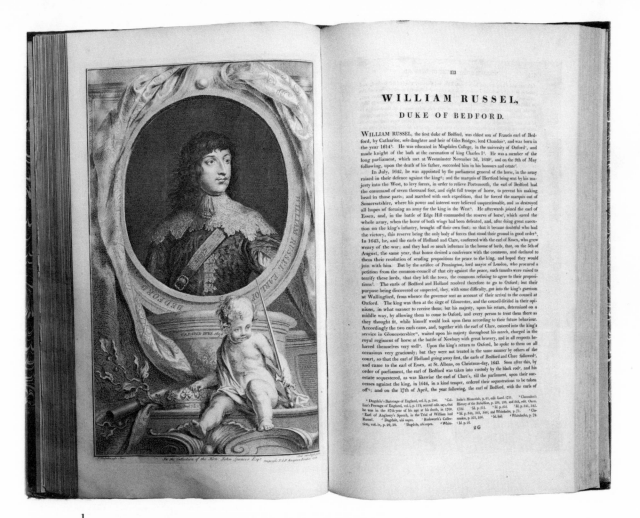

1

William Russell, duke of Bedford, 1613-1700. Engraving, circa 1738, by
Jacobus Houbraken after Anthony Van Dyck, 35.9 × 22.4 cm. From Thomas Birch, *Heads of Illustrious Persons of Great Britain* (London, 1813). (*Library Company of Philadelphia*)

Neglected even in their own time (in spite of contemporary critical praise),
each project quickly passed out of print in its original form. And when the
last two of the three series were revived, their original creators would not
have recognized them.

The wedding of heroic biography and patriotic art was not financially
successful. Part of the problem was the competition from the English
book-export industry, for which America long had been considered a
captive market. American publishers and printers, particularly those of
literature and "art books," complained bitterly of artificially cheap British
editions flooding the market and undercutting their domestic productions.
Exports such as Thomas Birch's new folio edition of *Heads of Illustrious
Persons of Great Britain* (London, 1813) engulfed all competition (fig. 1).
Even though the plates had first been engraved in the late 1730s and 1740s
and had been revived and reworked for this edition, they were still superior

to any similar American production. At the other end of the price spectrum were ugly but cheap chapbooks, such as *Biography Illustrated* (London, 1828), which were dumped on the market in large quantities. Often totally inaccurate and possessed of limited American content, they were none-theless cheaper and more widely available than many superior domestic productions.[5] Clearly something had to be done to enable publishers and artists to fulfill their post-Revolutionary promise of establishing a national literature on a firm commercial basis.

Joseph Delaplaine (1777-1824) and His *Repository*

A new type of businessman was needed to join the new, rising romantic nationalism of America's authors with the vision of its pictorial artists. Composed in equal parts of writer, artist, publisher, and dreamer—and seasoned with salesmanship and brass—he had to be the kind of man who could invent the coffee-table book before there was a coffee table. Such a man was Joseph Delaplaine (fig. 2).

Born in Philadelphia into the moderately wealthy family of James and Mary Keen Delaplaine on December 20, 1770, Joseph moved to Cincinnati in 1805 on the recommendation of his friend John Fanning Watson.[6] By the time he returned to Philadelphia in 1809, his successful business activities and an advantageous marriage to Jane Livingston, the grand-daughter of William Livingston, the first governor of the state of New Jersey, had brought him a fortune of twenty thousand dollars. With John Hellings as a partner, he launched the firm of Delaplaine and Hellings, Publishers in September 1810, and before the end of the year they had

5 For particular notice of English publishers' sales practices in America and a protest against "dumping," see [Draft memorial to the Chairman and the Committee on U.S. Manufactures, U.S. Congress, from the New York Committee of Book-sellers], Jan. 1820, enclosed in J. Hart to Matthew Carey, Feb. 8, 1820, folder 6, box 88, vol. 1, no. 90, Edward Carey Gardiner Collection, Historical Society of Pennsylvania (hereinafter PHi). See also Samuel G. Goodrich, *Recollections of a Lifetime, or Men and Things I Have Seen . . .*, 2 vols. (New York and Auburn, 1857), 1:99–113; William Charvat, *The Profession of Authorship in America, 1800–1870: The Papers of William Charvat*, ed. Matthew J. Bruccoli (Columbus, Ohio, 1968), pp. 29–48.

6 I would like to express my special appreciation to Mr. Bernard Heinz of Guilford, Conn., who is at work on a biography of Joseph Delaplaine, for sharing his notes, ideas, and writings. Unless otherwise credited, all information on Delaplaine is derived from Heinz's unpublished article "The Picture Found in the Attic: A 'Promote America' Planner Revealed."

Joseph Delaplaine, 1777-1824. Oil on canvas, date unknown, by John Wesley Jarvis, 84 × 66 cm. (*National Portrait Gallery, Smithsonian Institution*)

issued three new Latin schoolbooks. Delaplaine's flair for promotion quickly surfaced. Securing written prepublication reviews from every teacher of rhetoric or Latin within two hundred miles of Philadelphia, he had them printed as a laudatory preface to one of the volumes, perhaps the first example of a publisher submitting advance page proofs to a select audience for favorable comments.[7]

Following the success of the schoolbooks, publishing ideas and projects flowed from Delaplaine's volcanic brain like molten lava. Shedding Hellings as a partner, he joined forces with a well-established publisher, Edward Parker, in April 1811 and published an American edition of the *New Edinburgh Encyclopaedia.* It was equal in length to the original but with new articles written for the American market. Delaplaine evidently was the primary editor for the project, soliciting famous and knowledgeable Americans to adapt the English text to the American audience. Massive and costly, the work eventually ran to eighteen full, or thirty-six half, volumes and was not completed until 1831. The restless Delaplaine remained with the project through the publication of volume six, part two (1815), when other projects and possibly strained financial resources forced him to leave.[8]

The *Encyclopaedia* was not his only enterprise during these years. In May 1812 he issued, as sole publisher, an eighty-page monthly magazine, the *Emporium of Arts and Sciences,* edited by John Redman Coxe and illustrated with serviceable engravings of technical subjects by Cornelius Tiebout. Under Delaplaine and Coxe, the *Emporium* stressed the latest advances in practical knowledge and applied technology with particular attention to their influence on the arts. Its contents included the first etchings done on glass in America and in the April 1813 issue perhaps the earliest technical description of lithography in America. Interestingly, there had been a proposal to include short biographical sketches of the scientists and inventors whose portraits accompanied accounts of their

7 Responses to the advance sheets of Charles Francis [or François] L'Homond's *Epitome historiae sacrae . . . editio prima Americana . . .* (Philadelphia, 1810) were published in the introduction to the book.

8 For Delaplaine's role as editor-solicitor, see Delaplaine to R. R. Livingston, May 6, May 7, Nov. 13, 1811, Jan. 8, 1812, Charles Roberts Autograph Letters Collection, Quaker Library, Haverford College, Haverford, Pa.

work, but John Redman Coxe replied with a tartly worded notice, appended to the first volume, "Biography does not comport with the intention of the work." The *Emporium* ran through April 1813, when it was sold to the firm of Kimber and Richardson.[9]

To the two major projects he already had under way, Delaplaine ambitiously added a third—Bible publishing. In February 1813, in conjuction with Murray, Draper, Fairman and Company, he proposed the publication of a "splendid hot-pressed edition of Macklin's celebrated Bible." The American work was to be issued in fifty numbers, royal quarto, and was to contain two hundred engravings after "pictures and designs by the most eminent foreign and American artists."[10] One part was to be issued every six weeks, and the price was to be $3.50 an issue. On September 17, 1813, Delaplaine reported to New York friends that he wanted "about ninety subscribers more in Philadelphia" before the Bible was put to press.[11] Apparently he never got them; but, undaunted by this failure, Delaplaine issued in association with Edward Parker and Kimber

9   *To the Public* . . . (broadside prospectus, caption title), [March 1812], Joseph Downs Manuscript Collection, Winterthur Museum, Del.; *Prospectus of the Emporium of Arts and Sciences* . . . [Philadelphia, 1812], box 2, no. 22, miscellaneous items 1795–1806, Bradford Papers, PHi; and the two-page broadsheet, [Joseph Delaplaine], *The Publisher Respectfully Informs* . . . (caption title), [Philadelphia, 1812], in folder 1813–17, Correspondence 1796–1881, Bradford Papers, PHi. Just before the change in ownership, the *Emporium* had a listed circulation of 1,109, not unusually low considering the type of magazine. Quotation from "Notice," *Emporium* 1 (May 1812): [2].

10 "Proposed American Publications," *Analectic Magazine* 1 (Feb. 1813): 184. Delaplaine's edition of Macklin's Bible is noted as "not executed" in E. B. O'Callaghan, *A List of Editions of the Holy Scriptures and Parts Thereof, Printed in America Previous to 1860* . . . (Albany, 1861), p. 111. For the English edition of Thomas Macklin's Bible, see A. S. Herbert, *Historical Catalogue of Printed Editions of the English Bible, 1525–1961* (London and New York, 1968), pp. 320–21.

11 Delaplaine to Jacob and Paul Rapelye, Sept. 17, 1813, National Portrait Gallery, Washington, D. C. (hereinafter DSiP). Delaplaine's edition of Macklin's Bible came very close to being issued, as is evident from an 1813 type specimen sheet, *Binny and Ronaldson's New Columbian,* which is footnoted "Originally cut for the splendid Bible intended to be published by Delaplaine, Murray, Draper, & Co. and is now ready to be cast for such Printers as may order it." Binny and Ronaldson Specimen Book, vol. 2, General Manuscript Collection, PHi.

and Richardson a more modest proposal in October 1813 for a two-volume royal octavo edition of the Bible. Its unique selling point was to be sixty engravings, the subjects chosen by Rembrandt Peale and Thomas Sully and executed by America's best engravers. Unfortunately, Delaplaine apparently neglected to inform Rembrandt Peale that he was to be so employed.[12] The enterprise failed. But competition, rather than the Peale episode, was probably the major reason for the failure. The Bible market was one of the most cutthroat and competitive in all of publishing, and only the most established and financially secure firms could afford the gamble. Delaplaine was either wise or lucky not to have entered these troubled waters.

Simultaneous with his attempted venture in Bible publishing, Delaplaine became a wholesale and retail printseller. Some of the prints he sold, like those of Antoine Laurent Lavoisier, Isaac Newton, David Rittenhouse, and Benjamin Franklin, all by David Edwin, already had appeared as frontispieces in issues of the *Emporium*. Others, such as William S. Leney's *DeWitt Clinton*, were newly commissioned works meant solely for the print trade. Delaplaine sent fifty copies of Leney's *Clinton* to the New York merchant firm of Jacob and Paul Rapelye, who were to handle the distribution to the actual sellers.[13] Such an indirect system of distribution, using personal friends and firms not in the book or print business, did not bode well for his other publishing ventures, however well it served him in the short run.

In addition to domestically produced prints, Delaplaine imported engravings from the English firm of Boydell and Harrison and the London-based artist James Heath. He took orders for the large "furniture" prints of

12   For the announcement of the proposals, see *Analectic Magazine,* n.s., 2 (Oct. 1813): [350], and O'Callaghan, p. 117. O'Callaghan had contacted Rembrandt Peale about the proposal and stated that "Mr. Peale knows nothing about this work, and is of the opinion that it has never been published in whole or in parts" (p. 117). A search of the Peale family papers, kindly undertaken by Assistant Editor of the Peale Papers Sidney Hart, revealed no mention of the project by either Rembrandt or Charles Willson Peale.

13   The actual sellers were Eastburn, Kirk and Co., book publishers, and a Mr. Killpatrick, Delaplaine's agent for Bible subscriptions. See Delaplaine to Jacob and Paul Rapelye, Sept. 17 and Nov. 4, 1813, DSiP; and Delaplaine to Rapelye, Oct. 20, 1813, personal collection of the author.

James Fittler and, later, for the expensive large historical prints, by John Burnet, of Atkinson and Devis's painting of the Battle of Waterloo.[14]

Delaplaine also planned to produce his own large prints patterned on English models. He entered into an agreement with Thomas Birch on April 13, 1813, to issue a series of engravings celebrating American naval actions in the war with Great Britain. Expenses were to be shared equally between the partners. Birch was to furnish the original sketches or paintings, and Delaplaine was to secure subscriptions and to distribute and sell the finished work. The expenses of engraving and printing were to be borne equally by the partners. Somewhere along the process of creation, Delaplaine, as usual, transformed the modest offering into a grandiose series of large engravings entitled "Delaplaine's National Prints." The first publication of the series, Thomas Birch's *Commodore Perry's Victory on Lake Erie,* engraved by Alexander Lawson, was announced in the *Aurora* on September 28, 1815, and received a glowing seven-page review in the October issue of the *Port Folio.*[15] Other prints were planned for the series, but only one, John Lewis Krimmel's genre picture *Election Scene, Philadelphia,* is known to have progressed as far as the engraving stage.[16] Perhaps because of massive competition from other publishers for the naval print market, Delaplaine's weakened financial condition, or the lack of subscribers, the full series was not completed.[17]

14 Delaplaine, *Repository,* vol. 1, part 2 (Philadelphia, 1817), rear printed wrapper, Library Company of Philadelphia copy (hereinafter PPL).

15 "Articles of Agreement," April 13, 1813, case 7, box 39, Thomas Birch Papers, Gratz Collection, PHi. For notice that Lawson was to engrave Birch's painting of Perry's victory, see *Port Folio,* 3d ser., 4, no. 1 (July 1814): 96–97. *Aurora and General Advertiser* (Philadelphia), Sept. 28, 1815; *Port Folio,* 3d ser., 6, no. 4 (Oct. 1815): 364–70.

16 See *Thomas Birch, 1779–1851: Paintings and Drawings, March 16–May 1, 1966,* exhibition catalogue (Philadelphia, 1966). An unfinished plate by Alexander Lawson after John Lewis Krimmel's *Election Scene, Philadelphia* also probably was intended for this series. This may be the print mentioned in the *Aurora* announcement as *American Election Ground.* The Krimmel painting is exactly the same size as Birch's painting of Perry's victory.

17 For other naval prints of 1813–14, see *Analectic Magazine* 1, no. 5 (May 1813): rear wrapper and advertising pages; ibid., 3, no. 14 (Feb. 1814): extra unnumbered

3

Frontispiece and engraved title page. Engravings, circa 1814 and 1815, by Alexander Lawson after Thomas Birch and Gideon Fairman. From *Delaplaine's Repository,* vol. 1, pt. 1 (Philadelphia, 1816). (*National Portrait Gallery, Smithsonian Institution*)

Never one to stand still, the peripatetic publisher had already embarked on his most ambitious project: *Delaplaine's Repository of the Lives and Portraits of Distinguished Americans.* First announced in early 1814 (probably April or May), the *Repository* was to be a fine example of the bookmaker's art, the equal to anything Europe had produced, and the finest book published in America. It was to be a quarto in format and a royal quarto in size (i.e., 11¾″ × 9½″), with a fine, wove, off-white paper, generous uncluttered margins, and a clean, modern type style. The talented William Brown, already responsible for some of the finest books printed in Philadelphia, had been chosen to be its printer. Each half volume was to be issued "neatly put in boards," with an elegant vignette title page designed and engraved by Gideon Fairman and an embellished frontispiece engraved by Alexander Lawson (fig. 3). The price was to be four dollars a half volume for subscribers and six dollars to subsequent buyers.[18]

pages. Murray, Draper, and Fairman announced a series of naval prints in 1813, and the publisher John Melish announced two prints of Perry's victory by Benjamin Tanner in the *Aurora and General Advertiser,* Dec. 28, 1814, p. 4.

18 The first announcement appeared in the *Analectic Magazine,* n.s., 3 (June 1814): [522], where, even though the editor found the title "ostentatious" and felt that the proposals contained "too much of that wordy profession and wide-mouthed promise ... still we are of the opinion that a work of this kind ably and modestly executed, would deserve and receive the universal patronage of the nation."

As befit such a grand conception, Delaplaine issued, in June or July 1814, a sumptuous prospectus, thirty-three pages in length, with three portraits, a long introduction, and a sample biography of Christopher Columbus. Two previously printed broadside announcements were inserted, and the whole elaborate prospectus (cum salesman's sample) was bound in hard covers. It reflected Delaplaine's optimistic frame of mind, for most publishers issued only the simplest prospectus to minimize their cost in case there were not enough subscribers. As he intended, his prospectus attracted attention and even softened the hostile attitude of the *Analectic Magazine*'s critic, who, while still expressing doubts about the fundamental concept of the project, admitted that "for beauty of presswork and graphical embellishment, [the specimen] certainly surpasses anything of the kind that has yet been produced in this country."[19]

As the editor of the biographies, Delaplaine secured the services of Dr. Charles Caldwell, a splenetic and aristocratic editor of the *Port Folio* magazine, who seemed like an ideal choice.[20] Aside from his proven editorial talents, he was the author of several biographical sketches in the *Port Folio* that Delaplaine admired. In addition, as one of the growing circle interested in the new "science" of phrenology, Caldwell brought with him an attitude to biography oriented toward the manner in which facial characteristics display inner character. Everything seemed poised for the project to move ahead rapidly.[21]

19 Two copies of the pamphlet prospectus, one of which was a presentation piece to Benjamin West, are in the collections of the New-York Historical Society with the title *Proposals for Publishing* . . . [Philadelphia, 1814] and contain a sample biography and three plates. The text of the long introduction is the same in both the *Proposals* and the *Repository,* although set in different typefaces, and the sample biography of Columbus was rewritten for the *Repository.* For the review of this pamphlet prospectus-sample, see the *Analectic Magazine,* n.s., 4 (Aug. 1814): 174.

20 Delaplaine had first approached Robert Walsh (1784–1859) to be his editor but turned to Caldwell when Walsh asked a salary of fifteen thousand dollars. See Delaplaine to Jacob and Paul Rapelye, Sept. 17, 1813, DSiP.

21 For Charles Caldwell (1772–1853), see Emmet Field Horine, *Biographical Sketch and Guide to the Writings of Charles Caldwell, M.D.* (Brooks, Ky., 1960), and Charles Caldwell, *Autobiograpy,* ed. Harriot W. Warner (Philadelphia, 1855), pp. 314–15.

But an easy path from conception to existence was not to be. The *Repository*'s first problem was procuring the engravings. Original portraits of sufficient quality to survive copying and engraving and still resemble the subject proved difficult to secure. Although several were already done when the first broadside announcement was issued, others proved to be poorly executed, and Delaplaine insisted that they be done over. The painstaking care which Delaplaine exercised in the choice and execution of the image is exemplified in his statement:

> As there are many persons who believe that the most faithful likeness of George Washington is that which was painted by Stuart, while others, equally numerous, perhaps, prefer that of his bust by Houdon, the publisher has thought proper, in order to render universal satisfaction, and to enable our citizens to possess the best resemblances of the great and good man, to have an engraving executed from Stuart's portrait of Washington, and another from Houdon's bust of the General by Leney, from a drawing by Wood [fig. 4]. The last is finished, and has been submitted to the inspection of Judge [Bushrod] Washington, who has pronounced it an accurate likeness of his uncle.[22]

Both engravings were eventually included in volume one, part one, of the *Repository*.

Efforts to please everyone caused mounting delays. By 1815 faint-hearted subscribers began to withdraw, and Delaplaine was forced to issue a broadside to plead for patience. But, even while he was busy explaining, he reaffirmed "his determination never to suffer this work to appear, til he became satisfied that its execution would be honourable to himself and do credit to the country." Delaplaine also recirculated his full thirty-three-page prospectus, but it was difficult to counteract the charge that the *Repository* was an often-announced and never-seen project.[23]

Multiple biographies presented unique problems not encountered in other fine art books. Some of the subjects proved unable or unwilling to supply the necessary documentation for the accurate historical account of

22 *Lives and Portraits. Joseph Delaplaine, Philadelphia, Proposes to Publish...*, broadside [Philadelphia, 1815], case 14, box 31, Charles Thomson Papers, Gratz Collection, PHi.

23 This charge was a major complaint of the reviewers of the *Repository* when the first part of vol. 1 did appear in 1816 and further hurt the already flagging sales.

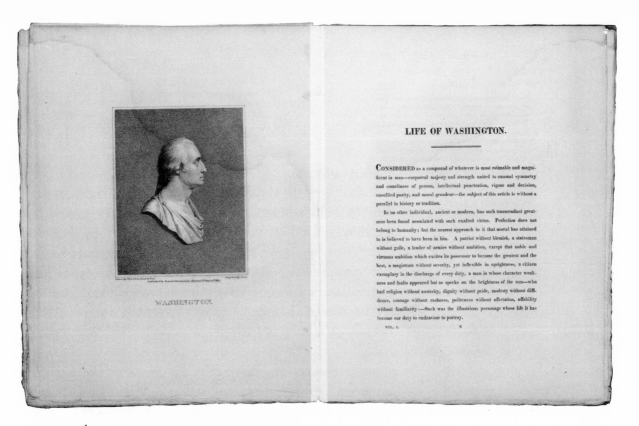

LIFE OF WASHINGTON.

CONSIDERED as a compound of whatever is most estimable and magnificent in man—corporeal majesty and strength united to unusual symmetry and comeliness of person, intellectual penetration, vigour and decision, unsullied purity, and moral grandeur—the subject of this article is without a parallel in history or tradition.

In no other individual, ancient or modern, has such transcendant greatness been found associated with such exalted virtue. Perfection does not belong to humanity; but the nearest approach to it that mortal has attained to is believed to have been in him. A patriot without blemish, a statesman without guile, a leader of armies without ambition, except that noble and virtuous ambition which excites its possessor to become the greatest and the best, a magistrate without severity, yet inflexible in uprightness, a citizen exemplary in the discharge of every duty, a man in whose character weakness and faults appeared but as specks on the brightness of the sun—who had religion without austerity, dignity without pride, modesty without diffidence, courage without rashness, politeness without affectation, affability without familiarity:—Such was the illustrious personage whose life it has become our duty to endeavour to portray.

4

George Washington, 1732-1799. Engraving, copyright 1814, by William S. Leney after Joseph Wood after Jean-Antoine Houdon, 13 × 10.6 cm. From *Delaplaine's Repository,* vol. 1, pt. 1 (Philadelphia, 1816). (*National Portrait Gallery, Smithsonian Institution*)

their life that Delaplaine insisted must accompany his exact likenesses. Charles Thomson, with whom Delaplaine conducted a number of interviews and carried on an extensive correspondence, was unable to supply details of his political career because he had destroyed his papers. With other subjects, Delaplaine labored to overcome false modesty, genuine disinterest, or distrust of biographers in general, and occasionally an article had to be written totally without the subject's cooperation. Both before and after the biographies were published, relatives, admirers, or the subjects themselves demanded revisions. Delaplaine tried to avoid, as would Longacre and Herring, some of these difficulties by keeping his biographies short.[24]

24 To answer criticisms of errors in the biographies in the *Repository,* even Delaplaine planned to issue "a Supplement to the lives every 3, 4 or 5 or 6 vol[umes] so as to make each life perfect." See "Joseph Delaplaine's Notes on the Repository, vol. 1" pasted inside vol. 1 of the National Portrait Gallery's copy. For problems of securing biographical details, see Delaplaine's Notes, DSiP; seven letters to Charles Thomson, May 24, 1816–Feb. 26, 1817, case 14, box 31, Charles Thomson Papers, Gratz Collection, PHi; and Delaplaine to Major Barker, June 17, 1817, McAllister Collection, PPL. For insistence on changes, see William Coleman to Rufus King, Feb. 5, 1817, in Charles R. King, ed., *The Life and Correspondence of Rufus King,* 6 vols. (New York, 1894–1900), 6:52–53.

The *Repository* became controversial when Charles Caldwell's personal and scientific dispute with the Reverend Samuel Stanhope Smith, the former president of Princeton, spilled over into Smith's reviews of the work with which Caldwell was now associated.[25] Other reviewers without a personal grudge suggested that the biographies were too long or too short. For some the whole concept was too ostentatious and therefore not fitting for a country of simple republican virtues. Although by the time of Longacre and Herring it was acceptable to include living subjects, Delaplaine was criticized for including both living celebrities and foreigners resident in America.[26]

Other more favorable reviews helped to counteract the negative impact of the long delays, controversy, and sweeping criticisms. In addition, Delaplaine, as he had done with his schoolbook series, used favorable comments from the correspondence of public figures in his *Repository* publicity. A few other public figures, among them Thomas Jefferson (fig. 5), aided Delaplaine's project in more concrete ways. The sage of Monticello removed engravings from books in his personal library to provide the basis for the *Repository*'s plates of Amerigo Vespucci and Christopher Columbus.[27] By the means of such direct aid, Delaplaine was

25   "S" [i.e., Samuel Stanhope Smith], "Original" (review of the *Repository*), *Analectic Magazine*, 1st ser., 8, no. 3 (Sept. 1816): [193]–209; and reply by [Charles Caldwell], *The Author Turned Critic; or the Reviewer Reviewed Being a Reply to a Feeble and Unfounded Attack on Delaplaine's Repository . . .* [Philadelphia, 1816], pp. 1–34. This pamphlet is often erroneously attributed to Delaplaine. His contribution in fact consisted of five pages of advertising matter and testimonials to the worth of the *Repository* appended to the end of Caldwell's ad hominem attack.

26   For advice not to include famous foreigners then resident in America, see Portuguese naturalist Joseph [Francisco] Correa de Serra to Delaplaine, Nov. 5, 1818, American Philosophical Society, Philadelphia (hereinafter PPAmP); and "American Biographical Works," *Analectic Magazine*, 1st ser., 4, no. 1 (Aug. 1814): 174; for lack of "republican simplicity," see the review of the prospectus for the *Respository* entitled "Domestic Literature," ibid., 3, no. 6 (June 1814): [522]; for more constructive reviews of vol. 1, part 1, see *Portico* (Baltimore) 2, no. 4 (October 1816): 282–93, and no. 6 (Dec. 1816): 506–21. The reviews of vol. 1, part 2 and vol. 2, part 1 in the *Analectic Magazine* were only slightly less hostile; see 1st ser., 10, no. 6 (Dec. 1817): 483–88 and 13, no. 2 (Feb. 1819): 89–92.

27   See E. Millicent Sowerby, *Catalogue of the Library of Thomas Jefferson* (Washington, D.C., 1952–59), 4:166, item 12, regarding Vespucci print; also 4:170–72, item 15, part 5, regarding the three versions of the portrait of Columbus; and 4:297–99, item

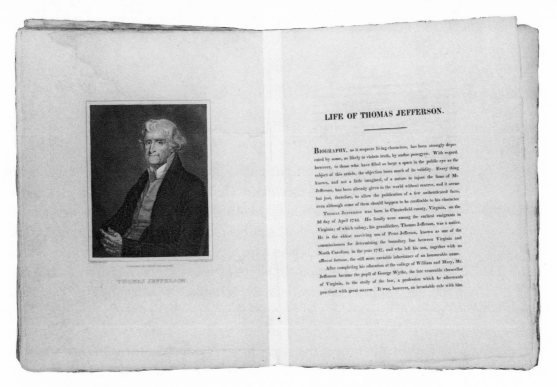

LIFE OF THOMAS JEFFERSON.

BIOGRAPHY, as it respects living characters, has been strongly deprecated by some, as likely to violate truth, by undue panegyric. With regard, however, to those who have filled so large a space in the public eye as the subject of this article, the objection loses much of its validity. Every thing known, and not a little imagined, of a nature to injure the fame of Mr. Jefferson, has been already given to the world without reserve, and it seems but just, therefore, to allow the publication of a few authenticated facts, even although some of them should happen to be creditable to his character.

THOMAS JEFFERSON was born in Chesterfield county, Virginia, on the 2d day of April 1743. His family were among the earliest emigrants to Virginia; of which colony, his grandfather, Thomas Jefferson, was a native. He is the eldest surviving son of Peter Jefferson, known as one of the commissioners for determining the boundary line between Virginia and North Carolina, in the year 1747, and who left his son, together with an affluent fortune, the still more enviable inheritance of an honourable name.

After completing his education at the college of William and Mary, Mr. Jefferson became the pupil of George Wythe, the late venerable chancellor of Virginia, in the study of the law, a profession which he afterwards practised with great success. It was, however, an invariable rule with him.

5

Thomas Jefferson, 1743-1826. Engraving, circa 1816, by John B. Neagle after Bass Otis, 13.7 × 11 cm. From *Delaplaine's Repository*, vol. 1, pt. 2 (Philadelphia, 1817). (*National Portrait Gallery, Smithsonian Institution*)

able to publish the second part of volume one in the fall of 1817 and the first part of volume two in the following year, although both were late.

Contemporary opinion and controversy aside, how well did Delaplaine accomplish his goal? Given his personal circumstances and the economic and artistic conditions of the period, Delaplaine produced a work remarkable in its conception, design, and execution. The *Repository* is one of a half-dozen American works published in the first quarter of the nineteenth century worthy of being called fine printing. Delaplaine was also the first publisher to create a purposely limited edition of his plates, stating in 1816 that the *Repository* "shall never be sold at auction [and] when the number of impressions required are struck off, the plates are destroyed."[28] Insofar as can be determined, he lived up to his promise. No later uses of the plates from the *Repository*, over which he still had control after 1819, have been found. Delaplaine's success in blending log-cabin patriotism and European cultural tastes was extraordinary and pioneering.

Although Delaplaine's *Repository* project was not completed in the

165, 4:393, item 16, and 5:213. For a brief and partisan account of the Delaplaine-Jefferson friendship, see Gordon Hendricks, "A Wish to Please, and a Willingness to Be Pleased." *American Art Journal* 2, no. 1 (Spring 1970): 16–29. Bernard Heinz plans to tell this episode in detail in his biography.

28 [Caldwell], *Author Turned Critic*, Delaplaine's advertising pages, p. [5].

normal sense of that word, he had so planned it. Delaplaine, as later would Jared Sparks and Longacre and Herring, saw his series of illustrated biographies as never-ending. In April 1818 he stated that he had "made arrangements to continue the publication for years. It ought, indeed never to be discontinued." Such an expansive ambition could only end in failure. Delaplaine also failed to implement his plan, announced at the end of volume two, part one, to include facsimiles of each subject's handwriting, but both Sanderson and Longacre and Herring incorporated this idea into their projects.[29]

Why, then, was the *Repository* a financial failure? In part, Delaplaine was paying the price for being first to coordinate the production of accurate biographies with accurate likenesses based on paintings from life. In addition, he failed to establish a distribution network within the publishing industry. He used as his agents personal friends and previous associates in the mercantile field who could not do the type of promotion and selling that such a great project needed. And he failed because he overestimated his potential audience. As a one-man shop, he simply could not afford—as many European publishers could—to bear the financial burden until the project slowly gained sales and critical acceptance. This problem was to plague every publisher of multiple-volume fine art books before the Civil War. The capital investment involved, combined with the long development, execution time, and slow sales, would doom every large-format publication to be a millstone around the neck of its creator.

The final blow, in Delaplaine's case, was the depression and financial panic of 1819. With his resources already stretched before the onset of the depression, he could not survive extended pressure on his finances. Delaplaine had claimed in 1816 that he had already spent more than eleven thousand dollars on the *Repository* project, an amount which would have taxed even the largest American publisher.[30]

Oblivious to the danger, Delaplaine announced his final grandiose idea—a national gallery for the portraits of America's heroes. With typical

---

29   "Delaplaine's Notes on the Repository, vol. 1," DSiP copy, p. [1]; *Repository,* vol. 2, part 1, rear printed wrapper; [Caldwell], *Author Turned Critic,* Delaplaine's advertising pages, p. [5]; and Delaplaine to E[zra] Ames, April 10, 1818, case 6, box 21, American Literary Miscellaneous, Gratz Collection, PHi.

30   The eleven-thousand figure was contained in a letter, Delaplaine to Ashbel Green, Sept. 24, 1816, case 6, box 21, American Literary Miscellaneous, Gratz Collection,

romantic brash, he called it "Delaplaine's National Panzographia for the Reception of the Portraits of Distinguished Americans." He issued a prospectus for it in December 1818 and opened his gallery to the public on January 1, 1819, using the portraits collected for the *Repository*. But it was not the success he had hoped it would be. Facing stiff competition from the long-established Peale Museum, as well as half-a-dozen other galleries and viewing rooms in Philadelphia, the Panzographia limped along until 1823 when Joseph Reed, recorder of the city of Philadelphia, took it over, probably in payment for a loan to Delaplaine. Reed sold it to Rubens Peale, who had plans to move it to a city with less competition for the limited museum audience. Delaplaine, his health declining, was reduced to doing odd editorial jobs for Mathew Carey. Bills were paid, if at all, by bartering engravings for services. Finally, his body racked with tuberculosis, Joseph Delaplaine died, probably penniless, on May 31, 1824.[31]

Sanderson's Biography of the Signers to the Declaration of Independence, 1820-27

The true story of John and Joseph Sanderson's *Biography of the Signers to the Declaration of Independence* is so complex that one wonders if the participants knew what was happening themselves. But the traditional accounts of its almost decade-long birth struggle reads more like a simple morality play. Dr. James Rush recorded one version of the story in an undated pencil note inside the first volume of his set.[32] In the good doctor's

---

PHi, and referred only to vol. 1, part 1. Later, in a letter to James N. Barker, Nov. 23, 1819, case 6, box 21, Gratz Collection, PHi, Delaplaine claimed that the cost of his portrait gallery and the *Repository* was twenty-three thousand dollars. This larger figure may be the total cost of all of his many print, book, and gallery projects. In the same letter to Barker, Delaplaine reported he was so poor that he had "frequently for two days together, not sufficient money to go to market."

31   Heinz, pp. 20–22; *Prospectus of Delaplaine's National Panzographia, for the Reception of the Portraits of Distinguished Americans* (Philadelphia, 1818); Delaplaine to Mathew Carey, Feb. 20, 1823, folder 17, box 85, Carey Manuscripts, Edward Carey Gardiner Collection, PHi. Delaplaine paid a dental bill with a print or a painting, *The Dream of Lord Nelson;* see Dr. Edward Hudson to Delaplaine, April 28, 1823, Society Manuscript Collection, PHi; and obituary of Delaplaine in *American Daily Advertiser* (Philadelphia), May 31, 1824.

32   James Rush, manuscript pencil note inside vol. 1 of PPL copy of Sanderson's *Biography*. The correct title of the work is "Biography of the Signers *to* the Declaration of Independence." The word "of" was not used in place of the "to" until the 1847 one-volume edition, revised and edited by Robert T. Conrad and published by Thomas, Cowperthwait and Company.

6

Left to right: John Sanderson, 1783-1844; Henry D. Gilpin, 1801-1860; and
Robert Waln, Jr., 1794-1825. Lithograph, circa 1830, by Albert Newsam,
12.2 × 10.5 cm.; engraving, date unknown, by H. W. Hodson after Henry
Inman, 11.2 × 9.2 cm.; and anonymous wood engraving, date unknown,
11.5 × 9.7 cm. (*Historical Society of Pennsylvania, Philadelphia*)

version, John Sanderson (fig. 6), a Philadelphia schoolteacher and manager of the Clermont Seminary who had originated the idea and conducted
the work through volume two, was forced out of the project by "one of those
Yankee missionaries of impudence and trick." Sanderson's financial resources were limited, and the Yankee trickster, sensing the potential profit
of the project, induced the originator to give up his share in it. Rush was so
upset by the turn of events, he wrote, that he refused to accept the third
volume when it was sent to the subscribers. Years later, he had to complete
his set with odd volumes.

To contradict Dr. Rush, the project originated with Joseph M.
Sanderson, John's brother, a printer-publisher in Philadelphia since 1815
who had moved to Baltimore in late 1817. In 1818 Joseph announced in a
broadside that he would publish by subscription a work entitled A *Biography of the Signers to the Declaration of Independence,* edited by Paul Allen
and accompanied by plates.[33] Evidently, Joseph did not get a sufficient

33 H. Glenn Brown and Maude O. Brown, *A Directory of the Book-Arts and Book Trade
in Philadelphia to 1820* (New York, 1950), p. 105, locates Joseph M. Sanderson in
Philadelphia only in 1817. But for proof that he was in the city earlier, see *Circular.*

response in Baltimore, for he moved back to Philadelphia in October 1819, issuing a new prospectus there in pamphlet form.[34] The engraver of the "upwards of fifty portraits" was to be James Barton Longacre (fig. 7), who had just finished his indenture with George Murray; the printer, known for his fine presswork, was to be James Maxwell. The influence of Delaplaine's *Repository* was evident, for Joseph Sanderson planned to publish his biographies in numbers or half volumes of two hundred pages each, with ten issues completing the series. The price was to be $2.50 per number. Joseph assured his potential subscribers that the first number was then in press and would be published in January 1820.

This first volume was actually a 224-page history of the American colonies written by Joseph's brother, John Sanderson, with an engraved title page and four plates of autographs copied from John Binn's 1818 facsimile of the Declaration of Independence.[35] Appended was a 43-page sample biography of John Hancock with an engraved portrait by Longacre after a painting by John Singleton Copley. The text was disjointed, repetitious, and poorly worded. John Sanderson apologized to his readers

---

Philadelphia, October 2d, 1815 ... (caption title) [Philadelphia, 1815], 3 pages, Stauffer Collection, no. 2477, PHi. For Sanderson in Baltimore, see Rollo Silver, *The Baltimore Book Trade, 1800–1825* (New York, 1953), p. 49. The broadside is listed as entry no. 45632 in Ralph R. Shaw and Richard H. Shoemaker, *American Bibliography: A Preliminary Checklist for 1818* (New York, 1963). The Library of the National Archives is cited as possessing the broadside, but it cannot be located. That it was printed is proved by Caesar A. Rodney's letter to Joseph M. Sanderson, Dec. 13, 1818, vol. 79, Henry D. Gilpin Papers, Gilpin Family Collection, PHi, in which the proposals are mentioned, and in Sanderson to Thomas Jefferson, Dec. 9, 1818, in "The Jefferson Papers," *Collections of the Massachusetts Historical Society*, 7th ser., 1 (1900): 273–74.

34 Joseph M. Sanderson, *Proposals by ... for Publishing by Subscription A Biography of the Signers to the Declaration of Independence. Accompanied with Plates, and the Declaration Itself with Fac-simile Engravings of the Signatures. By John Sanderson. To the Public ...* [Philadelphia: 1819], PPAmP copy.

35 Anna Lane Lingelbach, "John Sanderson," *DAB;* Rufus Griswold, *The Prose Writers of America...*, 2d ed., rev. (Philadelphia, 1847), pp. 239–40. For the relationship between John and Joseph M. Sanderson, see James M. Sanderson, *My Record in Rebeldom, as Written by Friend and Foe ...* (New York, 1865), p. 94. The plates of autographs were made by John Warr, Jr., who specialized in design and signature engraving. Longacre frequently used other engravers to do lettering and decorative borders, which he disliked doing himself.

7

James Barton Longacre, 1794-1869. Watercolor, circa 1845, self-portrait,
26 × 20.2 cm. (*National Portrait Gallery, Smithsonian Institution*)

in the preface that "this number is offered under disadvantages, which may not exist with the succeeding ones." He explained that it had been written during the evenings and that he had been deprived of the chance of revision or correction. He promised that this would not happen with the second number.[36]

Work on the second volume proceeded more smoothly. It did not appear until August 1822 and contained but four biographies. The Sandersons tried to avoid the criticism leveled at previous projects, that they were mere collections of unrelated fragmentary sketches, by connecting the individual biographies to form a narrative history of the winning of American independence. But, even with the additional editorial time devoted to the second volume, it was necessary to append eight pages of notes, corrections, and additions.

The conception of chronological history told through individual biographies did not meet with universal critical approval.[37] The most damaging criticisms were made by Robert Walsh in the *National Gazette and Literary Register* on August 19, 1822. Characterizing John Sanderson's literary style as "extremely pedantic and awkward," he also found little evidence of the use of primary sources in the biographies: "Here, are no *Lives* properly so called, but, for the most part, only loose outlines and meagre notices, possessing no peculiar merit of arrangement, diction or general observation." After first admiring the fine typography and the engravings, he then declared that the portraits could never approach the beauty of the impression and engraving in Delaplaine's work. Longacre's use of a George Wythe portrait from a magazine called the *American Gleaner* as a source for his own engraving suggested to Walsh that the images lacked authenticity. His final and most serious charge was that "almost the whole substance" of the 153-page biography of Benjamin Franklin in volume two had been taken from Delaplaine and was clearly an "absolute and resolute case of plagiarism."

This vituperative attack began a round robin of acrimony in the newspapers. In the August 22 issue of John Binns's *Democratic Press*, two

---

36 Sanderson, *Biography* 1:[2].

37 The critic for the *American Quarterly Review* was generally approving of the project but added: "Looseness of style, and unnecessary repetition of historical narratives and political reflections, are the faults with which some of the later volumes must be taxed." "Art. I. American Biography," *American Quarterly Review* 1, no. 1 (March 1827): 6–7.

anonymous writers pointed out that Walsh himself was the author of the *Repository* biography of Franklin, which he had offered to the Sandersons for sixty dollars without Delaplaine's consent. Walsh's enmity had been aroused when the unethical offer was refused. On August 29 John Binns printed Walsh's reply. He asserted that permission to offer the work had been obtained from Delaplaine and that, even if it had not, he had never been fully paid by Delaplaine and was thus free of any obligation. John Sanderson responded two days later in the same paper, charging that Walsh had willfully distorted the negotiations between Joseph Sanderson, Delaplaine, and himself. While asserting that straightforward chronological biographies were bound to have parallels when the authors used the same published memoirs, he did admit to borrowing "three or four incidents, and those of very trivial importance." In a final volley, he accused Walsh of disregarding the bounds of normal criticism by engaging in character assassination.

Despite the controversy, the first two volumes were apparently popular. But in late 1822 and early 1823 drastic changes were made in the project. John Sanderson left, just as James Rush had said. His replacement was not, however, some Yankee interloper, but Robert Waln, Jr. (see fig. 6), the talented son of a Philadelphia mercantile family.[38] Joseph M. Sanderson's place as publisher was taken by Ralph W. Pomeroy, a former Baltimore printer recently arrived in Philadelphia.[39] The exit of the two Sandersons was probably caused by a gradual slide into economic difficulty rather than one sudden financial shock. The project had been underfinanced from the beginning and had always taken a back seat to John Sanderson's more lucrative ventures. By the time he began to consolidate his business affairs in the spring of 1822, he had already turned over half of the editorial chores to Waln. When volume three finally was issued in July 1823, after further delays caused by the bankruptcy in May of James

38   John C. Mendenhall, "Robert Waln, Jr." *DAB*; and William S. Hastings, "Robert Waln, Jr.: Quaker Satirist and Historian," *Pennsylvania Magazine of History and Biography* 76 (1952): 71–80.

39   Pomeroy announced his move to Philadelphia in the (Baltimore) *Federal Gazette*, Oct. 2, 1819; see Silver, pp. 46–47, and Emily Ellsworth Ford Skeel, ed., *Mason Lock Weems: His Works and Ways*, 3 vols. (New York, 1929), 1:106, 128, 243, 398, and 3:114 n.2, 162, 302, 348.

Maxwell, the printer, Waln was listed on the title page as the only editor.[40]

By this time, the pretext of partial volumes (or numbers) had been dropped, and the number of biographies included in each volume had increased to seven. Waln is credited with writing only one of the biographies in volume three, but we know from his notes that he did more than just edit the copy which came in from Hugh McCall, DeWitt Clinton, Arthur Middleton, Edward Everett, William Wolcott, and Henry Stockton. Sometimes he received only the barest outline of a life and had to put the flesh on the bones himself. Often he had to verify all of the assertions made by his authors, who frequently worked from memory and family tradition.[41]

In a preface to the third volume, the new publisher, Pomeroy, assured his subscribers that there would be an improvement in the series. Volumes would now appear with greater frequency and would be edited with "a more careful attention than Mr. [John] Sanderson's limited leisure has permitted him to bestow on the first volumes." For a time the promise was upheld. By the end of 1823, despite publishing a book on his experiences in China at the same time, Robert Waln had completed the draft of eight biographies for volume four.[42] Through sheer persistence, he had overcome the paucity of original, reliable sources, the reluctance of relatives to lend manuscripts, and the inability of his authors to write a coherent account of their common experience and produced the texts for two full volumes within a year.

40   Waln to Timothy Pitkin, Aug. 12, 1822, Sterling Memorial Library, Yale University, New Haven (hereinafter CtY); Maxwell's assignment of assets to Thomas Bradford, Jr., dated May 22, 1823, in *Aurora and General Advertiser*, June 5, 1823. See also Waln to Roger S. Baldwin, July 28, 1823, CtY.

41   Robert Waln, "Memoranda and Notes," vol. 79, Henry D. Gilpin Papers, Gilpin Family Collection, PHi.

42   In his letter to the Rev. Ashbel Green, Dec. 10, 1823, case 6, box 13, Gratz Collection, PHi, Waln refers to the text of the fourth volume as "having been, for some time, prepared, & now on the eve of publication." Although the imprint on vol. 4 reads 1823 and the copyright notice is dated May 1, 1823, this letter proves that actual printing of this volume did not begin until December. Waln's book *China: Comprehending a View of the Origin of That Empire and a Full Description of American Trade to Canton* (Philadelphia, 1823) was published in four parts, quarto, and totaled 475 pages in length.

Pomeroy, too, had been busy. In addition to reorganizing the whole project and refinancing James Maxwell so that he could continue as the project's printer, Pomeroy spent the summer and fall of 1823 publicizing the series to secure new subscribers and to counteract any adverse effects which the change in editor and publisher might have had. He succeeded in both his aims, necessitating the reprinting of volumes one and two. Consequently, volume four was delayed until mid-1824, and new postponements were projected for the fifth and sixth volumes. Waln, a hired editor on salary with little concern for sales and promotion, was annoyed, and he began to devote increasingly more time to other projects. He finished the last biographies for volume five in the fall of 1824 but began to fall behind in his work on volume six. Furthermore, he persuaded Maxwell to set aside the Pomeroy series to print his own full-length biography of Lafayette. Finally, under pressure from Pomeroy, he began again, in the spring of 1825, to send in copy, submitting in June his essay on Stephen Hopkins, the eleventh of the twelve biographies for volume six. One month later, before he could finish the last biography, he suddenly died.[43]

A long suspension ensued while Pomeroy tried to find another man with equal literary talents. He finally settled on Henry D. Gilpin (see fig. 6), a lawyer and friend of Waln and, although only twenty-four, already the author of several short biographies serialized in Philadelphia magazines.[44] Gilpin set to work immediately. He completed the revisions of Waln's biography of Layfayette and saw it the remaining way through the press. Next he began the thankless task of sifting through his friend's papers. Gilpin found volume six almost done, lacking only one biography, that of Benjamin Harrison. Rather than take the time to finish the missing biography, Gilpin cut Waln's original number to nine, holding back the biographies of John Hurt and Francis Lightfoot Lee already printed. Gilpin

43   [Robert Waln], "Daily Mem[oranda] continued from No. I," and John Farmer to Waln, Sept. 28, 1824, vol. 79, Henry D. Gilpin Papers, Gilpin Family Collection, PHi; Waln to Samuel W. Dana, Jan. 6, 1825, Boston Public Library; Waln to Timothy Pitkin, Jan. 6 and Jan. 30, 1825, Henry E. Huntington Library, San Marino, Calif.; R. W. Pomeroy to Waln, May 27, 1824, vol. 79, Henry D. Gilpin Papers, PHi; and the letters between Waln and Thomas McKean, March 14, 1824–June 14, 1825, vol. 5, pp. 22–33, Thomas McKean Papers, PHi.

44   Ralph D. Gray, "Henry D. Gilpin: A Pennsylvania Jacksonian," *Pennsylvania History* 36, no. 4 (Oct. 1970): 340–51; Gilpin to P. Paca, April 29, 1826, vol. 79, Henry D. Gilpin Papers, Gilpin Family Collection, PHi.

had only to do some proofreading, and volume six was ready for the subscribers.

Within a year and a half of Waln's death, the last three volumes began to appear. Gilpin had the ninth, and final, volume completed near the end of 1827. Twenty-one biographies were encompassed in volumes seven through nine. Waln had already written two of these and had begun work on a third. In Gilpin's new scheme, these biographies would not be used until the last volume. Gilpin needed help, and he found it in the person of Edward Ingersoll, a fellow lawyer and published poet and author. With the help of Henry B. Latrobe and J. C. Hooper, Gilpin and Ingersoll brought out the seventh volume of six biographies in record time. Gilpin is credited with writing nine, and Ingersoll six, of the biographies in the last three volumes.[45]

But the difficulty of maintaining quality while producing so much text so fast was evident. Readers expecting Robert Waln's measured and mildly "heroic" prose must have found the style in the Gilpin volumes hurried and sketchy. Several biographies appear to have been assembled with scissors and paste rather than written, particularly the nine biographies crammed into volume nine. William Ellery's biography, although credited to Gilpin, was largely Waln's draft cut up and rearranged; the biography of Samuel Adams contained more than eight pages from Delaplaine's *Repository* and at least two from the second volume of Richard Henry Lee, Jr.'s biography of his father. While it was usual in this period for authors to quote from other works without credit, Gilpin appears to have exceeded common practice.[46]

45 For Ingersoll, see *Appleton's Cyclopedia of American Biography* (New York, 1888–89), 3:348. Gilpin had read law in the office of Joseph R. Ingersoll. A list of the authors of the biographies in the Sanderson-Pomeroy series first appeared in the *New York Times* and was copied into the *Daily Cincinnati Gazette* of Aug. 11, 1827. This list was reproduced without correction in the *Proceedings of the Massachusetts Historical Society* 15 (1876–77):393. A similar list was published in William Brotherhead, ed., *The Book of the Signers* (Philadelphia, 1861), pp. iii–iv. However, all of these lists are incorrect in at least one respect: the biography of George Wythe was not written by Thomas Jefferson but by William R. Smith. See Smith to John W. Forney and Smith to John A. McAllister, Nov. 20, 1860, box 75 (7381.F.23), McAllister Collection, PPL. See also Appendix 2.

46 Based on an analysis of two manuscript volumes labeled "Biographies of Signers of the Declaration of Independence," vols. 1–2, Henry D. Gilpin Papers, Gilpin Family Collection, PHi.

The stress of the increased production schedule also became evident in the portrait engravings. Through volume six, James Barton Longacre had produced seventeen plates unaided and one, that of Francis Hopkinson, in conjunction with another engraver. Only three had to be turned over to other engravers to meet the publication deadlines. Simeon S. Jocelyn was asked to do the engravings for Roger Sherman's portrait, because the painting from which it was to be copied was in New Haven, Connecticut. Asher B. Durand did the plate of William Floyd from a painting in Joseph Delaplaine's gallery; and Durand's friend Charles Cushing Wright, an engraver-diesinker in Charleston, South Carolina, was asked to do the plate of Francis Lewis from a local painting.

But the bulk of the labor for the illustrations fell upon Longacre, alone and unaided. Not only did he supervise all the other artists and engravers as well as the actual printing of the plates, but he also began the practice, in the later volumes, of supplying the drawing from which the plate was engraved, a tactic he would use more frequently in his own series. Though smaller than the plates in Delaplaine's *Repository,* his portraits for the Sanderson-Pomeroy series, quickly engraved in stipple or line, were generally satisfactory as likenesses if uninspired as images (fig. 8).

In the portrait of Elbridge Gerry (fig. 9), the subject's family cooperated with Longacre on condition that the plate could also be used as the frontispiece to another Gerry biography. Using a drawing by John Vanderlyn owned by the family and following the suggestions and advice of Elbridge Gerry, Jr., and Thomas Russell Gerry, Longacre engraved and printed the plate for Pomeroy. Afterward, he reworked the same plate for James T. Austin's biography.[47]

Whether Longacre frequently found secondary uses for his Sanderson plates is not known, but he was involved simultaneously in other multiple-plate projects and particularly in marketing his own large engravings for the commercial art market. He was often forced to take shortcuts

47 Elbridge Gerry, Jr., to Longacre, Oct. 4, 1826, folder 18, box 1, Longacre Collection, PPL. Compare the plate of Elbridge Gerry that Longacre did for vol. 8 of Sanderson-Pomeroy and the frontispiece in vol. 1 of James T. Austin, *The Life of Elbridge Gerry, with Contemporary Letters, to the Close of the Revolution,* 2 vols. (Boston, 1828).

JEFFERSON.

THE great tragic poet of antiquity has observed, and historians and philosophers in every age, have repeated the observation, that no one should be pronounced happy, till death has closed the period of human uncertainty. Yet if to be happy, is to descend into the vale of years, loved and honoured; to enjoy in life, that posthumous fame, which is usually bestowed only beyond the tomb; to see the labours of our earlier years, crowned with more than hoped for success; and to find those theoretic visions which untried, could offer nothing more than expected excellence, exceeding in practical utility their promised advantages; if these can confer aught of happiness on this side the grave, then may the subject of our memoir be esteemed truly happy.

He has indeed outlived those who were the partners of his toils, and the companions of his earlier years; but in so doing, he has not experienced the usual fate of mortality, in outliving the sympathy, the kindness and the love of his fellow creatures. A new race of companions has risen around him, who have added to those feelings the deeper ones of admiration, respect, and gratitude; and he still lives in the bosom of his country, which is

VOL. VII.—B

8
Thomas Jefferson, 1743-1826. Engraving, circa 1827, by James B. Longacre after Robert Field after Gilbert Stuart, 10 × 8.4 cm. From *Biography of the Signers to the Declaration of Independence,* vol. 7 (Philadelphia, 1827) (*National Portrait Gallery, Smithsonian Institution*)

ELBRIDGE GERRY.

ELBRIDGE GERRY was born in the small town of Marblehead, in the province of Massachusetts Bay, in the month of July, 1744. Of his family and early history, we have been able to obtain but few particulars, and indeed in recording the history of his life, important and interesting as it is, we have greatly to regret the difficulty of obtaining materials, beyond the common and temporary records which are open to the public inspection.

The father of Mr. Gerry is said to have been a respectable merchant of Marblehead, and to have acquired a considerable fortune by his commercial pursuits. His son was placed at Harvard University, where he passed through the usual collegiate studies with much literary reputation and success; he there received the degree of bachelor of arts in the year 1762. After leaving college, he turned his attention to that line of life in which his father's prosperity seemed to hold out the greatest inducements to a young and enterprising mind; and he plunged at once into the most active pursuits of commerce. His fairness, correctness and assiduity, and the extensive knowledge of commercial con-

9
Elbridge Gerry, 1744-1814. Engraving, circa 1827, by James B. Longacre after John Vanderlyn, 10 × 8.4 cm. From *Biography of the Signers to the Declaration of Independence,* vol. 8 (Philadelphia, 1827). (*National Portrait Gallery, Smithsonian Institution*)

with the illustrations to stay on schedule.[48] Frequently a plate for the Sanderson-Pomeroy series was copied from one engraved earlier for a different publisher. The portrait of Franklin for volume two was from the same plate, retouched and slightly changed, that he had engraved for Delaplaine's *Repository*. His image of Francis Hopkinson, engraved with the help of J. Nesmith, was based on J. Heath's engraving in the *Repository* rather than the original painting by Robert Edge Pine. Altering the face slightly, particularly around the mouth, and dropping out part of the chair and a large vertical book, he published it as his own.

This was not the way Longacre preferred to work. He considered himself an original artist rather than a mechanical copyist. It was a matter of personal pride for him to make his own interpretive drawing on which to base his engraving. But he was forced to adopt the "borrowing" expedient because of the number of plates to be done, the difficulty of locating a suitable original oil portrait, the reluctance of owners to allow copying, and the wide geographical dispersal of those portraits.

By the end of 1827 Longacre could look back with pride, if not entirely with pleasure, at eight years of labor during which he engraved, did the original drawing, or supervised the printing of thirty-one portrait engravings, one engraved title page, and four pages of facsimile autographs. The early plates were, on the whole, workmanlike and competent likenesses. By the end of the series, his ability as an artist and engraver had grown to the extent that even a hurried effort demonstrated his command of the medium.

The project had taken nine years to complete and had consumed the talents of seven men. Pomeroy had paid $2,700 in authors' fees alone, and the final monetary cost of the project, including engraving, printing, paper, and binding, may have exceeded $10,000.[49] Although he had

---

48 Among Longacre's other portrait engravings for a series were ones for Mathias Lopez and Francis C. Wemyss, eds., . . . *Acting American Theatre, Containing the Most Popular Plays* . . . , 4 vols. (Philadelphia, 1826–27); and for Matthew Henry, *An Exposition of the Old and New Testaments* . . . , 6 vols. (New York and Philadelphia, 1828–29). Among his large, special "art" portrait engravings were *Charles Carroll of Carrollton*, after Chester Harding, and *Andrew Jackson*, after Thomas Sully.

49 The author's fees were $1 for each printed page (R. W. Pomeroy's note, Oct. 3, 1825, vol. 79, Henry D. Gilpin Papers, PHi). The engravers' fees were $75 per

probably made a reasonable profit from the venture, he hurriedly sold the rights and plates for the series in 1827 to William Brown and C. Peters, who issued a five-volume abridged edition in 1828. Pomeroy remained a publisher but preferred thereafter the safety of common editions of the Bible, the classics, and English literature. After the Brown and Peters edition of the *Biography,* there were six later versions. But each successive new edition was abridged and edited until the original content was barely recognizable. And the style of illustration and its execution became increasingly ugly and ornate.

The contemporary critical reaction to the Sanderson-Pomeroy series underwent a similar transformation. In the beginning, except for the harsh judgments of Robert Walsh, it had been uniformly warm and laudatory. Noting in 1822 that "the praises of editors and other individuals throughout the union have been profuse but gratuitous; they have not been bought by extortion or bribery," John Sanderson was understandably amazed by Walsh's criticism and implied that it was not in the best interests of American letters. After the exchange between the two, John Binns, in the *Democratic Press,* began to impugn Walsh for anglophilia and anti-American attitudes. It was difficult for any critic to pass fair judgment on any of these collected illustrated biographies given the noble intent of the publishers and the patriotism of the editors, artists, and writers. John Everett even began his 1823 review with the statement: "We feel it a kind of national duty to recommend to our readers any publication of respectable claims, which has for its end to commemorate the great events in our history."[50]

By 1832, however, the critical tide had turned against the Sanderson-Pomeroy series. A new spirit of history was taking hold, and its practitioners demanded accuracy above all else. When Jared Sparks informed John Quincy Adams of his plans for a series of biographies, Adams commented: "[Sanderson's] 'Lives of the Signers' are all eulogies, is it

---

copperplate (Peter Maverick to Longacre, March 8, 1827, Longacre Collection, PPL). By my calculations, based on known costs (approximately $10,000), the publisher would have to sell 444 sets at full retail price ($22.50) to break even.

50 John Sanderson, "To the Editor," *Democratic Press* (Philadelphia), Aug. 31, 1822, p. 2, cols. 1–2; the attack on Walsh's other writings is in the September 18, 1822, and following, issues of the same newspaper. John Everett, "[Review] Art. XII," *North American Review,* n.s., 16, no. 13 (January 1823): 182–96.

intended that your 'Library of Biography' should be so?" The new critical standards that were evolving, when fully developed, would mean the end of the age of heroic biography.[51]

James Barton Longacre and James Herring's National Portrait Gallery, 1833–39

Issued in four volumes between 1833 and 1839, James Barton Longacre and James Herring's *National Portrait Gallery* was the literal descendant of the Delaplaine and Sanderson-Pomeroy series.[52] Though intimately aware of the difficulty and expense of undertaking a large and complex work, Longacre chose to ignore the potential problems and launch his own project. A collection of illustrated biographies was a natural ambition for him; the focus of his career had been portraiture. When he was a nineteen-year-old apprentice of George Murray, his friend and mentor John Fanning Watson had assured him that his future lay in the engraving of portraits.[53] In a letter to James Herring in October 1831, Longacre stated that he had been dreaming and planning his gallery of portraits for nearly seven years. These dreams had helped to "beguile the tediousness and disappointments of [his] professional career," and only a lack of financing had prevented his undertaking the project before. Business successes in the years 1829–31 finally gave him the personal capital he needed to begin.[54]

Longacre, however, had already commenced work before full financing was assured. Late in 1829 or early in 1830, letters were sent to famous politicians and statesmen to secure their promise of cooperation well in advance of the formal series announcement. Longacre had learned from

51   John Quincy Adams to Sparks, Dec. 1, 1832, in Herbert B. Adams, ed., *The Life and Writings of Jared Sparks*, 2 vols. (Boston and New York, 1893), 2:193.

52   The basic history of the project, including a detailed discussion of each portrait, has been recounted in Robert G. Stewart, *A Nineteenth-Century Gallery of Distinguished Americans. Exhibition 22 February–1 May 1969* (Washington, D.C., 1969). Unless otherwise indicated, all information about Longacre, Herring, and the *National Portrait Gallery* series is from this source.

53   Watson deviated only once from this opinion, when he recommended Longacre as the engraver of the historical painting *Penn's Treaty with the Indians* in Watson to Longacre, Nov. 21, 1826, in interleaved manuscript copy of Watson's *Annals*, pp. 178–79, PHi, and Watson to Robert Vaux, Nov. 24, 1826, box 4, Robert Vaux Papers, PHi.

54   Longacre to Herring, Oct. 28, 1831, Longacre Letterbook, 1830–37, box 4, Longacre Collection, PPL.

his involvement with the Sanderson-Pomeroy series that there was no such thing as too much advance planning. In Delaplaineian fashion, Longacre engraved several portraits as samples of the finished work, and by mid-1830 he had at least one biographical sketch in hand, written by Robert Y. Hayne.[55]

Even at this early stage, Longacre's peculiar artistic nationalism was evident. Because he intended his series to include only living subjects, it was vital to its success that everything about the series be nonpartisan. To be able to sell in all parts of the country, it was mandatory that the series not be tainted by the rising tide of sectionalism brought on by the nullification controversy of 1828–32. Longacre therefore edited the Hayne essay to remove any "expressions calculated to give a [political] party aspect to the narrative." Further, he planned to give greater emphasis to the engravings than any previous series had done. The biographies would be little more than filler between slices of heroic art. He also stated that impartiality was of the utmost importance because the book was "calculated to produce a community of feeling, most desirable at this period— It introduces the Arts, as a peace offering to the angry and jealous passions, that are striking at our Nation's heart."[56]

Late in 1830 or early 1831, Longacre signed a contract with Samuel F. Bradford to supply fifteen hundred copies of a work to be called the *American Portrait Gallery*. Sales agents were engaged, subscription papers issued, publicity circulars mailed to all parts of the country, and a thousand dollars of Longacre's own funds invested in engraving plates before he saw the prospectus for a similar undertaking that James Herring issued in October 1831.[57]

---

55 Longacre to Hayne, July 24, 1830, to [William] Wirt, June 29, Oct. 22, 1831, Longacre Letterbook, 1830–37, box 4, Longacre Collection, PPL; Longacre to ? (possibly a circular letter to journalists or reviewers), circa 1836–39, folder 37 "Undated letters and Fragments," box 2, Longacre Collection, PPL.

56 Ibid.

57 Longacre to ?, circa 1836–39, folder 37, box 2, and Longacre to Herring, Oct. 28, 1831, Longacre Letterbook, 1830–37, box 4, Longacre Collection, PPL. An advertisement for "The American Portrait Gallery" first appeared in the *Washington Daily National Intelligencer*, Feb. 12, 1831, p. 3, stating that the size was to be royal octavo, that each of four yearly numbers was to contain four plates, and that the first number would be issued in the summer of 1831. The cost was to be five dollars a year. No trace of this first number has been found.

Following the shock of discovering a rival in a field he thought was his alone, Longacre joined forces with his New York counterpart.[58] Both men were the same age, thirty-seven, and both were artists. But there the similarity ended. Where Longacre had always been an artist, James Herring came to art later in life and was a largely self-taught portrait painter. Herring began his career in a commission merchant firm and in 1809 found employment in his father's brewery. He ran away in 1810 to become a teacher in Wantage, New York, but returned to the brewery within a year. The business failed in 1812, and his father died two years later. Herring was now free to pursue a career in the arts, first as a colorer of prints in New York City and Philadelphia and later as a maker of profiles. When he returned to New York in 1822, it was as a portrait painter and art entrepreneur. His fascination with art and literature led him to found, in 1830, a large private circulating library, the Enterprise Library.[59] The following year, while he was secretary of the American Academy of Fine Arts, Herring proposed that the academy sponsor the publication of his work *The National Portrait Gallery of Distinguished Americans* and the formation of a National Portrait Gallery. An academy committee was to superintend the selection of paintings for the gallery, their execution as engravings, and "the literary part of the work."[60]

Herring's 1831 plan was markedly different from Longacre's. More closely following Delaplaine's lead, the New Yorker planned a "national monument." Portraits of figures from America's past as well as the present, with a longer biographical record of their contributions to the rising nation, would be included. Herring took as his model the English

58   Samuel F. Bradford was probably very happy to void his contract with Longacre, because he had just become the publisher for Thomas L. McKenney and John Hall's massive *History of the Indian Tribes of America*, which would prove to be among the causes of his bankruptcy within two years. See Herman J. Viola, *The Indian Legacy of Charles Bird King* (Washington, D.C., and New York, 1976), p. 74.

59   Stewart, p. 1; George C. Groce and David H. Wallace, *The New-York Historical Society's Dictionary of Artists in America, 1564–1860* (New Haven, 1957), p. 311; James Herring, "Autobiography," and biographical notes by George T. Mortimer, Jr., Manuscript Collection, New-York Historical Society; William Dunlap, *History of the Rise and Progress of the Arts of Design in the United States,* ed. Alexander Wyckoff, 3 vols. (1834; rev. ed., 1918; new ed., New York, 1965), 3:73–76.

60   Stewart, p. 1; Mary Bartlett Cowdrey, *American Academy of Fine Arts and American Art-Union: Introduction, 1816–1852,* (New York, 1953), p. 50.

The National Portrait Gallery, 12 parts in yellow wrappers. By James B. Longacre and James Herring. Vol. 1, pts. 1-12 (Philadelphia, [1833]-1839). (*Library Company of Philadelphia*)

work by William Jerdan entitled the *National Portrait Gallery,* which was then enjoying rapid sales in the United States.[61]

Longacre, having garnered only fifteen or twenty subscribers for his *American Portrait Gallery,* was willing to adapt his ideas to Herring's. The final form of the book, originally issued in twelve numbers per volume (fig. 10), "has lost something in unity of design," Longacre noted, "but has gained in becoming more national, historical, and less egotistical, and perhaps better adapted to the present condition of taste and information

61 William Jerdan, *National Portrait Gallery of Illustrious and Eminent Personages of the Nineteenth Century, with Memoirs* . . . , 5 vols. (London, 1830–34). See also William Jerdan, *Autobiography* . . . , 4 vols. London, 1852–53), 4:302. Both the Jerdan series and Charles Knight, *Gallery of Portraits, with Memoirs* (London, 1833), followed the trail blazed by Edmund Lodge, *Portraits and Memoirs of the Most Illustrious Personages of British History,* which began to be published in 1821 and was already into a third edition by 1829. Many other English portrait series were being issued in this period. See Henry M. Hake, *Catalogue of Engraved British Portraits Preserved in the Department of Prints and Drawings in the British Museum* (London, 1925), 6 (Supplement and Indexes): 721–38.

amongst that portion of society, to whose support, the enterprise must chiefly look.''[62] By this he meant that if Americans would not buy a product of their own country's design and conception, perhaps a Yankee Doodle project dressed up in John Bull's clothes would be more acceptable.

The new partners followed Herring's English model in giving each biography its own pagination, so that it could be issued as a fascicle when ready and later combined into volumes when enough were finished. They sought to avoid Delaplaine's fate by issuing their portrait series in several formats: royal quarto, imperial octavo, and royal octavo. Different-quality papers would be used for each size, and special proof copies of the engraved plates would also be available. Volumes could be purchased unbound in parts, bound in cloth, or, for the discriminating bibliophile, a special embossed plaque binding (fig. 11) of long-grained green or red morocco by Benjamin Gaskill, Jr., was available. Longacre and Herring planned to appeal to every aspect of the book market—from those interested in the finest art book to those concerned with procuring a serviceable biographical reference tool.[63]

James Herring seems to have been the smarter businessman of the two. His duties in the project were limited to promoting, supervising, writing some biographies, and occasionally sketching copies of the portraits from which the engravings were made. His main function was to secure subscribers, which he did with great success, obtaining nearly a thousand in New York City and another thousand in the New England states. Philadelphia, according to Longacre, "with all her fame for science and refinement," returned less than two hundred subscribers.[64] All of the

62   Longacre to ?, circa 1836–39, folder 37, box 2, Longacre Collection, PPL.

63   Longacre and Herring, National Portrait Gallery *Prospectus*, [circa 1836], folder 11, box 3, Longacre Collection, PPL. For Gaskill, see [Edwin Wolf 2nd], *The Annual Report of the Library Company of Philadelphia for the Year 1976* (Philadelphia, 1977), p. 56, and *The Annual Report of the Library Company of Philadelphia for the Year 1977* (Philadelphia, 1978), pp. 23–25. Also *Bibliothèque Raphäel Esmerian*, 4:11–12, item no. 2. Gaskill was the binder of the large, royal-quarto special edition only.

64   Longacre to ?, circa 1836–39, folder 37, box 2, Longacre Collection, PPL. For Longacre's growing concern over poor subscriptions, sales, and collections in the South and West, see Longacre to James Greenleaf, Aug. 24 and Oct. 3, 1836, and to Mr. Taylor, Aug. 30, 1836, Longacre Letterbook 1830–1837, box 4, Longacre Collection, PPL.

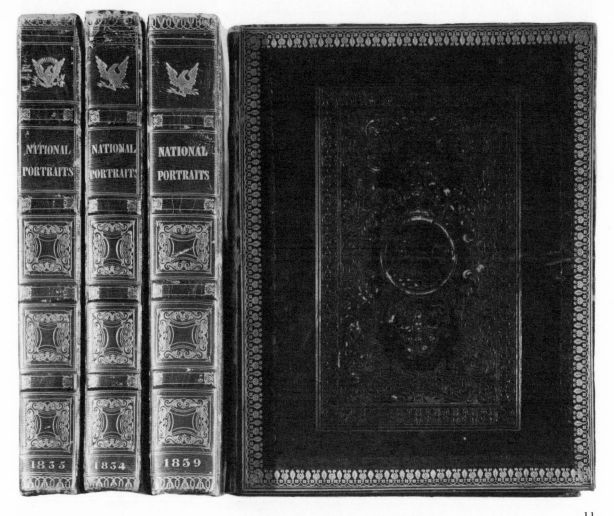

11

Green morocco leather embossed plaque bindings by Benjamin Gaskill, Jr. On royal quarto edition, 28.3 × 23 cm., of James B. Longacre and James Herring, *National Portrait Gallery*, 4 vols. (Philadelphia, 1834-39). (*Library Company of Philadelphia*)

plates from the New York half of the partnership bore the line "copyright James Herring." Not so astute a businessman, Longacre never found the time to copyright many of his engravings—which was clearly an oversight, since many were also issued separately.

Longacre had other details on his mind. The task of coordinating 144 plates done by twenty-six different engravers was awesome, even with Herring's assistance. Locating and copying original portraits was difficult and involved time-consuming travel. Longacre himself drew both copies and original life portraits in quick but accurate watercolor sketches (fig. 12). He also engraved a number of the plates and supervised their printing (fig. 13). Despite the enormity of the task, he achieved a standard of quality in these illustrations that far surpassed the two previous publications. Perhaps because he had full responsibility for the project, the engravings for the *National Portrait Gallery*—both his own and those he supervised (fig. 14)—are far better and more interesting images than his

12
Daniel Webster, 1782-1852. Watercolor, 1833, by James B. Longacre,
22.5 × 16.2 cm. (*National Portrait
Gallery, Smithsonian Institution*)

illustrations for the Sanderson-Pomeroy series. Longacre claimed that if
he "had any model at that time it was in the work of Robert Nanteuil
executed in the seventeenth century."[65] The dense texture of the *National
Portrait Gallery* prints, the simplicity of framing, and the clarity of image as
well as the accuracy of likeness and indication of character are reminiscent
of the great French portrait engraver. That Longacre could require such a

65 Longacre to ?, circa 1836–39, folder 37, box 2, Longacre Collection, PPL. See also
    T. H. Thomas, *French Portrait Engraving of the XVIIth and XVIIIth Centuries*
    (London, 1910), pp. 34–59.

13
Daniel Webster, 1782-1852. Engraving, copyright 1833, by James B. Longacre, 11.2 × 8.8 cm. From *National Portrait Gallery,* vol. 1 (Philadelphia, 1834). (*National Portrait Gallery, Smithsonian Institution*)

14
John Trumbull, 1756–1843. Engraving. copyright 1833, by Asher B. Durand after Samuel Lovett Waldo and William Jewett, 12 × 9.3 cm From *National Portrait Gallery,* vol. 1 (Philadelphia, 1834). (*National Portrait Gallery, Smithsonian Institution*)

level of technical quality and accuracy from his team of engravers was indeed an achievement of American arts.

The first bound volume of the series came out on schedule in 1834; the second appeared the following year. However, Longacre and Herring began to encounter the inevitable problems that had plagued their predecessors: delays in delivery, flagging subscription sales, difficulties in collecting remittances, and the necessity of training engravers to meet the quality demanded. In addition, a series of fires at the bindery in 1835 postponed the publication of volume three; and the Panic of 1837 delayed the fourth volume until 1839. These calamities and their attendant expenses pushed James Longacre into voluntary bankruptcy. He had incurred huge debts in his missionary pursuit of the perfect book, not the least of which was the amount owed to James Herring. Benjamin Gaskill, Jr., who had made the fine morocco embossed plaque bindings, was another major creditor. The bankruptcy helps to explain why some copies of the royal quarto volume four bear the publication date 1839 while others have 1840. Those with the latter date were issued to satisfy the demands of creditors using the original stereotyped plates. It is also probable that the creditors began the practice of selling an elegantly bound set of the plates without the text for twenty-five dollars.[66]

But even this final disaster did not break the spirit or the faith that Longacre had in the *National Portrait Gallery*. Until 1842 he was engaged in selling, for his creditors, the copies already printed. In this capacity he undertook numerous sales trips to the South and West to peddle his wares personally like the commonest saddlebag drummer, while his family acted as shipping agents and kept the accounts of sales and expenses.[67] Everything was sacrificed to pay his *National Portrait Gallery* debts, including

66 Indenture of assignment of assets to creditors, July 18, 1839, folder 7, box 3, Longacre Collection, PPL; "Assignees of the Estate of James B. Longacre Account Current Shewing the Results of all Business; First—from October to Aug. 12 1842. Second—from August 12 1842 to Jan. 1 1844," 5 pp., folder 2, box 3, Longacre Collection, PPL; undated memorandum in JBL's handwriting, undated letters and fragments, folder 37, box 2, Longacre Collection, PPL. His bankruptcy was ended by court order on Aug. 16, 1842, U.S. District Court Certificate no. 839, folder 7, box 3, Longacre Papers, PPL.

67 Sarah Longacre (daughter) to Longacre, Jan. 21, Feb. 21, 1841, Sarah and Eliza (wife) Longacre to Longacre, June 14, July 28, 1841, April 9, April 11, July 7, 1842, folders 38 and 39, box 2, Longacre Collection, PPL.

other engraved and stereotyped plates he had in his shop at the time of bankruptcy. His faith in his creation persisted through everything. Even when the plates had passed from his control and new, somewhat inferior editions were issued by others, Longacre voluntarily offered advice on how to rework the plates in order to extend their useful printing life. He never lost interest in the fate of the *National Portrait Gallery,* advising the later publishers in the 1850s on their choice of additional persons to include and on how best to use the plates that were still serviceable.[68]

In evaluating Longacre and Herring's *National Portrait Gallery,* it is only possible to echo Robert Stewart's judgment that it "was a monumental event" in the book arts, and the arts in general, in a country only fifty years old. It was the only major multivolumed portrait series with text to be completed true to its original conception. Longacre and Herring had realized Delaplaine's dream, and in a fashion he would have appreciated.

The Successors

The field of collected illustrated biographies, after Longacre and Herring's *National Portrait Gallery,* fell increasingly into the hands of more commercially minded men. A few, however, tried to surpass the efforts of the first three decades of the nineteenth century. One of the most ambitious was William H. Brown's *Portrait Gallery of Distinguished American Citizens,* published in Hartford in 1845 by the Kellogg brothers. Brown revised the standard formula of the previous projects. His biographies were even shorter, and the size of the page even larger, now a royal folio (i.e., 17″ × 13″) in size and format. Portraits were reproduced using what was by that time an old process, lithography, but they were based on Brown's silhouettes, cut from life with some characteristic aspect of the person's surroundings included in the picture (fig. 15). A full-page facsimile of the honored person's handwriting was included. Although Brown had avoided the problems of locating and copying oil paintings, his work was not a success; only one volume was published, although he clearly intended to continue.[69]

68 Longacre to L. J. Cist, Aug. 18, 1851, vol. 85, pp. 29–30, part 1, F. J. Dreer Collection, PHi; Longacre to Mr. Rogers, fragment, June 12, 1858, folder 37, box 2, Longacre Collection, PPL.

69 In his preface, Brown stated that he had wanted to publish fifty-four plates rather than the twenty-seven he finally issued. See William Henry Brown, *Portrait Gallery*

John Randolph, 1773-1833. Lithograph with tintstone, copyright 1844, by
Edmund Burke Kellogg and Elijah Chapman Kellogg after William Henry
Brown, 34 × 25.2 cm. From William Henry Brown, *Portrait Gallery of Distinguished American Citizens* (Hartford, 1845). (*Library Company of Philadelphia*)

More success was to come to those like Benson J. Lossing who "adapted" the work of the pioneers and issued cheap, small-format, single-volume editions with crude illustrations. In all, Lossing issued three works of collected illustrated biography. The first, *Biographical Sketches of the Signers,* published in 1848, was a scissors-and-paste job using Jared Sparks and the Sanderson-Pomeroy series as its construction material. The other two works, *Our Countrymen* (1855) and *Eminent Americans* (1857), used the same successful formula: stereotyped wood engravings for illustrations, crown octavo format (i.e., 7½" × 5" or smaller), narrow margins, undistinguished typography, and cheap paper. All the corner-cutting showed in the final product. But Lossing achieved what no one else had—large sales and a healthy income from his productions.[70]

Before the Civil War, one man, Abner Dumont Jones, tried to blend the two approaches. Beginning in 1853, he issued his *Illustrated American Biography* (sometimes bearing the spine or cover title "American Portrait Gallery") as an annual, using stereotyped wood engravings by William Orr. He used a larger format than Lossing, a medium quarto (10¾" × 8") But, to insure sales, he used various grades of paper, ranging from the mediocre to the awful. Whatever the quality of the insides, he packaged the whole production in a handsome binding (fig. 16). Jones did one unique thing—he sold advertising on a regional basis and alternated leaves of ads with his one-leaf biographies (fig. 17). Thus the Reverend Lyman Beecher might find himself facing an ad for McPherson's elixir in one edition and a girdle advertisement in the next. Paul McPharlin speculated, in a brief notice of these books in the *New Colophon,* that Jones's volumes issued with advertisements were probably not sold but placed in hotels, steamships, and other public places, free of charge, to achieve maximum

---

of Distinguished American Citizens, with Biographical Sketches, and Facsimiles of Original Letters (Hartford, 1845), PPL copy. This work was reissued at Troy, N.Y. in 1925 and in New York City in 1931.

70 David D. Van Tassel, "Benson J. Lossing: Pen and Pencil Historian," *American Quarterly* 6 (Spring 1954): 32–44. For other successful popular biographers like Lossing, see Van Tassel, *Recording America's Past: An Interpretation of the Development of Historical Studies in America, 1607–1844* (Chicago, 1960), pp. 66–76.

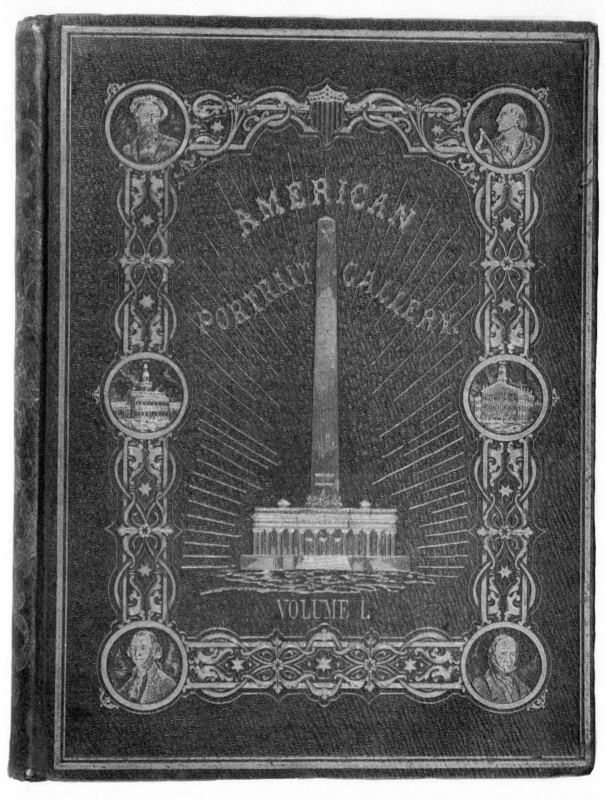

Front cover, blue cloth binding with gold blocking, by B. Bradley and Co. of Boston. On large-margin copy, 27.5 × 21.5 cm., of Abner Dumont Jones, *Illustrated American Biography*, vol. 1 (New York, 1853). (*Library Company of Philadelphia*)

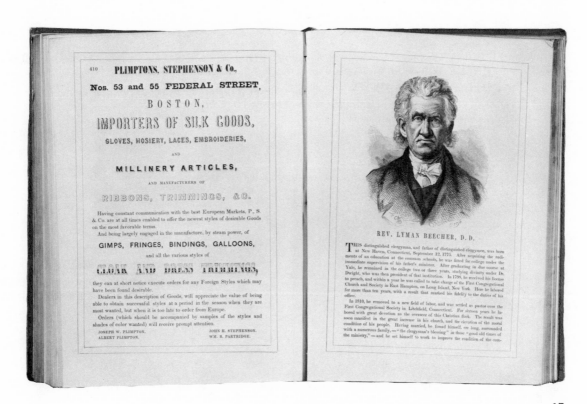

Lyman Beecher, 1775-1863. Stereotyped wood engraving, 1853, by John William Orr, 11.6 × 10 cm. From Abner Dumont Jones, *Illustrated American Biography,* vol. 2 (New York, 1854). (*Historical Society of Pennsylvania, Philadelphia*)

circulation for his advertisers. Surely not all the subjects so honored were happy about achieving such exposure.[71]

From the likes of Jones, Brown, and Lossing, series biography with portraits degenerated to the post–Civil War "mug" books in which, to be included, one merely had to pay a fee.[72] No attempt was made to create heroes for emulation or a fine art book to last the generations. The motive was narrowly commercial, and it showed. The days of both heroic biographies and patriotic ambitions for publishing them were over.

71   Paul McPharlin, "A Scrap Book of Strays [Mug Books]," *New Colophon* 1, no. 2 (April 1948): 202–4. Jones published three volumes between 1853 and 1855 with the title *Illustrated American Biography* in conjunction with J. Milton Emerson & Co. of New York City. The basic contents of these three volumes reappear in various formats (one volume and two volumes), issued by various publishers, with and without advertisements, and even without portraits. No complete bibliography of Jones's many editions exists.

72   McPharlin, pp. 202–3. See also Oscar Lewis, "Mug Books," *Colophon* 5, pt. 17 (1934); Archibald Hanna, Jr., "Every Man His Own Biographer," *Proceedings of the American Antiquarian Society* 80, pt. 2 (Oct. 1970): 290–98; and R. W. G. Vail, "The First New York State Mug Book: Portraits of the Legislature of 1798," *New-York Historical Society Quarterly* 35, no. 1 (Jan. 1951): 5–13.

APPENDIX 1:   Engravings in *Delaplaine's Repository*

Volume I, Part 1   Wrapper: *Delaplaine's Repository of the Lives and Portraits of Distinguished Americans*. Philadelphia: William Brown for the Proprietor, Joseph Delaplaine, 1816.

Engraved title page: *Delaplaine's Repository of the Lives and Portraits of Distinguished American Characters*. Philadelphia, 1815. Engraved by G. Fairman.

Subject	Engraver
Frontispiece (allegory)	A. Lawson after T. Birch
Columbus	P. Maverick after M. Maella
Americ[*sic*] Vespuccius	G. Fairman
Benjamin Rush	D. Edwin after T. Sully
Fisher Ames	J. Boyd after G. Stuart
Alexander Hamilton	W. S. Leney after G. Ceracchi
George Washington	W. S. Leney after J. Wood after J. A. Houdon

Volume I, Part 2   Wrapper: *Delaplaine's Repository of the Lives and Portraits of Distinguished Americans*. Philadelphia: William Brown for the Proprietor, Joseph Delaplaine, 1817.

Subject	Engraver
Peyton Randolph	G. Goodman and R. Piggot after C. W. Peale
Thomas Jefferson	J. Neagle after B. Otis
John Jay	W. S. Leney after G. Stuart
Rufus King	W. S. Leney after J. Wood
DeWitt Clinton	W. S. Leney after J. Trumbull
Robert Fulton	W. S. Leney after B. West

Volume II, Part 1   Wrapper: *Delaplaine's Repository of the Lives and Portraits of Distinguished Americans*. Philadelphia: William Brown for the Proprietor, Joseph Delaplaine, 1818.

Engraved title page: *Delaplaine's Repository of the Lives and Portraits of Distinguished Americans*. Engraved by J. Heath after G. Fairman.

Subject	Engraver
Samuel Adams	G. Goodman and R. Piggot after J. S. Copley
George Clinton	P. Maverick after E. Ames
Henry Laurens	J. Neagle after C. W. Peale
Benjamin Franklin	J. B. Longacre after D. Martin
Francis Hopkinson	J. Heath after R. E. Pine
Robert Morris	J. Heath after R. E. Pine.

APPENDIX 2:   Authors and Engravings in Sanderson's *Biography of the Signers*

Volume I   *Biography of the Signers to the Declaration of Independence* by John Sanderson. Vol. I. Philadelphia: Published by Joseph M. Sanderson for the Proprietor, J. Maxwell printer, 1820. (Engraved title page: coiled snake on rock device; engraving by J. B. Longacre after C. A. Lesueur, lettering by J. Warr, Jr.)[73]

---

73   In this series, binders or printers occasionally have mixed engraved title pages of various dates with the incorrect printed half titles. This practice has led some authorities to assume variant issues when there are no textual or typographic changes evident.

2d edition: *Biography*... by John Sanderson. Philadelphia: R. W. Pomeroy, 1823. (Engraved title page as above but without volume number.)

Subject[74]	Author[75]	Engraver
Introduction	John Sanderson	4 plates of autographs by J. Warr, Jr. (after John Vallance)
John Hancock	John Adams	J. B. Longacre after J. S. Copley

Volume II   *Biography*... By John Sanderson. Vol. II. Philadelphia: Joseph M. Sanderson, 1822. (Same engraved title page as in vol. 1, with number altered.)

2d edition: *Biography*... by John Sanderson. Philadelphia: R. W. Pomeroy, 1823. (Engraved title page as in vol. 1, without volume number.)

Subject	Author	Engraver
Benjamin Franklin	John Sanderson	J. B. Longacre after D. Martin
George Wythe	William R. Smith[76]	Drawn and engraved by J. B. Longacre after portrait in *American Gleaner*
Francis Hopkinson	R. Penn Smith	J. B. Longacre and J. H. Nesmith after R. E. Pine
Robert Treat Pine	A. Bradford	Engraved and drawn by J. B. Longacre after E. Savage

Volume III   *Biography*... by John Sanderson. Vol. III. Philadelphia: R. W. Pomeroy, 1823. (Engraved title page as in vol. 1 with new imprint and volume number.)

Printed title page: *Biography*...by Robert Waln, Jr.

Subject	Author	Engraver
Edward Rutledge	A. Middleton	Drawn and engraved by J. B. Longacre after Earle
Lyman Hall	Hugh McCall	*No portrait*
Oliver Wolcott	W. Wolcott	J. B. Longacre after painting in Delaplaine's Gallery
Richard Stockton	H. Stockton	*No portrait*
Button Gwinnet	Hugh McCall	*No portrait*
Josiah Bartlett	R. Waln, Jr.	*No portrait*
Philip Livingston	DeWitt Clinton	J. B. Longacre after painting
Roger Sherman	Edward Everett	S. S. Jocelyn after Earle

---

74   The subjects are listed in the order in which they occur in each volume.

75   Attribution of authorship of the biographies is based on the sources cited in note 45, on notes by R. Waln, Jr., and on notes on the manuscript drafts of the biographies themselves. See two volumes, "Biographies of Signers . . .," and vol. 79 in Henry D. Gilpin Papers, Gilpin Family Collection, PHi.

76   This essay has usually been attributed to Thomas Jefferson, but for positive reattribution to William R. Smith, see note 45.

Volume IV   *Biography*...by John Sanderson. Vol. IIII. Philadelphia: R. W. Pomeroy, 1823. (Engraved title page as in vol. 1 with new imprint and volume number.)

Printed title page: *Biography*...by Robert Waln, Jr.

Subject	Author	Engraver
Thomas Heyward, Jr.	John Hamilton	J. B. Longacre after miniature
George Read	Mr. Read of Del.	J. B. Longacre after R. E. Pine
William Williams	R. Waln, Jr.	*No portrait*
Samuel Huntington	R. Waln, Jr.	*No portrait*
William Floyd	Aug. Floyd	A. B. Durand after painting in Delaplaine's Gallery
George Walton	Hugh McCall	*No portrait*
George Clymer	R. Waln, Jr.	J. B. Longacre after B. Trott
Benjamin Rush	John Sanderson	J. B. Longacre after T. Sully

Volume V   *Biography*... [no author stated]. Philadelphia: R. W. Pomeroy, 1824. (New engraved title page with figure of woman, by F. Kearny after T. Underwood, no volume number.)

Printed title page: *Biography*... by Robert Waln, Jr. Vol. V.

Subject	Author	Engraver
Thomas Lynch, Jr.	James Hamilton	J. B. Longacre after an enamel painting
Matthew Thornton	R. Waln, Jr.	*No portrait*
William Whipple	R. Waln, Jr.	*No portrait*
John Witherspoon	Ashbel Green	J. B. Longacre after C. W. Peale
Robert Morris	Edward Ingersoll	J. B. Longacre after painting

Volume VI   *Biography*... [no author stated]. Philadelphia: R. W. Pomeroy, 1824. (Engraved title page, figure of woman, as in vol. 5, no volume number.)

Printed title page: *Biography*... by Robert Waln, Jr. Vol. VI.

Two issues: one with copyright notice within ornamental border and one with no border, no priority established; variant texts begin at p. 341.

Subject	Author	Engraver
Arthur Middleton	H. M. Rutledge	J. B. Longacre after T. Middleton after B. West
Abraham Clark	R. Waln, Jr.	*No portrait*
Francis Lewis	M. Lewis	C. C. Wright after painting
John Penn	John Taylor of N.C.	*No portrait*
James Wilson	R. Waln, Jr.	J. B. Longacre after miniature
Carter Braxton	Wm. Brockenbrough	*No portrait*
John Morton	R. Waln, Jr.	*No portrait*
Stephen Hopkins	R. Waln, Jr.	*No portrait*
Thomas McKean	R. Waln, Jr.	J. B. Longacre after G. Stuart

Volume VII   *Biography*... [no author stated]. Philadelphia: R. W. Pomeroy, 1827. (Engraved title page, figure of woman, as in vol. 5, no volume number.)

Printed title page: *Biography*... [no author stated]. Vol. VII.

Subject	Author	Engraver
Thomas Jefferson	H. D. Gilpin (assisted by G. W. Crabbe)[77]	J. B. Longacre after R. Field after G. Stuart
William Hooper	J. C. Hooper (or A. M. Hooper) (assisted by Mr. Ashburner)	*No portrait*
James Smith	Edward Ingersoll	*No portrait*
Charles Carroll of Carrollton	Henry B. Latrobe (assisted by G. W. Crabbe)	J. B. Longacre after R. Field
Thomas Nelson, Jr.	H. D. Gilpin	*No portrait*
Joseph Hewes	Edward Ingersoll	F. Kearney after J. B. Longacre after painting

Volume VIII *Biography*. . . [no author stated]. Philadelphia: R. W. Pomeroy, 1827. (Engraved title page, figure of woman, as in vol. 5, no volume number.)

Printed title page: *Biography*. . . [no author stated]. Vol. VIII.

Subject	Author	Engraver
Elbridge Gerry	H. D. Gilpin	J. B. Longacre after J. Vanderlyn
Caesar Rodney	H. D. Gilpin (assisted by G. W. Crabbe)	*No portrait*
Benjamin Harrison	H. D. Gilpin (assisted by G. W. Crabbe)	*No portrait*
William Paca	Edward Ingersoll	P. Maverick after J. B. Longacre after J. S. Copley
George Ross	H. D. Gilpin	*No portrait*
John Adams	Samuel Adams	Drawn and engraved by J. B. Longacre after B. Otis after G. Stuart

Volume IX *Biography*. . . [no author stated]. Philadelphia: R. W. Pomeroy, 1827. (Engraved title page, figure of woman, as in vol. 5, no volume number.)

Printed title page: *Biography*. . .[no author stated]. Vol. IX.

Subject	Author	Engraver
Richard Henry Lee	Richard H. Lee, Jr.	P. Maverick and J. B. Longacre after J. B. Longacre after miniature
George Taylor	H. D. Gilpin	*No portrait*
John Hart	R. Waln, Jr.	*No portrait*
Lewis Morris	Edward Ingersoll	*No portrait*
Thomas Stone	Edward Ingersoll	G. B. Ellis after J. B. Longacre after R. E. Pine
Francis Lightfoot Lee	R. Waln, Jr.	*No portrait*
Samuel Chase	Edward Ingersoll	(J. B. Longacre?) after J. B. Longacre after J. W. Jarvis
William Ellery	H. D. Gilpin (and R. Waln, Jr)	*No portrait*
Samuel Adams	H. D. Gilpin	Drawn and engraved by J. B. Longacre after J. S. Copley

---

77 G. W. Crabbe was a newspaper editor and writer.

Volume I	Subject[78]	Author[79]	Engraver[80]
	George Washington (engraved title page: anaglyptograph of obverse of "Washington before Boston" medal)		C. Gobrecht or A. Eckfeldt after Du Vivier
	George Washington (frontispiece)		A. B. Durand after J. Trumbull
	George Washington	James Herring	J. B. Longacre after G. Stuart
	Martha Washington	G. W. P. Custis	J. B. Longacre after W. Robertson
	Charles Carroll of Carrollton	James Herring	A. B. Durand after C. Harding
	Nathaniel Greene	James Herring	J. B. Forrest after J. Trumbull
	Anthony Wayne	James Herring	J. F. E. Prud'homme after J. Herring after J. Trumbull
	William Moultrie	James Herring	E. Scriven after J. Trumbull
	Israel Putnam	James Thacher	W. Humphreys after J. Trumbull
	Timothy Pickering	Rev. C. W. Upham	T. B. Welch after J. B. Longacre after G. Stuart
	Isaac Shelby	Charles G. Todd	A. B. Durand after M. H. Jouett
	Aaron Ogden	Autobiography adapted by J. Herring	Painted and engraved by A. B. Durand
	John Marshall	Hon. Joseph Story	A. B. Durand after H. Inman
	Edward Shippen	Hon. Joseph Hopkinson	E. Wellmore after G. Stuart
	Jonathan Williams	Samuel Rush	R. W. Dodson (after W. E. West?) after T. Sully
	Daniel D. Tompkins	W. P. Crosby	T. Woolnoth after J. W. Jarvis (printed by Illman & Pilbrow)[81]
	Henry Clay	James Herring	J. B. Longacre after W. J. Hubard

---

78 Subjects are arranged in the order in which they occur in the large paperbound copy of the first edition of each volume.

79 Attribution of authorship of the biographies is based primarily on a list published in the *Philadelphia Press,* circa Nov. 1, 1873, which was supplied by John Jay Smith (one of the authors) and verified by Mrs. John F. Keen (Longacre's daughter). Additional material—complete names or initials, etc.—in parentheses comes from a variety of sources, including initials at the ends of the biographies themselves, Longacre's correspondence, and Stewart.

80 The basic information for this list comes from the engravings themselves. Additional material in parentheses is supplied from Stewart; standard reference works; and Longacre's correspondence. Minor errors in the information contained on the engravings have been corrected without acknowledgment.

81 Unless indicated, all prints are presumed to have been printed by, or to have had the printing supervised by, J. B. Longacre. However, certain plates were printed by commercial copperplate printers and were identified as such on some copies of the prints.

Subject	Author	Engraver
Andrew Jackson	Rev. John Hall	Drawn and engraved by J. B. Longacre
Daniel Webster	Prof. George Ticknor	Drawn and engraved by J. B. Longacre
William Wirt	P. Cruse	Drawn and engraved by J. B. Longacre
Lewis Cass	Autobiography	T. B. Welch after J. B. Longacre
Thomas Macdonough	Samuel L. Knapp	J. B. Forrest after J. W. Jarvis
Alexander Macomb	Unidentified	J. B. Longacre after T. Sully
Joel R. Poinsett	Robert Walsh	Drawn and engraved by J. B. Longacre
Josiah S. Johnston	Henry D. Gilpin	J. B. Longacre after C. B. King
Edward Livingston	Henry D. Gilpin	E. Wellmore after J. B. Longacre
Louis McLane	Autobiography	T. Kelly after G. S. Newton
William White	Rev. Dr. Schroeder after sketch by Rev. James Montgomery	T. B. Welch after J. B. Longacre
Timothy Dwight	W. P. Crosby	J. B. Forrest after J. Trumbull
Joel Barlow	W. P. Crosby	A. B. Durand after R. Fulton
John Trumbull	James Herring	A. B. Durand after S. L. Waldo and W. Jewett
Gilbert C. Stuart	William Dunlap	A. B. Durand after S. Goodrich
Samuel L. Mitchell	J. W. Francis, M.D.	S. H. Gimber and A. L. Dick after H. Inman
Theodric Romeyn Beck	Unidentified	J. F. E. Prud'homme after R. W. Weir
Washington Irving	Prof. Kenwick of Columbia College	M. J. Danforth after C. R. Leslie
Catharine M. Sedgwick	Autobiography	A. B. Durand after C. C. Ingham
James F. Cooper	James E. Dekay, M.D.	E. Scriven after J. W. Jarvis (printed by Illman & Pilbrow)

Volume II	Subject	Author	Engraver
	Benjamin Franklin (engraved title page)		E. Wellmore after J. B. Longacre after Houdon; lettering engraved by J. and W. W. Warr
	Benjamin Franklin (frontispiece)[82]		R. W. Dodson after J. B. Longacre (after Antoine Noel Benoit Graincourt after Joseph-Siffred Duplessis)

---

82 The two Franklin plates, Dodson's and T. B. Welch's, were used interchangeably as the frontispiece for vol. 2, and their relative position has no significance as to "issue" or "edition."

Subject	Author	Engraver
Benjamin Franklin	John Jay Smith	T. B. Welch (after C. W. Peale and J. Peale) after D. Martin
Thomas Jefferson	Henry D. Gilpin	J. B. Forrest after G. Stuart
John Hancock	Benjamin Bussey Thatcher	J. B. Forrest after J. Herring after J. S. Copley
John Jay	James Herring	A. B. Durand after G. Stuart and J. Trumbull
Patrick Henry	Thomas A. Budd	E. Wellmore after J. B. Longacre (after T. Sully)
Joseph Warren	James Herring	T. Illman (after?) after J. S. Copley
Henry Knox	Benjamin Bussey Thatcher	J. F. E. Prud'homme after J. Herring after G. Stuart
Benjamin Lincoln	Benjamin Bussey Thatcher, adapted by J. Herring	T. Illman after J. Herring after H. Sargent
David Wooster	Timothy Pitkin	J. B. Longacre (after English mezzotint) after painting
Philip J. Schuyler	Chancellor James Kent	T. Kelly after J. Trumbull
Alexander Hamilton	Chancellor James Kent	J. F. E. Prud'homme after A. Robertson
John E. Howard	Benjamin C. Howard	J. F. E. Prud'homme after C. Harding (after R. Peale)
Otho H. Williams	Gen. Samuel Smith	J. B. Longacre after C. W. Peale
John Brooks	Edward Everett	A. B. Durand after J. Herring after G. Stuart
Francis Barber	Major (W. C.?) of Elizabethtown, N.J.	S. H. Gimber after J. Herring after sketch
John Barry	Thomas A. Budd	J. B. Longacre after G. Stuart
Daniel Boone	Dr. (W. A.) Caruthers of Virginia	J. B. Longacre after C. Harding
David Rittenhouse	John Jay Smith	J. B. Longacre after C. W. Peale
David Humphreys	Mr. (Ebenezer) Baldwin of New Haven	G. Parker after J. Herring after G. Stuart
Edward Preble	Benjamin Bussey Thatcher	T. Kelly (after J. B. Marston) after painting
Oliver H. Perry	Samuel L. Knapp	J. B. Forrest after J. W. Jarvis (printed by Miller)
Jacob J. Brown	John Adams Dix	A. B. Durand after J. Herring after J. W. Jarvis
DeWitt Clinton	Dr. S. R. Beck	A. B. Durand after C. C. Ingham
James A. Bayard	R. H. Bayard	E. Wellmore after A. U. Wertmuller
John C. Calhoun	F. Markoe	T. B. Welch after J. B. Longacre
Robert Y. Hayne	M. L. Pinckney and C. Raquet	J. B. Forrest after J. B. Longacre

Subject	Author	Engraver
William Gaston	Jo. Seawell Jones	A. B. Durand after G. Cooke
Levi Woodbury	R. Ella	J. B. Longacre after J. B. Longacre[83]
Mrs. Marcia Van Ness	C. Middleton	T. B. Welch after F. Alexander
Noah Webster	Prof. (Chauncey A.) Goodrich	G. Parker after J. Herring
Caspar Wistar	W. E. Horner, M.D.	J. B. Longacre after B. Otis
David Hosack	James Herring	A. B. Durand after T. Sully
James Kent	W. S. Johnson	A. B. Durand after F. R. Spencer
Charles Ewing	Hon. S. L. Southard	E. Wellmore after J. B. Longacre after C. B. Lawrence
George Wolf	Hon. Ellis Lewis	E. Wellmore after A. B. Rockey

Volume III

Subject	Author	Engraver
Montpelier, Va., seat of James Madison (engraved title page)		J. F. E. Prud'homme after J. G. Chapman
James Madison (frontispiece)		T. B. Welch after J. B. Longacre
James Madison	Charles J. Ingersoll	W. A. Wilmer after D. Edwin after G. Stuart
Dolley P. Madison	Mrs. S. H. (Mary?) Smith	J. F. E. Prud'homme after J. Herring after J. Wood
James Monroe	S. L. K. (Samuel L. Knapp?)	A. B. Durand after J. Vanderlyn
John Dickinson	Thomas A. Budd	J. B. Forrest (after J. B. Longacre?) after C. W. Peale
Francis Hopkinson	Joseph Hopkinson	J. B. Longacre after R. E. Pine (printed by H. Quig)
Elias Boudinot	Dr. B. McCready	J. W. Paradise after S. L. Waldo and W. Jewett
Benjamin Rush	Samuel Rush	R. W. Dodson after T. Sully
David Ramsay	Hon. Robert Y. Hayne	J. B. Longacre after C. Frazer after C. W. Peale (i.e., R. Peale)
Arthur St. Clair	E. D. Ingraham	E. Wellmore after J. B. Longacre after C. W. Peale (printed by H. Quig)
Lachlan McIntosh	T. Spalding of Sapelo Island	H. Meyer after J. B. Longacre after painting
Daniel Morgan	Major (Morgan) Neville	J. F. E. Prud'homme after J. Herring after J. Trumbull

83 Many of the plates were reworked or touched up in the later editions. For example, Levi Woodbury in vol. 2 was originally "Drawn and engraved by J. B. Longacre," but in later versions of the same plate the caption reads "Drawn from life by J. B. Longacre and engraved by R. E. Whitechurch." Some of these reworked plates may be found in first editions as later replacements for the geniune first issue of the print.

Subject	Author	Engraver
Francis Marion	James Herring	T. B. Welch after J. B. Longacre after T. Stothard (printed by B. Rogers)
Andrew Pickens	Hon. F. W. Pickens	J. B. Longacre after T. Sully after painting
Henry Lee	Dr. (B.) McCready	J. F. E. Prud'homme after J. Herring after G. Stuart
William A. Washington	John Jay Smith	J. B. Forrest (after J. B. Longacre) after C. W. Peale
Morgan Lewis	James Herring	A. B. Durand and J. W. Paradise after J. Herring
Benjamin Tallmadge	James Herring	G. Parker after E. Ames
James Jackson	Col. Joseph Jackson	W. A. Wilmer after J. B. Longacre after C. B. J. F. de Saint-Mémin
William R. Davie	A. H. Davie	J. B. Longacre after J. Vanderlyn
John Paul Jones	Th. McK. Pettit	J. B. Longacre after C. W. Peale
Richard Dale	Th. McK. Pettit	R. W. Dodson after J. B. Longacre after J. Wood
William Bainbridge	James Herring	G. Parker after J. W. Jarvis
Stephen Decatur	James Herring	A. B. Durand after J. Herring after T. Sully
Fisher Ames	Dr. (B.) McCready	J. F. E. Prud'homme after D. Edwin after G. Stuart
Rufus King	James Herring	T. Kelly after G. Stuart
Stephen Van Rensselaer	N. B. Blunt	G. Parker after C. Fraser
William Pinckney	J. H. Lamman	E. Wellmore after C. B. King
Lindley Murray	John Griscom	S. H. Gimber after E. Westoby
Charles Brockden Brown	William Dunlap	J. B. Forrest after W. Dunlap
Robert Fulton	N. B. Blunt	G. Parker after B. West
Joseph Story	Prof. (Simon) Greenleaf, Cambridge	G. Parker after C. Harding
William H. Harrison	Morgan Neville of Cinn.	R. W. Dodson after J. R. Lambdin
Martin Van Buren	Henry D. Gilpin	E. Wellmore after H. Inman
Mahlon Dickerson	Autobiography adapted by James Herring	G. Parker after J. Vanderlyn
Felix Grundy	Virgil Maxcey	T. B. Welch after W. B. Cooper

Volume IV

Subject	Author	Engraver
Eastern front of the Capitol, Washington City (engraved title page)		J. and W. W. Warr
John Adams (frontispiece)	John Quincy Adams	J. B. Longacre after B. Otis after G. Stuart (printed by H. Quig)

Subject	Author	Engraver
Abigail Adams	John Quincy Adams	G. F. Storm after G. Stuart
Samuel Adams	James Herring	G. F. Storm after J. B. Longacre after J. S. Copley
Jonathan Trumbull	James Herring	E. MacKenzie after J. Trumbull
John Rutledge	Dr. Ramsay	G. F. Storm after J. Herring after J. Trumbull
Henry Laurens	James Herring	T. B. Welch after W. G. Armstrong (after mezzotint) after J. S. Copley (printed by H. Quig)
Thomas Sumter	Dr. (B.) McCready	G. Parker after W. G. Armstrong after C. W. Peale (i.e., R. Peale)
Richard Montgomery	John Jay Smith	E. MacKenzie after C. W. Peale
Charles C. Pinckney	Col. James Lynab	E. Wellmore after E. G. Malbone
Thomas Pinckney	James Herring	W. G. Armstrong after J. Trumbull
Oliver Ellsworth	Mrs. L. H. Sigourney	E. MacKenzie after J. Herring
Thomas Mifflin	Thomas A. Budd	E. Wellmore after G. Stuart (printed by H. Quig)
Thomas McKean	Thomas A. Budd	T. B. Welch after G. Stuart (printed by H. Quig)
Robert Morris	James Herring	T. B. Welch after J. B Longacre after R. E. Pine
Joseph Habersham	Richard W. Habersham	J. Gross after G. W. Conarroe after Douglass
Mordecai Gist	Dr. J. P. Cockey	W. A. Wilmer (after L. Terry after C. W. Peale)
George R. Clarke	James Herring	T. B. Welch after J. B. Longacre after J. W. Jarvis (printed by H. Quig)
Simon Kenton	John Jay Smith	R. W. Dodson after L. M. Morgan
Joshua Barney	E. D. Ingraham	J. Gross after W. G. Armstrong after J. B. Isabey (printed by H. Quig)
Luther Martin	J. H. Lanman	W. A. Wilmer after painting
Samuel Chase	C. F. Mayer	J. B. Forrest after J. B. Longacre after J. W. Jarvis
Abraham Baldwin	Joel Barlow and Hon. H. Baldwin	J. B. Forrest after E. G. Leutze after R. Fulton
Robert R. Livingston	Dr. J. W. Francis	E. MacKenzie after J. Vanderlyn
John Quincy Adams	Rev. Charles W. Upham	J. W. Paradise after A. B. Durand
Louise Catherine Adams	Autobiography	G. F. Storm after C. R. Leslie (printed by H. Quig)

Subject	Author	Engraver
William H. Crawford	(Charles Edward or Edward Bishop) Dudley	S. H. Gimber after J. W. Jarvis
Hugh Lawson White	James Herring	T. B. Welch after E. G. Leutze
John Randolph	E. D. Ingraham	T. B. Welch after J. Wood
William C. C. Claiborne	W. C. C. Claiborne (Jr.)	J. B. Longacre after A. Duval
John McLean	Unidentified	W. G. Armstrong after T. Sully
Edward Everett	Rev. C. W. Upham	G. Parker after A. B. Durand
Thomas Say	Dr. B. M. Coates	H. Meyer after J. Wood
Nathaniel Bowditch	James Herring	J. Gross after J. B. Longacre after J. Frazee
Philip S. Physick	W. E. Horner, M.D.	R. W. Dodson after H. Inman (printed by H. Quig)
John W. Francis	Autobiography	J. F. E. Prud'homme after J. Herring
Lydia H. Sigourney	Mrs. S. J. Hale	G. Parker after J. Herring
Winfield Scott	Dr. (B.) McCready	W. G. Armstrong after C. Ingham (printed by Butler & Long)
Edmund P. Gaines	Col. (John Goddard) Watmough	J. B. Longacre after J. W. Jarvis
Nicholas Biddle	Hon. R. T. Conrad	J. B. Longacre and T. B. Welch after R. Peale (printed by Butler & Long)

Portraits for Every Parlor

Albert Newsam and American Portrait Lithography

WENDY

WICK

REAVES

From the time of her arrival in New York in May 1840, the ballerina Fanny Elssler was a sensation. The throngs who cheered her at each performance crowded the print stores demanding images of their new ballet idol. Charles Hart, working for George Endicott's lithography company, recalled that their firm was hard pressed:

> *The demand for Fanny Elssler's portrait was increasing day by day. My master, being in the picture business was besieged for a likeness of the dancer. But none was to be had. . . . William A. Coleman. . . at length obtained from London a picture of the divine Fanny. . . as she was irreverently called. [As] soon [as] it became known that such a picture was on exhibition, the sidewalk in front of his store was blocked for many days. . . . It remained however for Mr. George Endicott to issue the grandest of all the portraits of Fanny Elssler. None of the cheap pictures having satisfied the serious demand for the portrait of the famous danseuse. Henry Inman, one of the principal portrait painters of that time obtained sittings. . . . The scene represented was the dancer resting in her chair, after the long and fatiguing "Tarantella" dance. . . . When the first proof was taken and pronounced "good" a load was lifted from our minds. . . . Henry Inman, the painter, Henri Heidemans, the lithographer, myself as assistant to Louis Nagle the printer, and only one or two others were allowed to be present on that important occasion.[1]*

1 Charles Hart, "Lithography: Its Theory and Practice Including a Series of Short Sketches of the Earliest Lithographic Artists, Engravers, and Publishers of New York," unpublished memoir (1902), New York Public Library, pp. 107–15.

Hart's account gives a good idea of how prevalent the lithographic portrait was at that time—when the public could demand and expect to buy, immediately and inexpensively, images of their idols. The lithographed likeness was the parlor ornament, souvenir, T-shirt, and bumper sticker of its day. Every group wanted its portrait-emblem—the congregation, its minister; the cause, its martyr; the organization, its spokesman; the audience, its idol.

Lithography had become commercially feasible in America in the mid-1820s. Not only was it cheaper, quicker, and easier to draw on stone than to engrave a copperplate, but the number of images that could be printed was virtually limitless. The commercial potential was quickly seized upon by that concoction of engravers, painters, and publishers who formed the country's first lithographic firms. Inexpensive pictorial material of all kinds, available to everyone, poured from the presses. "Scarcely a cottage or hamlet can be found," reported the *Connecticut Courant* in 1849, "however obscure and isolated, but what displays upon its walls more or less specimens of this art."[2]

The lithographic grease crayon was regarded by the print scholar Frank Weitenkampf as the "most flexible agent for the rendering of the artist's desired effect"; it could be "particularly adapted to the delineation of the human face, both through its softness of texture and the suave force of its lines in reflecting character and mood."[3] But it was lithography's adaptation to commercial needs—the cheapness and speed of its production—that caused it to flourish in America. Louis Prang, a preeminent American lithographer, summed up its advantages:

> *Lithography is the most versatile of all known methods of reproduction. It will admit of flat, even tints, and of tints graduated from the darkest shade to the highest light, while it can equally as well imitate a crayon-drawing, a line-engraving, or a stipple-engraving. . . . Lithography amply deserves the high place as the most facile medium for artistic expression and reproduction which it has been accorded by the foremost artists of a past*

2 *Connecticut Courant* (Hartford), Feb. 1849, quoted in Frances Phipps, "Connecticut's Printmakers: The Kelloggs of Hartford," *Connecticut Antiquarian* 21 (June 1969): 21.

3 Frank Weitenkampf, "Portraits in Lithography," *New York Public Library Bulletin* 34 (Jan. 1930): 11.

generation. . . . The commercial product in this country has reached an artistic development which makes it certainly equal to the best that is produced in Europe.[4]

On the popular level, American art was still dominated by portraiture; and pictures of the famous—and infamous—were stock items in every lithographer's shop. They were the sure sellers, the bread and butter, of the print stores and were sometimes published in larger editions than any other category of lithograph. In 1849 a Hartford newspaper reported that the Kellogg company presses "run off daily from 3000 to 4000 copies of various popular prints. . . . More than 100,000 copies have been sold from a single design. The portrait of Washington takes the lead and next to him stands Old Rough and Ready."[5]

One expects to find, and does find, the most famous names of the day. The luminaries of the stage—Edwin Forrest, perhaps, or Fanny Kemble—shared the printshop windows with ballerinas, such as Amalia Taglioni, who often floated gracefully and weightlessly through their pictures balanced on one tiny pointed toe. On sale for every partisan were the politicians, such as presidential candidate Henry Clay with his running mate, John Sargeant, and the military heroes en route to being politicians, such as General William Henry Harrison. An elder statesman such as Charles Carroll had his public, as did frontier congressman David Crockett (fig. 1) and Supreme Court Justice John Marshall. Popular writers—Fitz-Greene Halleck, for example, or James Fenimore Cooper—were salable commodities, as were the wealthy merchant and financier Stephen Girard and the respected surgeon Philip Syng Physick.

Portraits of the famous were published by the firm as commercial ventures, but there were also outside commissions for lithographs of the less famous. Any face with a following was potential for a picture. Notwithstanding their anonymity today, these men and women in their brief moments of glory captured the public imagination. Joseph Markle (fig. 2) did not get very far in Pennsylvania politics, but in his portrait lithograph he achieves a commanding presence, promising to uphold

---

4 The Grolier Club, *Catalogue of an Exhibition Illustrative of a Centenary of Artistic Lithography, 1796–1896* (New York, 1896), pp. 7, 10, 9.

5 *Connecticut Courant*, Feb. 1849, quoted in Phipps, p. 23.

DAVID CROCKETT.

I am happy to acknowledge this to be the only correct likeness that has been taken of me.

David Crockett

1
David Crockett, 1786-1836. Lithograph, 1834, by Newsam after Samuel S. Osgood, 22.7 × 18.1 cm. (*National Portrait Gallery, Smithsonian Institution*)

democratic Whig principles and protect the manufacturers and agriculturists of his state. The print of a stern-faced Philip White seemed to inspire his fellow sons of temperance; and a group of doctors commissioned a picture of J. D. White, an apparently distinguished professor of anatomy and physiology at the Philadelphia College of Dental Surgery. Of course, one is curious whether there was a run on the printshops after the publication of sour-looking William D. Lewis, "collector of the Philadelphia customs."

With the exception of Fanny Elssler, all the likenesses just mentioned were drawn by Albert Newsam (fig. 3), whose work exemplifies, in many ways, the lithographic portrait in America. Newsam's early life reads

Painted by Wm Cogswell.   Drawn on stone by A Newsam   Lith of P S Duval Philad

RESIDENCE.

JOSEPH MARKLE,
DEMOCRATIC WHIG PRINCIPLES.

Joseph Markle

Joseph Markle. Lithograph, 1844, by Newsam after William Cogswell,
43.6 × 35.6 cm. (*National Portrait Gallery, Smithsonian Institution*)

3
Albert Newsam, 1809-1864. Photograph, circa 1855, by Walter Dinmore, 18.6 × 13.5 cm. (*Library Company of Philadelphia*)

like a nineteenth-century novel.[6] A deaf-mute born in 1809 in Steubenville, Ohio, Newsam was raised by an innkeeper. When he was ten years old, a "mendicant-impostor" calling himself William P. Davis ran off with the boy, promising to take him to Philadelphia to be educated. Davis's real purpose, in fact, was to use the age and drawing talents of his young companion to elicit sympathy and contributions; making a substantial sum of money on the journey, he finally arrived, with his young charge, in Philadelphia in May 1820.

6   The primary source of biographical material on Newsam is Joseph O. Pyatt, *Memoir of Albert Newsam (Deaf Mute Artist)* (Philadelphia, 1868). Pyatt mentions a brief biographical sketch of Newsam prepared by Colonel Francis H. Duffee for the *Sunday Dispatch* (Philadelphia) and reissued in 1862 as a circular to raise money for the "Newsam fund."

According to his biographer, Newsam was drawing a picture in chalk of the square between 5th and 6th streets when he was noticed by Bishop William White, then president of the newly established Pennsylvania Institution for the Deaf and Dumb. The young boy was placed in the care of the institution, and his older companion departed, ostensibly to get money from relatives. When relatives, money, and Davis failed to reappear, Newsam was accepted as a state pupil.

During his six years at the institution, from 1820 to 1826, Newsam studied with George Catlin and Hugh Bridport and had as good an education in the rudiments of drawing as was available at the time. In 1827 he was placed with Colonel Cephas G. Childs to learn the art of engraving. Within a year, he was producing illustrations for the *Casket* magazine. One of these was of Queen Dido, and he had visited the Pennsylvania Academy of the Fine Arts to make a sketch for the engraving. Newsam was an occasional exhibitor and frequent visitor to the academy throughout his life. An avid collector of French and English prints, he became recognized, also, for his broad knowledge of art history.

Newsam's apprenticeship coincided with the beginnings of Philadelphia's first lithography firms. Although the city could claim some of the earliest American lithographs—particularly Bass Otis's experiments in 1819—it was almost a decade before the first firms were launched. Significantly, one of the artists who began to draw on stone for these early shops was Hugh Bridport, Newsam's former teacher.[7] In 1829 Colonel Childs joined with two other artists, John Pendleton and Francis Kearny, to begin the most successful of Philadelphia's early lithography firms. The peripatetic Pendleton had already started a company in Boston with his brother William, and before the year was out he had moved on to New York; but he left behind him a knowledge of the business.

Recognizing Newsam's talent for chalk and crayon drawing, Childs soon took the engraver's burin from his hands and started him on what was to be a lifelong career—lithography. On September 9, 1829, the editors of

---

7 George Catlin, Newsam's other teacher, was also an early lithographer, having drawn some plates for Cadwallader Colden's *Canal Book* (1826), produced by Anthony Imbert's New York firm. The history of Philadelphia lithography in general and of the successive partnerships of Childs, Inman, Lehman, and Duval is well documented in Nicholas B. Wainwright, *Philadelphia in the Romantic Age of Lithography* (Philadelphia, 1958).

the *United States Gazette,* having accepted a personal invitation from Childs to visit the shop, reported: "We were particularly struck with the exquisite work of a young man 'deaf and dumb,' who was engaged in drawing a Sioux warrior in full speed, on a fleet horse. There was a degree of expression in the figure which, while we fully admire it, asked an artist to appreciate its excellence. Some of the exquisite specimens of this young man's lithographic drawings were shown to us, that had a softness and beauty that appeared to belong only to the nicest graver." A few weeks later, the *Gazette* continued its enthusiastic commentary: "The pretty picture of the Sioux Warrior, we have already noticed, having seen it while under the hand of the deaf and dumb artist. From the same crayon, and executed on Messrs. P. [K.] and C.'s press, is a beautiful picture called the Twins—a copy [after Thomas Sully]. It has two youthful heads, of exceeding beauty; and the execution is of the first kind—calculated to enhance the estimation of the lithographic art."[8]

Newsam had only been drawing on stone for a few months when Childs encouraged him to direct his talents principally toward portraiture. Newsam contributed three small lithographic illustrations to the little volume of portraits and biographies, published in Philadelphia in 1829, called *Cabinet.* They were not particularly distinguished; in fact they seemed consciously to imitate the stipple engravings of the rest of Jackson's cabinet officers. One critic, who found the portrait of John Berrien uninspired, called it "anything but a likeness; the original being strikingly handsome."[9] But Cephas Childs, who knew the print-selling business, had more ambitious projects in mind for Newsam. Having seen how successfully fine engraved copies after the leading portrait painters could be sold, he planned to tap the same market with lithography. Henry Inman, writing to him from New York, approved of the scheme. "I like your enterprise in getting up a collection of full length pictures and trust that nothing will prevent your success."[10] Childs's plan was "to publish a series of lithographic likenesses of distinguished Americans,"[11] and, though he

8   *United States Gazette* (Philadelphia), Sept. 9, Oct. 15, 1829.

9   Ibid., Jan. 22, 1830.

10   Inman to Childs, Aug. 19, 1829, Henry Inman Papers, American Antiquarian Society, Worcester, Mass. (hereafter MWA).

11   *United States Gazette,* April 22, 1830.

abandoned his original intention to make them all full-lengths, he did begin the project within the firm's first year of operation.

By November 1829 the Philadelphia newspapers were advertising subscriptions to Newsam's portrait of Henry Clay after a painting by Joseph Wood. "It will be printed at the lithographic establishment of Messrs. Pendleton, Kearny, and Childs," reported one newspaper, "on the best paper and in their very best style. We have seen the likeness from which the drawing is to be made, and think it very beautiful."[12] Childs did not rely solely on the amiable editors of his local papers for promotion of the print. Henry Inman had seen an advertisement either in New York or in the *New Jersey Mirror.* "I perceive by the papers," he wrote, "that you are publishing a lithographic print by the deaf and Dumb boy. I wish you would consider me as a subscriber."[13] In a later state of the print, probably published at the end of the year, the inscription was changed to "C. G. Childs Lith.," indicating that the original partnership had dissolved and Cephas Childs was in business on his own.

Just a few months later, in May 1830, Childs announced plans to publish "an accurate whole length portrait of the President of the United States."[14] Following a practice sometimes used by engravers, he commissioned the painting, sending William James Hubard down to Washington to get sittings from President Jackson.

The *Andrew Jackson* lithograph (fig. 4) after Hubard's painting was the most ambitious project Newsam had ever undertaken. It was larger than the *Henry Clay,* and Newsam had to deal with much more complex problems, such as the delineation of the interior space and differentiation of textures of wood, cloth, marble, and flesh. The perspective of the picture frame is not perfect; and the floor, with its decorative rug patterns, tilts up to the point where the President seems to be bracing himself with his tiny feet to keep from sliding straight out of the picture; but these may have been faults copied from the painting, which is now lost. On the whole, the result was remarkably successful for a young man who had been

12 Ibid., Nov. 4, 1829.

13 *New Jersey Mirror* (Mount Holly), Dec. 2, 1829, cited in George C. Groce, Jr., "The First Catalogue of the Work of Joseph Wood," *Art Quarterly,* Supplement to 3 (1940): 394; Inman to Childs, Nov. 18, 1829, MWA.

14 *United States Gazette,* May 10, 1830.

Andrew Jackson, 1767–1845. Lithograph, 1930, by Newsam after William James Hubard, 49.8 × 35.5 cm. (*National Portrait Gallery, Smithsonian Institution*)

drawing on stone for about one year. The various textures are well differentiated, and it is a sensitive portrait, giving Jackson a solemn, dignified appearance which might have counteracted the backwoods crudeness his detractors promoted. Childs was undoubtedly pleased with the work. It seems to be the first lithograph to which he allowed the young man to sign his name: "Drawn by A. Newsam, Pupil of C. G. Childs."

Although lithographed images of the famous had an obvious market, they faced heavy competition from engravings. In view of this, Childs developed another scheme, the reproduction of private portraiture. On April 15, 1830, the *National Gazette* announced that his firm would supply "twenty-five impressions and the stone, of any portrait, at the moderate price of twenty-five dollars. The copy is exact and beautiful. We hope to see made in this way collections of likenesses of Americans distinguished for their public merits, or esteemed for their private virtues by a large circle of acquaintance." While images of Jackson, Clay, and Kemble hung in the windows of the printshops, Childs was encouraging Philadelphia's citizenry to bring in their Inman, Neagle, or Sully portraits and go home with reproductions to distribute to their friends: "Col. Childs has been engaged for some time past in executing some likenesses of our citizens for private distribution—a very cheap and certainly rational mode of gratifying the feelings of friends. We looked at two or three, and find them remarkably exact likenesses, although reduced from a full size portrait."[15]

Newsam had a magic touch. The lithographs of his early period, sometimes embellished with curling lines at the periphery as in *James Page* (see fig. 13), are generally small and have a delicacy and charm that are missing from his later, less carefully drawn portraits. With crispness, clarity, and confidence, he copied portraits by John Neagle, such as those of the architect William Strickland and the publisher Mathew Carey; by Joseph Wood, such as that of the engraver William Kneass; by Rembrandt Peale, such as that of William Henry Harrison; and, of course, by Philadelphia's leading portrait painter, Thomas Sully, such as those of Jared Sparks and Robert Walsh, Jr. (fig. 5).

But, more than any of these other painters, Newsam copied the work of Childs's future partner, Henry Inman. The lithographs of John G. Watmough (fig. 6) and William Rawle (fig. 7), both after Inman, were two

15 *National Gazette or Literary Register* (Philadelphia), April 15, 1830; *United States Gazette*, April 22, 1930.

94

5
Robert Walsh, Jr., 1784-1859. Lithograph, circa 1830, by Newsam after Thomas Sully, 11.1 × 13 cm. (*National Portrait Gallery, Smithsonian Institution*)

of Newsam's most admired portraits. "No American portrait we have seen, equals that of colonel John G. Watmough," reported a newspaper in 1831. Critical praise of the lithograph helped to publicize the original painting on exhibition at the Pennsylvania Academy. *W Rawle* was equally appreciated: "The likeness of the eminent jurist and truly excellent man is striking. . .and the ensemble has a remarkable effect. . . . Specimens of the kind are from week to week issued at the establishment of Messrs. Childs & Inman which entitles those gentlemen to claim for it an equality at least with any in our country."[16]

The portraits of Rawle and Watmough have been singled out by Frank Weitenkampf as representing a French lithographic style. And in 1830 the newspapers, admiring another Newsam print, *The White Plume*, after a painting by Charles Ingham, commented that it "may be compared with almost any print that has issued from the lithographic press at Paris."[17] It was not an idle comparison. The dominant artistic heritage of the first

16   *National Gazette or Literary Register*, April 20, 1831, March 21, 1832. The lithographs of Watmough and Rawle were praised both at the time when they were published and in later years. *William Rawle* was included in the 1896 Grolier Club lithography exhibition with the comment: "One of his most important works. A vigorous drawing, freely handled" (Grolier Club, *Catalogue*, p. 43). See also Weitenkampf references in note 17.

17   Frank Weitenkampf, *American Graphic Art* (1912; rept. New York, 1974), p. 186; and Weitenkampf, "Portraits in Lithography," pp. 14–15; *United States Gazette*, April 22, 1830.

6
John Goddard Watmough,
1793-1861. Lithograph, 1831, by
Newsam after Henry Inman, 31.2 ×
31.5 cm. (*Private collection*)

American shops came primarily from Paris, where the lithography market
was thriving. In 1816 the firms of Englemann and Lasteyrie had opened
there and had started to attract leading French artists to the medium.
Competing firms—Delpech, Gihaut, Motte, and Lemercier—followed
shortly thereafter, and almost overnight artists' lithographs, as well as
lithographic copies of paintings, flooded the market.

French prints (and French printers) had made their way to America
when lithography was just beginning. Philadelphia's *Analectic Magazine* in
July 1819 reported that "the prints from stone that have reached us, here
are chiefly by M. Engelmann. . .and by M. de Lestayrie [*sic*] at Paris."[18]
Just before he came to Philadelphia, John Pendleton had gone to France to
have Gilbert Stuart's paintings of the first five Presidents copied on stone.
Printed and published by the Pendleton brothers in Boston in 1828, the

18 *Analectic Magazine* (July 1819) quoted in Joseph Jackson, *Some Notes towards a
History of Lithography in Philadelphia* (Philadelphia, 1900), p. 13.

7

William Rawle, 1759-1836. Lithograph, 1832, by Newsam after Henry Inman, 26 × 21.3 cm. (*National Portrait Gallery, Smithsonian Institution*)

French-made "American Kings" were widely distributed and imitated and became, in fact, a standard format for presidential portrait series throughout the century.[19]

For the Childs firm, imported prints from Paris clearly represented the highest achievement in the medium. "It is proof of Mr. Child's love of the arts," the editors wrote, "and of his intention to make improvements in his own establishment, that he exhibits to visitors specimens of Parisian lithographs superior to those of his own drawing."[20] In 1829 Pendleton, Kearny, and Childs had hired a French printer about whom little is known, and in 1831 Childs returned from Europe with a second French

19 Mabel M. Swan, "The American Kings," *Antiques* 19 (April 1931): 278–81; "The Editor's Attic," ibid., 20 (July 1931): 11–13. Newsam copied these images for the first five prints of his own presidential series in 1846.

20 *United States Gazette*, Sept. 9, 1829.

printer and lithographer, Pierre S. Duval, who eventually became partner and then sole proprietor of the firm. Newsam seems to have been surrounded by French influence in lithography. His former teacher, Hugh Bridport, produced for Pendleton, Kearny, and Childs a portrait of John Vaughan also drawn in a French style.

Exactly which French portrait prints served as models is unknown, but Philadelphians may well have been seeing the work of an artist like Achille Devéria, one of the important portrait lithographers of Paris. Another prolific portraitist, and one whom Newsam claimed to admire, was Henri Grevedon,[21] whose crayon style does seem similar to his.

French prints had an effect on Newsam, and American lithography in general, primarily in the early stages. Certainly there were other influences, too: English sources were predominant in lithographic book illustration and music sheets, and the artistic influence of the German immigrants of the late 1840s was substantial. Local artists had their own impact on lithography, since portraits, along with views, were mostly copied from American work and often reflect the style of the painter much more than that of the lithographer.

Because of the role of the painter, it is sometimes difficult to recognize a "Newsam style." Although *The White Plume, Jn. G. Watmough,* and some of his prints after daguerreotypes are drawn with rich contrasts, and the small, early images have distinctive, curling lines at the periphery, many of Newsam's lithographs are drawn with an almost lineless tint, a perhaps consciously nondescript crayon style that does not interfere with the translation of the original image. Frequently it is easier to tell that the original is by Sully, Inman, or Hubard than that the print itself is drawn by Newsam. It is both his strength and his primary weakness.

Cephas Childs's friendship with Philadelphia artists had a major effect on the development of his business. Engraving was still the respected medium for reproduction, and Childs had to compete with well-established stipple engravers such as David Edwin and James Barton Longacre and the talented new mezzotinter John Sartain. Nevertheless, he was able to interest Philadelphia's leading painters in lithography. Between Childs's personal connections and Newsam's talent, lithography

21 Pyatt (pp. 52–53) mentions that Newsam spoke highly of Lecompte and Grevedon and thought that Richard Lane was the greatest lithographic artist in Great Britain.

acquired some respectability as a graphic medium, just as it had in Boston through the efforts of William Pendleton. New York could not claim a similar personality among its early lithographers, and, in fact, it was Childs who drew that city's leading painter, Henry Inman, into the lithography fold.

Childs's partnership with John Pendleton and Francis Kearny had lasted only through 1829. In 1830 he was on his own, and in December of that year, the newspapers announced his partnership with Inman. Although well established as a painter and serving as vice-president of the National Academy of Design, Inman remained very conscious of the graphic reproduction of his work and frequently sold paintings, specifically to be engraved, to publishers of annuals and giftbooks. This was probably how he first came into contact with Cephas Childs, who during 1823 and 1824 had engraved his illustrations of James Fenimore Cooper's stories for publication in the magazine *Port Folio*. Although Inman admired Childs's abilities,[22] he was occasionally disappointed by the work of other engravers. He complained about one of Asher B. Durand's illustrations of his work in a January 1829 letter to publisher Mathew Carey: "It is my wish to have a place in your next year's Annual in order to redeem some reputation which I have lost by the unfortunate engraving of the Sisters: (I do not censure Mr. Durand, but only lament that he had not more time to devote to that subject.)"[23]

Perhaps discouraged with engraving, Inman became intrigued by lithography—particularly that of Albert Newsam. When, in August 1829, Childs asked him to paint some portraits for the young artist to lithograph, Inman replied: "It will be impossible for me, owing to my present engagements, to supply you with any of the sketches of character you speak of, which I regret the more, in as much as I shall thereby miss the pleasure of obliging you and the satisfaction of having my drawings lithographed by your young prodigy."[24] A few months later, Inman was subscribing to Newsam's lithograph of Henry Clay. Eventually, he did start sending his

22 Inman to Childs, March 27, 1829, MWA.

23 Inman to Carey, Jan. 18, 1829, Harriet Sartain Papers, Historical Society of Pennsylvania, Philadelphia (hereafter PHi).

24 Inman to Childs, Aug. 19, 1829, MWA.

own sketches, and he was pleased with the results. Reacting to a proof he had been sent, he wrote to Childs in June 1830, "I have seen your lithograph of Dr. Godman. It is excellent." The following month he requested that Godman's widow send two or three proof impressions for the library of the academy.[25]

Although their partnership was not announced until December 1830, and although Inman did not arrive in Philadelphia until April of the following year, lithographic stones, sheets of India paper, letters, portrait sketches, and proofs were shuttled back and forth, with Inman's energetic and impatient personality sometimes one step ahead of practicality: "I have been expecting to hear from you every day. . . . Have you any of them ready yet? I want as I said before the head of Bishop Dubois lithographed. Shall I send it on at once or bring it on with me? Have you done anything to Halleck?" In another letter: "Have you done Vaux? Don't fail to send me one of the earliest impressions as well as of Watmough when done." "Yours in a hell of a hurry," he sometimes signed himself.[26]

Inman also did his best to market the prints in New York City. At first he was skeptical about the chances of selling Newsam's lithograph of DeWitt Clinton (fig. 8), writing to Childs on June 30, 1830: "I should have written you a day sooner but I could not find at home some of the printsellers and booksellers upon whom I called to show the Clinton. Bleecker was the only one of them that gave me a distinct order for any and he only wished 12—Browne makes a poor mouth and says they won't sell. Bliss don't want any, Gilley says he don't deal in prints, and thus far I do not see the vast prospect of sale in this city that I once imagined." But he was not discouraged: "However they all say with emphasis that it is the best likeness of the man they have seen. I have set the editors at work praising it and in that way curiosities will be excited in the public to see it. You may as well send on whatever number you think advisable and I will place them in the different stores on commission."[27]

The following day, the prospects began to improve. Inman wrote that he had shown the print to "Verplanck, Stone, and other gentlemen that

25   Inman to Childs, June 11, July 16, Aug. 28, 1830, MWA.

26   Inman to Childs, July 11, 1830, Jan. 28, 1831, Dec. 7, 1829, MWA.

27   Inman to Childs, June 30, 1830, MWA.

100

8

DeWitt Clinton, 1769-1828. Lithograph, 1830, by Newsam after Henry Inman, 13 × 13.8 cm. (*Historical Society of Pennsylvania, Philadelphia*)

DEWITT CLINTON.

knew him well, and they say it is the only likeness of him extant." He added that he thought it would be wise to send on "a good number." Advertisements had already appeared in some of the New York papers. On July 11 Inman wrote to Childs that the "book and print sellers are waiting for the Clintons. Have you any ready yet?" The package he awaited arrived on the sixteenth. Of the forty impressions of the *Clinton,* Inman kept one for himself, sent three to newspaper editors to review, and deposited thirty-six at various bookstores and printshops in the city. By August he could tell Childs "many fine things respecting the success of your head of Clinton." When Childs sent him the lithograph of Robert Vaux, Inman returned it with the comment: "I presume you will understand the marks I have made on the sketch you sent me. Indeed I saw no necessity for sending it on at all. The Clinton might generally serve as a model for heads where hands are not introduced."[28]

While Inman was always impatiently demanding more lithographs, he felt that a new commission should take instant priority—as was the case

28 Inman to Childs, July 1, 1830, MWA. Inman's statement was untrue: there were several paintings of Clinton; an engraving by Leney after Trumbull which was published in *Delaplaine's Repository*, 1817, and in the *Casket*, 1827; and a 1796 engraving by Saint-Mémin (Inman to Childs, July 11, July 16, Aug. 1830, Jan. 12, 1831, MWA). Inman eventually sold his sketch of Clinton to Asher B. Durand for fifty dollars, and Durand engraved a portrait for Harpers Family Library in 1830 (Inman to Childs, Oct. 21, 1830, MWA).

with "the celebrated Dr. Broussais, the French Physician." For a translated edition of his works, the publishers needed his likeness to use as the
frontispiece: "They wish a copy made of the head of the same size done in
our best style. . .and they wish as soon as possible 550 Impressions. The
dress may be done in a much more sketchy style with a little more
background.—All this of course on stone. As it is important to make an
impression in this city with respect to our establishment, I would beg of
you to let Albert put everything aside to do it."[29] The irrepressible Inman
embellished this directive with a crude sketch of the portrait and added the
instruction "Terminating like the Clinton." Within two-and-a-half
weeks, Inman could report that the publishers had already received the
prints. Although peevish that the paper size did not match the speci-
fications, he did mention that "the execution of the Head is much approved
of."[30]

By the time Inman finally arrived in Philadelphia, in April 1831,
Childs had arranged sittings with prominent patrons and Newsam was
ready to lithograph the paintings. Inman even experimented briefly with
the medium himself. From his retreat in Mount Holly, New Jersey, near
the city, he wrote to Childs: "I shall by and by when the cold weather sets
in, want some Lithographic stones prepared for I intend to do something
funny to help make the 'mare go.' "[31]

Newsam was not the only lithographer in Philadelphia, but he had
quickly developed a devoted following. The drawing and printing skills of a
supposed competitor, M.E.D. Brown, just arrived from Boston, were
extolled by "Plain Truth," a newspaper correspondent, on May 31, 1832.
In the following week's paper, an irate reader challenged "Plain Truth" to
"mention what subject from the hands of Mr. Brown, he thinks worthy of
being classed with those of Newsam." The writer stressed that it would
"be difficult to supplant the 'pupil of Childs' in fulness of fame." Although

29 Inman to Childs, Jan. 5, 1831, Dreer Collection, PHi.

30 Inman to Childs, Jan. 22, 1831, MWA. Inman was generally enthusiastic about
    Newsam's work. He did, however, offer the following criticism: "Have you seen the
    head of Webster from Pendleton of Boston. Newsam must try to give the same kind
    of stipple looking grain to his drawing. The want of it is the only fault he has"
    (Inman to Childs, March 3, 1831, MWA).

31 Inman to Childs, Oct. 2, 1832, MWA.

Brown was a skilled lithographer, who produced a masterpiece in his print of William P. Dewees, he may have sensed the public's support of its adopted son, for he drew very few portraits and eventually left Philadelphia.[32]

There were other popular successes issued by the Childs and Inman firm besides Newsam's portraits, including the *Cabinet of Natural History* lithographed by Thomas Doughty, some views by George Lehman, and some cartoons by Edward Clay. In the precarious business world of the day, however, the firm was always on the financial brink. In April 1833 the partnership dissolved, and Inman returned to New York. For a time, Childs took on George Lehman as a partner, but he still found himself in debt. In 1834 he sold his part of the business to Peter Duval, who had been his printer for three years. Lehman left at the end of 1837, and P.S. Duval continued on for many years as Philadelphia's leading firm.

One connecting link throughout these changes was the firm's principal artist, Albert Newsam, and his portraits. An attempt at oil painting in 1855, under the tutelage of James Reid Lambdin, was short-lived. He continued to draw on stone until his eyesight failed in 1857; a partial recovery was set back by a stroke in 1859. After Newsam's death in 1864, Duval recalled his preeminence: "When I arrived in this country in 1831, to take charge of Messrs. Childs and Inman's lithographic establishment, Albert Newsam was their principal artist, and had exclusive charge of the drawing of portraits on stone, which was the main branch of the business in those days, and he was remarkably successful in obtaining resemblances."[33]

Duval went on to say that Newsam's great strength was as a copyist and that his life portraits lacked animation because his deafness precluded conversation with his sitters. This is perhaps a bit overstated. A comparison of two Newsam drawings, a pair of unidentified pencil portraits recently acquired by the Library Company of Philadelphia, which are undoubtedly taken from life, show both his strengths and his weaknesses. The *Unidentified Man* (fig. 9) is an example of the repetitive formula that he lapsed into because of the enormous quantity of pictures he was asked to

32 *United States Gazette*, May 31, June 8, 1832.

33 Pyatt, pp. 112–14, 147. Duval's statement is also quoted in Harry T. Peters, *America on Stone* (New York, 1931), pp. 297–98.

9

Unidentified man. Pencil drawing, 1843, by Newsam from life, 23.5 × 20 cm. (*Library Company of Philadelphia*)

produce. The drawing is competent, hard, and tight and gives the impression of having been done in record time. The features are very specific—one has the feeling that it is an accurate likeness—but they are unexciting. The coat is quickly drawn, the folds and wrinkles are suggested, but there is no care taken. The *Unidentified Woman* (fig. 10), on the other hand, is lovingly portrayed. The intricacy of the lace is rendered in detail, and highlights and shadows are carefully drawn on each minute gather of her bodice. Her face, with its weary eyes and serene and dignified expression, has many of the subtle and intriguing qualities that we might ask of a far more skilled and renowned portraitist. Newsam was not a Sully or a Neagle or an Inman, but it is still unfortunate that more of his life drawings have not survived.[34]

Although not a majority, a significant number of Newsam's litho-

34 The only other drawings by Newsam identified at present are a charcoal portrait of Edwin Forrest in the Hatch Collection of the National Gallery of Art, Washington, D.C., and a small landscape drawing owned by the Historical Society of Pennsylvania in Philadelphia.

10
Unidentified woman. Pencil drawing, 1843, by Newsam from life, 22 × 20 cm. (*Library Company of Philadelphia*)

graphs were based on his own life drawings. In 1841 Thomas Wagner started publishing his *U.S. Ecclesiastical Portrait Gallery*, with biographies and lithographs, most of them from life, by Newsam.[35] Like so many periodicals of the time, this one did not succeed, but it did leave us a number of Newsam's life portraits, of which Daniel Dodge is a striking example. The dramatic hand-colored portrait of John D. Bemo (fig. 11), the nephew of Osceola, is also inscribed "From Life on Stone by A. Newsam." A short biography is appended to the title: "Converted to christianity at sea, united to the Mariner's church, Philad, under the care

35 Wainwright, pp. 41–42. The *U.S. Ecclesiastical Portrait Gallery* was either very short-lived or never published. The only remaining evidences of its existence are the lithographic portraits and a few printed biographies in the Newsam collection of the Historical Society of Pennsylvania. Included among the Newsam portraits probably made for this series are *Albert Barnes, J. F. Berg, John Breckinridge, Charles Carroll, D. C. Carroll, Daniel Dodge, Robert Gerry, George Higgins, George B. Ide, J. Kennaday, Joseph H. Kennard, John McDowell, J. Gordon Maxwell,* and *Stephen H. Tyng.*

JOHN D. BEMO,
or HUSTI-COLOC-CHEE

Nephew of the celebrated Seminole Chief Osceola.
Converted to christianity at sea, united to the Mariner's church, Philad: under the care of Rev. O Douglass Sept 1842.
Preparing to return to his tribe to instruct them in the way of salvation.

11
John D. Bemo. Lithograph, 1842, by Newsam from life, 39.5 × 25.5 cm. (*Historical Society of Pennsylvania, Philadelphia*)

of Rev. O. Douglass Sept. 1842. Preparing to return to his tribe to instruct them in the way of salvation.''

Newsam played various roles in the production of Huddy and Duval's *U.S. Military Magazine* (1839–42)), drawing original portraits for others to lithograph or drawing them on stone himself.[36] His full-length illustration

36 See Frederick P. Todd, "The Huddy & Duval Prints: An Adventure in Military Lithography," *Journal of the American Military Institute* 3 (Autumn 1839): 166–76. Todd mentions several plates by or after Newsam. Missing from the list but also drawn by Newsam for this periodical are lithographs of *Colonel James Page* and *Peter Fritz*.

James Page, 1795-1875. Lithograph, circa 1840, by Newsam from life, 27 × 25 cm. (*Historical Society of Pennsylvania, Philadelphia*)

of Colonel James Page (fig. 12), done from life, makes an interesting comparison with his earlier lithograph of Page (fig. 13), copied after Inman. Newsam lacked the graceful elegance and refinement of the leading portrait painters, but his direct and forceful approach does give his somewhat wooden figures a certain liveliness.

Childs and Inman's newspaper promotions of their portrait lithographs may not have made the firm solvent, but it did solidly establish

13
James Page, 1795-1875. Lithograph, circa 1830, by Newsam after Henry Inman, 11.2 × 12 cm. (*Historical Society of Pennsylvania, Philadelphia*)

Newsam's reputation. Before long, his portrait commissions took on a life of their own, and the newspapers were not needed. Financial promoters outside the firm are indicated by the telltale copyright line on the bottom of the lithographs.

One group that often approached Newsam for lithographs was the portrait painters. Initially, Childs had approached them; but as lithography became more established, the artists began to seek out the best draftsmen and finance the lithographic work themselves. James Reid Lambdin had Newsam copy his portrait of Joseph Hopkinson just after the subject's death; and John F. Francis published several Newsam lithographs, including the one after his painting of Governor Joseph Ritner. The itinerant portrait painter Jesse Atwood published a Newsam lithograph of his likeness of Zachary Taylor, on which, in order to diminish the obvious shortcomings of the original portrait, he included an authentication of the image signed by several of the officers and a facsimile letter from Taylor himself.

Soon after the daguerreotype was introduced into Philadelphia, Newsam had a new portrait medium to copy and a new group of artists seeking his talents. His 1841 print of Fanny Elssler after a plate by Robert Cornelius may have been the first lithograph to be copied from a daguerreotype. After seeing Elssler dance, Newsam wrote: "As I sat in the theatre, I saw people around me clapping when she danced and mimed. I too was moved to applaud, for I understood every one of her movements. If everyone expressed themselves as clearly as Fanny, the world would no longer be veiled for us deaf-mutes."[37] Newsam's prints after the dag-

---

37 William Stapp, who has done extensive research on Robert Cornelius, has suggested that Newsam's *Elssler* may be the first lithograph after a daguerreotype. Ivor Guest, *Fanny Elssler* (Middletown, Conn., 1970), p. 176.

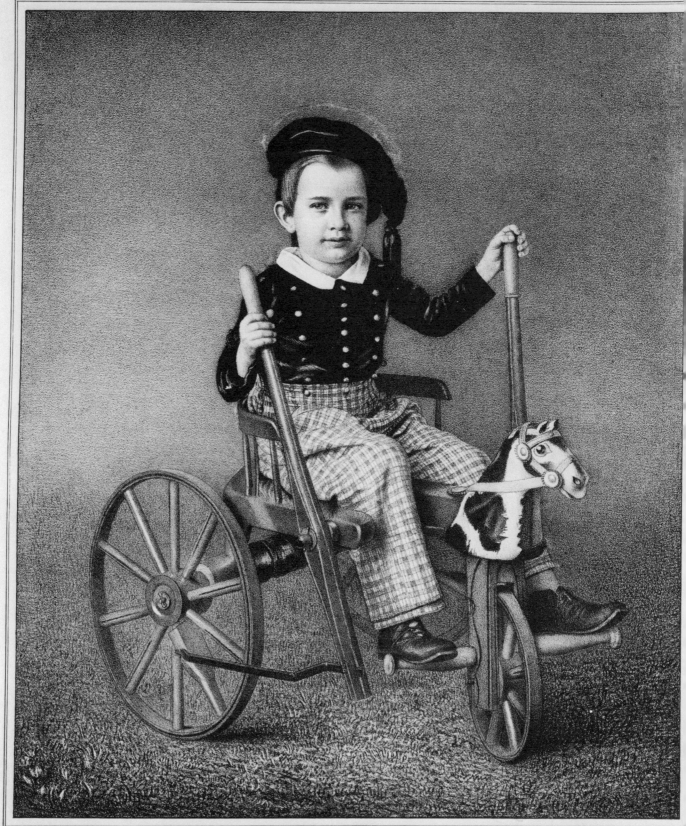

14

Child on velocipede. Lithograph, circa 1846, by Newsam after John Jabez
Edwin Mayall, 26.3 × 22 cm. (*Historical Society of Pennsylvania,
Philadelphia*)

CM Clay.
CASSIUS M. CLAY.

The daguerreotype (of which the above is a most exact copy) was taken of Mr Clay during his visit to Philadelphia,
in January 1846, and is considered by himself and friends one of the most faithful portraitures ever executed.

Philadelphia, Published by T.P Collins, N° 100 Chesnut St above 3ᵈ.

15
Cassius M. Clay, 1810-1903. Lithograph, 1846, by Newsam after Thomas P. Collins, 26.5 × 30 cm. (*Historical Society of Pennsylvania, Philadelphia*)

uerreotypist John Jabez Edwin Mayall, such as the proof of an unidentified child on a velocipede (fig. 14), were particularly striking and drawn with deep, rich blacks. "Published by J. E. Mayall at his daguerreotype Gallery," reads the inscription on two Newsam prints of *Charles Lyell Esqr.* and *Jamison as MacBeth,* both dated 1846. The daguerreotypist T. P. Collins had Newsam copy his plate of *Cassius M. Clay* (fig. 15), and just to make sure that everyone appreciated the original, he included the inscription line: "The daguerreotype (of which the above is a most exact copy) was taken of Mr. Clay during his visit to Philadelphia, in January 1846, and is considered by himself and his friends one of the most faithful portraitures ever executed."

A variation on the same practice was Newsam's "plumbeotype" of John Breckinridge, published in 1846 by John Plumbe, Jr.[38] Although the

38 See Alan Fern and Milton Kaplan, "John Plumbe, Jr., and the First Architectural Photographs of the Nation's Capitol," *Quarterly Journal of the Library of Congress* 31 (1974): 3–20. See also Ruel Pardee Tolman, "Plumbeotype," *Antiques* 8 (July 1925): 27–28.

"new art" of the plumbeotype was nothing more than a lithographic copy of one of Plumbe's daguerreotypes, the *John Breckinridge*—possibly the only non-Plumbe plumbeotype—was, in fact, from the same stone Newsam made for the *Ecclesiastical Portrait Gallery,* copied from a drawing by John Sartain. Whether Newsam drew any plumbeotypes that were after the daguerreotypes is unknown. The quality of most of them is so poor that one suspects he did not.

Book and music publishers, of course, had been another major source of commissions since the early days of lithography. Despite his exalted reputation, Newsam turned out his full share of hastily drawn, small illustrations, which rarely surpassed the accepted standards of mediocrity. His music titles varied from coarse copies of English sheet music to somewhat more interesting efforts based on daguerreotypes.

Newsam was also involved, however, in some ambitious publication projects that transcended the usual limits of illustration. His work for the *Ecclesiastical Portrait Gallery* has already been mentioned, as well as his contribution to Huddy and Duval's *U.S. Military Magazine.* Eclipsing both of these in scale and quality was McKenney and Hall's massive *History of the Indian Tribes of North America* (1837–44).

Thomas McKenney, the first head of the Bureau of Indian Affairs, had ventured very early into lithographic illustration. His *Sketches of a Tour to the Lakes,* published in Baltimore in 1827, had interesting but crude little Indian portraits and scenes drawn by Moses Swett and other artists of both the Pendleton and the Imbert firms. Less than a decade later, McKenney chose Childs and Inman to produce the large, hand-colored lithographs that illustrated his Indian biographies, and the contrast with his previous venture is spectacular. The McKenney-Hall lithographs—*Kai-Pol-E-Quah* (fig. 16), for example—were carefully and beautifully hand-colored, much larger, better drawn, and more accurate than the crude images from the earlier work. Most of the portraits in the first volume were originally painted by Charles Bird King, copied in oils by Inman, and then given to Newsam to lithograph. This may have been the final financial disaster of the firm. Having moved out to Mount Holly, Inman worked on painting copies of King's portraits and sent letters to Childs complaining about the delay in McKenney's payments.[39] After the firm had supplied most of the forty-eight stones for the first volume (the

39 Inman to Childs, Oct. 25, 1833, MWA.

KAI-POL-E-QUAH or WHITE NOSED FOX.

Kai-Pol-E-Quah. Lithograph 1833, by
Newsam after Charles Bird King,
31.2 × 23 cm. (*Historical Society of
Pennsylvania, Philadelphia*)

111

majority of which were probably drawn by Newsam), the project, beset with financial problems, was transferred to J. T. Bowen's lithography company.[40]

Although the McKenney-Hall lithographs were always meant to be accompanied by a text, other publishers were commissioning groups of separately issued prints. It was the era of the portrait series: every promoter hoped that subscribers, having succumbed to one image, would feel compelled to buy the entire lot. Newsam did several series, mostly for publishers outside of the firm. His handsome set of the Presidents, hand-colored and embellished with a printed gold border, was issued by C. S. Williams, who was, according to the city directories, a "map agent." Joseph M. Wilson commissioned a series portraying ministers of the Presbyterian church. Joseph How published an interesting set of lithographs of black ministers, mostly after paintings by Joseph Kyle.

Unquestionably, Newsam made some outstanding portrait lithographs, and his prints have appeared in many exhibitions of American lithography;[41] but the course of his career was by no means unique. His

40 Herman Viola, *The Indian Legacy of Charles Bird King* (Washington, D.C., 1976), p. 80; Wainwright, p. 33.

41 Grolier Club, *Exhibition of Artistic Lithography* pp. 43–44; Club of Odd Volumes, *Exhibition of Early American Lithographs, 1819–1859* (Boston, 1924); Boston Mu-

work, though of a consistently high quality, was exemplary of a whole genre of graphic art, indeed of a whole industry. His method of working, the variability of his style, the gradual change to photographic rather than painted sources, the publication procedures of the firm, all reflected common practice.

Newsam was not the best American artist to draw portraits on stone. Other more versatile, more skilled, or better-trained artists experimented with lithography. Rembrandt Peale, whom Newsam is said to have idolized,[42] won the silver medal at the Franklin Institute in 1827 for his lithograph of George Washington after his own painting. Though Peale thought of lithography as merely a reproductive process, he was one of the first American artists to transcend that limitation.[43] Even in his book illustrations, such as the likeness of John Kirkland, after Stuart, for James Thacher's *American Medical Biography* of 1828, he set a high standard for copy work that few other lithographers could match at the time.

Though numerous artists reproduced their own paintings on stone, there are few who qualify as portrait lithographers working from life. Charles Fenderich is one of those few.[44] His series of "Living American Statesmen" comprises strong, boldly drawn lithographs, with carefully defined facial characteristics. He achieved interesting effects with clothing, often using a fur-trimmed cloak, plaid vest or polka-dot cravat, or velvet collar to embellish his likenesses (fig. 17). Newsam copied Fenderich's *James K. Polk* for his own presidential series.

If Albert Newsam was not the best portrait lithographer, he was, at the least, thoroughly professional, especially in comparison to some of his less-skilled colleagues. *The Rev. Spencer H. Cone*—actor, journalist,

---

seum of Fine Arts, *An Exhibition of Lithographs* (Boston, 1937), p. 44; Cleveland Museum of Art, *Catalogue of an Exhibition of the Art of Lithography* (Cleveland, 1949), p. 53.

42 Pyatt, p. 124.

43 See John E. Mahey, "Lithographs by Rembrandt Peale," *Antiques* 97 (Feb. 1970): 236–42.

44 See Alice Lee Parker and Milton Kaplan, *Charles Fenderich: Lithographer of American Statesmen* (Washington, D.C., 1959).

P. P. Pitchlynn

P. P. PITCHLYNN.

Speaker of the National Council

OF THE CHOCTAW NATION

AND

CHOCTAW DELEGATE

to the

Government of the United States.

17
Peter Pitchlynn, 1806-1881. Lithograph, 1842, by Charles Fenderich from life, 28.2 × 27 cm. (*National Portrait Gallery, Smithsonian Institution*)

soldier, and Baptist clergyman—was published by a dentist; and with his hair standing on end, he looks as if he might well have been drawn from life as he sat in the dentist's chair.

The lithograph by John Landis of William Miller, originator of the Advent Movement, who predicted the second coming of Christ and the destruction of the world between 1843 and 1844, is equally crude. One suspects that it was the strength of Miller's oratory and the doom of his message, rather than the face in this lithograph, that struck terror into the hearts of thousands of his followers.[45]

Then there is the *Rev. Sylvanus Palmer* (fig. 18), drawn on stone by S. Palmer, Jr.: a devoted son's portrait of his father. He made a brave attempt at the background drapery, diligently crammed the spandrels with floral embellishment, and drew a charming little landscape in the distance with the rector's own church. Unfortunately, in his zeal to suggest wrinkles in the trousers, he seems to have amputated the poor man's leg. Beneath the

45 The lithograph of Miller was attributed to Landis by John Carbonell.

114

18
Sylvanus Palmer. Lithograph, 1844,
by Sylvanus Palmer, Jr., from life,
19.2 × 15.1 cm. (*Harry T. Peters
America on Stone Collection, National
Museum of American History, Smithsonian Institution*)

portrait is a marvelous biblical quotation, perfectly chosen for this image: "I am afraid of you, lest I have bestowed upon you labor in vain."

Perhaps it is not fair to compare Newsam's professional work to these charming, but obviously amateur, efforts. But even at his worst, his portraits are merely dull, lacking perhaps in inspiration. As likenesses, as documents, they have an integrity sometimes entirely missing in the cheap productions of other companies. We know very little about the early portrait artists of Nathaniel Currier's firm, and that is not surprising. His portraits were often so cheaply produced, so far from the original image, that no one would dare acknowledge them. Some of the likenesses published by the Sarony and Major company fall into the same class. Napoleon Sarony himself was such a talented portrait artist, as can be seen in his 1874 self-portrait lithograph, that it is hard to imagine prints such as the 1844 *James K. Polk* coming from his firm. Childs would never have allowed such mediocrity; neither would Duval. They did not have to. They had Albert Newsam, patiently and diligently turning out likenesses over a span of thirty years, leaving us an indelible record of the lithographic portrait.

It is at present impossible to do a complete and accurate checklist of Albert Newsam's portraits. An extremely prolific artist, he produced numerous book illustrations and sheet-music covers for which there are no records. In addition, he would often draw several versions of the same portrait, which differed only in minor details or in size. However, since the only checklist of the lithographs—David McNeely Stauffer's "Lithographic Portraits of Albert Newsam," *Pennsylvania Magazine of History and Biography* 24(1900): 267-89, 403-52, 25(1901): 109-13, 26(1902): 382-86—is woefully incomplete and somewhat inaccessible, this preliminary list has been assembled. Additions to Stauffer's list are based on the collections of the Historical Society of Pennsylvania, the Library of Congress, and the National Portrait Gallery, Smithsonian Institution. Information about original painter or photographer, date, lithography company, publisher, and publication in which the print appeared is given where available. The information in this checklist is based on the inscriptions on the prints and the letters and sources consulted for this essay.

A few of the pieces in the Historical Society of Pennsylvania's Newsam Collection have been left out of this list. Even though most of the early lithographs with Child's name on them seem to have been drawn by Albert Newsam, under his teacher's supervision, the prints of Issac Collins and Madame Malibran Garcia, whose inscriptions state specifically "C. G. Childs fecit" and "C. G. Childs on stone," have been excluded. Also excluded from this list are nonportrait lithographs and prints drawn on stone by August Koellner for the *U.S. Military Magazine* after Newsam's original drawings.

	Subject and Publication	Original Artist	Date	Lithography company / Publisher
1	Abd-El-Kader, *The Parlour Review*		1838	Lehman & Duval
2	Abd-El-Kader, *Abd-El-Kader Quick Step*		1844	Lehman & Duval
3	John Adams	G. Stuart	1846	P. S. Duval for C. S. Williams
4	John Adams	G. Stuart		P. S. Duval
5	John Quincy Adams		1846	P. S. Duval for C. S. Williams
6	John Quincy Adams	G. Stuart		P. S. Duval
7	James Allen	daguerreotype		P. S. Duval
8	Thomas G. Allen	photograph by M. P. Simons		P. S. Duval
9	Thomas G. Allen	photograph by M. P. Simons		P. S. Duval & Son
10	Amelia			Childs & Inman for S. M. Stewart
11	A-Na-Cam-E-Gish-Ca, *History of the Indian Tribes*	C. B. King	1836	Lehman & Duval for Key & Biddle
12	William J. B. Andrews, *U.S. Military Magazine*	from life		Huddy & Duval
13	Archbishops of Baltimore (Carroll, Neale, Marechal, Whitfield, Eccleston, Green)		1837	John T. Green

	Subject and Publication	Original Artist	Date	Lithography company / Publisher
14	R. Arthur			P. S. Duval & Son
15	Rose Atherton			P. S. Duval for C. H. Keith or for S. Colman
16	Edwin A. Atlee			P. S. Duval & Co.'s Steam Lith. Press
17	Alexander Dallas Bache			P. S. Duval
18	Mary Ann (Mrs. John) Bacon	daguerreotype by W. & F. Langenheim		P. S. Duval
19	Mary Ann Warder Bacon			Steam Lith. Press of P. S. Duval
20	William Badger	daguerreotype by M. A. Root		P. S. Duval & Co.
21	John C. Baker	daguerreotype by Johnson		P. S. Duval's Steam Lith. Press for Spangler & Brother
22	W. Baker			P. S. Duval's Steam Lith. Press
23	William Baldwin	C. W. Peale	1843	P. S. Duval
24	John Banks	J. B. Schoener	1840	P. S. Duval for J. B. Schoener
25	John Banks	J. B. Schoener	1841	P. S. Duval for J. B. Schoener
26	Albert Barnes	J. Neagle	c. 1831-33	Childs & Inman for R. H. Hobson
27	Albert Barnes, U.S. Ecclesiastical Portrait Gallery	from life	c. 1841	P. S. Duval for Thomas S. Wagner
28	John W. Bear	J. Eichholtz	1840	P. S. Duval for William M. Huddy
29	John W. Bear	from life	1844	P. S. Duval for Daniel McGinley
30	J. Beecher	Brewster		P. S. Duval
31	L. Van Beethoven (2 variants), The Parlour Review		1838	Lehman & Duval
32	Alan Beith	photograph	1858	P. S. Duval & Son for Joseph M. Wilson
33	Bellini, The Parlour Review		1838	P. S. Duval
34	John D. Bemo	from life	1842	P. S. Duval
35	J. F. Berg, U.S. Ecclesiastical Portrait Gallery	from life	c. 1841	P. S. Duval for Thomas S. Wagner
36	John M. Berrien, Cabinet	King	1829	Pendleton, Kearny & Childs
37	J. Porter Bewley			P. S. Duval's Steam Lith. Press
38	Clement C. Biddle	daguerreotype by McClees & Germon		P. S. Duval & Co.'s Steam Lith. Press

	Subject and Publication	Original Artist	Date	Lithography company / Publisher
39	Rebecca Cornell Biddle	T. Sully		Childs & Inman
40	Mrs. Nicholas Biddle	T. Sully		
41	William Bigler	daguerreotype by McClees & Germon		P. S. Duval's Steam Lith. Press for Harrison
42	William Bigler	daguerreotype by Van Loan & Co.	1851	P. S. Duval's Steam Lith. Press for S. T. Williams
43	Horace Binney			Childs & Inman
44	Robert M. Bird	daguerreotype by M. A. Root		P. S. Duval & Co.'s Steam Lith. Press
45	Anna Bishop, *Seeking Fortunes* or *On the Banks of Guadalquiver*	daguerreotype by McClees & Germon		P. S. Duval's Steam Lith. Press for A. Fiot
46	Anna Bishop, *V'era Un di Che il Cor Beata*			P. S. Duval's Steam Lith. Press
47	Andrew Blair	from life		P. S. Duval
48	Gustave Blessner			P. S. Duval for Lee & Walker
49	Will A. Blount			P. S. Duval & Co.
50	A. Bolmar			P. S. Duval & Co.
51	F. J. Bonduel			P. S. Duval
52	Daniel Boone	J. W. Berry after Chester Harding		Childs & Inman
53	James C. Booth	daguerreotype by M. A. Root		P. S. Duval & Co.'s Steam Lith. Press
54	George Boyd	Joseph B. Ord		Childs & Inman
55	Augustus Braham, *Never Despair*		1852	P. S. Duval & Co.'s Steam Lith. Press for A. Fiot
56	John Breckinridge, *U.S. Ecclesiastical Portrait Gallery*	J. Sartain	c. 1841	P. S. Duval for Thomas S. Wagner
57	John Breckinridge	J. Sartain	c. 1846	John Plumbe, Jr.
58	Henry H. Breen		1852	P. S. Duval for W. H. Freeman
59	A. G. Broadhead, Jr.	photograph by J. Brown		P. S. Duval & Son
60	William Francis Brough			P. S. Duval
61	F. J. V. Broussais, *Sketches of . . . Living Surgeons & Physicians*	H. Inman	1831	Childs & Inman
62	David Paul Brown	J. Neagle		P. S. Duval
63	W. H. Brown	from life		P. S. Duval
64	James Buchanan	J. Henry Brown		P. S. Duval's Steam Lith. Press
65	T. L. Buckingham			P. S. Duval & Son
66	James Burrows	J. Kyle	1842	P. S. Duval for Joseph How
67	William E. Burton as "Bob Acres"	T. Sully, Jr.		P. S. Duval

	Subject and Publication	Original Artist	Date	Lithography company / Publisher
68	Caa-Tou-See, *History of the Indian Tribes*	C. B. King	1836	Lehman & Duval for E. C. Biddle
69	William Camac (Carnac?)		1854	P. S. Duval & Co.'s Steam Lith. Press
70	James R. Campbell	Brewster		Lehman & Duval for Juvenile Foreign Missionary Society
71	W. S. Campbell	from life		P. S. Duval
72	Mathew Carey (2 variants)	J. Neagle	c. 1830	C. G. Childs
73	Mathew Carey	J. Neagle		Childs & Inman
74	Mathew Carey	J. Neagle		Lehman & Duval
75	Charles Carroll of Carrollton	T. Sully	1832	T. Sully, Childs & Inman
76	Daniel Lynn Carroll (2 variants), *U.S. Ecclesiastical Portrait Gallery*	from life	c. 1841	P. S. Duval for Thomas S. Wagner
77	Francis Xavier Cartland	daguerreotype by Brady		P. S. Duval's Steam Lith. Press
78	C. Stato Castani	daguerreotype by Collins		P. S. Duval
79	Ca-Ta-He-Cas-Sa, *History of the Indian Tribes*	C. B. King	1837	Lehman & Duval for E. C. Biddle
80	Mme. Catalini, *The Parlour Review*		1838	P. S. Duval
81	Rev. John Chambers			
82	Joseph R. Chandler	daguerreotype by McClees & Germon		P. S. Duval for McClees & Germon
83	Joseph R. Chandler	from life		P. S. Duval
84	Joseph R. Chandler	daguerreotype by McClees & Germon		P. S. Duval's Steam Lith. Press
85	Rt. Rev. Philander Chase	sketch by a young lady		C. G. Childs
86	L. Cherubini, *The Parlour Review*		1838	P. S. Duval
87	Child on velocipede	daguerreotype by J. J. E. Mayall		P. S. Duval
88	Chippeway Squaw & Child, *History of the Indian Tribes*	C. B. King	1837	Lehman & Duval for E. C. Biddle
89	Chon-Ca-Pe, *History of the Indian Tribes*	C. B. King	1837	Lehman & Duval for E. C. Biddle
90	Chon-Man-I-Case (Shaumonekusse), *History of the Indian Tribes*	C. B. King	1836	Lehman & Duval for E. C. Biddle
91	Thomas M. Clark	daguerreotype by T. P. & D. C. Collins	1847	P. S. Duval for T. P. & D. C. Collins

	Subject and Publication	Original Artist	Date	Lithography company / Publisher
92	Cassius M. Clay	daguerreotype by T. P. Collins	1846	P. S. Duval for T. P. Collins
93	Henry Clay	J. Neagle	1844	P. S. Duval for C. W. Bender & Co.
94	Henry Clay	J. Neagle	1844	P. S. Duval for John Neagle
95	Henry Clay	J. Wood	1829	Pendleton, Kearny & Childs; or C. G. Childs for D. Mallory
96	Henry Clay and John Sergeant		c. 1831	Childs & Inman
97	DeWitt Clinton	H. Inman	1830	C. G. Childs, Phila., & H. Inman, N.Y.
98	John Cole	H. Inman		P. S. Duval
99	Edmund Coles	H. Inman	c. 1831	Childs & Inman
100	George W. Colladay	daguerreotype by M. A. Root	1855	P. S. Duval's Steam Lith. Press
101	Nicholas Collin, *Annals of the Swedes*	Rev. H. G. Morton	1835	Lehman & Duval
102	Isaac Collins	James McClees		P. S. Duval & Son
103	John Collins as "McShane" (full-length)	daguerreotype by M. A. Root		P. S. Duval
104	John Collins as "McShane" (half-length)	daguerreotype by M. A. Root		P. S. Duval
105	Margaret Morris Collins, *The Hill Family*		1854	P. S. Duval & Co.'s Steam Lith. Press
106	John Colt	Henry Inman		P. S. Duval
107	Mr. Colt	T. Sully		Childs & Inman
108	Roswell G. Colt (2 variants)	T. Sully		Childs & Inman
109	Edmon S. Conner as "Romeo"	T. Sully, Jr.		P. S. Duval
110	Mr. & Mrs. F. B. Conway	daguerreotype by W. L. Germon		
111	Alexander Cook	W. H. Brown		P. S. Duval
112	James Fenimore Cooper, *Philadelphia Messenger*	J. Boilly	c. 1832	Childs & Inman
113	Joseph T. Cooper (2 variants)	daguerreotype by S. Broadbent	1858	P. S. Duval & Son for Joseph M. Wilson
114	Joseph T. Cooper	daguerreotype	1858	P. S. Duval & Son for Joseph M. Wilson
115	Com. John O. Creighton, U.S.N			Childs & Inman
116	David Crockett	S. S. Osgood	1834	Childs & Lehman for S. S. Osgood
117	George M. Dallas			
118	William Darlington, M.D.			P. S. Duval

	Subject and Publication	Original Artist	Date	Lithography company / Publisher
119	Samuel B. Davis	T. Sully		Childs & Inman
120	C. R. Demme	daguerreotype by W. & F. Langenheim		P. S. Duval
121	William R. DeWitt, D.D.	J. F. Francis		P. S. Duval for Sunday School Teachers of Presbyterian Church, Harrisburgh, Pa.
122	A. C. Dodge	daguerreotype		P. S. Duval & Co.'s Steam Lith. Press
123	Daniel Dodge, U.S. Ecclesiastical Portrait Gallery	from life	c. 1841	P. S. Duval for Thomas S. Wagner
124	Ex-Ameer Dost Mohamed	General Harlan		P. S. Duval
125	E. A. Douglas			P. S. Duval & Son
126	Rev. Orson Douglass	from life		P. S. Duval
127	I. S. DuSolle (2 variants)	T. E. Barratt		P. S. Duval
128	Luigi and Annibale Elena	P. Haas		P. S. Duval's Steam Lith. Press
129	Jesse D. Elliott	from life		P. S. Duval
130	Fanny Elssler, Danse Cosaque			P. S. Duval
131	Fanny Elssler	daguerreotype by Cornelius	c. 1841	
132	Fanny Elssler, La Cracovienne			P. S. Duval for A. Fiot
133	John England			P. S. Duval for Eugene Camminsky
134	Emperor of Brazil		1831	Childs & Inman for Samuel M. Stewart
135	Empress of Brazil		1831	Childs & Inman for Samuel M. Stewart
136	Esh-Tah-Hum-Leah, History of the Indian Tribes	C. B. King	1836	Lehman & Duval for Key & Biddle
137	James Ewell			P. S. Duval
138	Isaac Ferris			P. S. Duval
139	Millard Fillmore	daguerreotype by N. S. Bennett	1850	P. S. Duval's Steam Lith. Press for N. S. Bennett
140	Clara Fisher		c. 1830	C. G. Childs for R. H. Hobson
141	James C. Fisher	T. Sully	1830	C. G. Childs
142	Thomas B. Florence	M. Brady		Thomas S. Wagner Lith. Co.
143	L. Fornasari	G. Riboni		P. S. Duval

		Subject and Publication	Original Artist	Date	Lithography company / Publisher
	144	Edwin Forrest	T. Sully, Jr.	1836	Lehman & Duval for C. Alexander
	145	George Fox		1835	Lehman & Duval
	146	Peter Fritz, *U.S. Military Magazine*	from life	1835	P. S. Duval for Huddy and Duval
	147	Peter Fritz	Freeland		P. S. Duval
	148	Peter Fritz			Childs & Inman
	149	S. Gross Fry	daguerreotype		P. S. Duval & Co. for Beck & Lawton
	150	Henry M. Fuller			P. S. Duval's Steam Lith. Press
	151	James Gardette	Vanderlyn		P. S. Duval
	152	Charles W. Gardner	from life	1841	P. S. Duval for Joseph How
	153	William Lloyd Garrison	daguerreotype by T. B. Shaw		P. S. Duval
	154	Francis Xavier Gartland	daguerreotype		P. S. Duval
	155	Robert Gerry, *U.S. Ecclesiastical Portrait Gallery*		c. 1841	P. S. Duval for Thomas S. Wagner
	156	Mary Gideon	daguerreotype by J. H. Whitehurst		P. S. Duval & Co. Steam Lith. Press
	157	G. Musgrave Giger	daguerreotype		P. S. Duval & Co.
	158	E. W. Gilbert	A. B. Rockey		Childs & Lehman
	159	Capt. Gillis			P. S. Duval & Co.'s Steam Lith. Press for William Darton, London
	160	Bernard Gilpin			
	161	Stephen Girard	B. Otis	1832	Childs & Inman for John Y. Clark
	162	Stephen Girard, *Godey's Lady's Book*	Leon Noel from statue by Gevelot		P. S. Duval
	163	John D. Godman	H. Inman	1830	C. G. Childs
	164	W. Gordon			P. S. Duval
	165	L. M. Gottschalk	photograph		P. S. Duval & Co.'s Steam Lith. Press
	166	John L. Grant			Childs & Inman
	167	Stephen Grellet			P. S. Duval & Co.
	168	J. N. C. Grier	from life	1858	P. S. Duval for Joseph M. Wilson
	169	Robert C. Grier	ambrotype	1858	P. S. Duval & Son for Joseph M. Wilson
	170	Charles Grobe			P. S. Duval & Son
	171	Charles Grobe, *United States Grand Waltz*		1845	P. S. Duval for Lee & Walker

	Subject and Publication	Original Artist	Date	Lithography company / Publisher
172	Felix Grundy	W. B. Cooper		Lehman & Duval
173	Reuben Haines	J. Wood		P. S. Duval
174	John P. Hale	daguerreotype by England & Gunn		P. S. Duval for England & Gunn
175	Mrs. Sarah Hall (2 variants)		c. 1833	Childs & Inman
176	Fitz-Greene Halleck	H. Inman	c. 1831	Childs & Inman
177	Robert Hamilton	T. Sully, Jr.		P. S. Duval
178	James B. Hardenbergh	from life		P. S. Duval
179	Clarisse Harlowe, *Grand Valse pour le Piano*			P. S. Duval for A. Fiot & W. T. Mayo
180	William Henry Harrison	R. Peale	c. 1835-36	Lehman & Duval
181	William Henry Harrison	J. H. Beard	1840	J. T. Bowen for James Akin
182	William Henry Harrison	G. Upham	1840	P.S. Duval for George Upham
183	William Henry Harrison	T. Sully, Jr	1841	P. S. Duval for W. E. Tucker & Charles W. Bender
184	William Henry Harrison		1846	P. S. Duval for C. S. Williams
185	William Henry Harrison	silhouette by W. H. Brown		
186	William Henry Harrison (2 variants)			P. S. Duval
187	E. H. Drummond Hay	daguerreotype by W. H. Freeman	1852	P. S. Duval & Co.'s Steam Lith. Press for W. H. Freeman
188	Erskine Hazard	ambrotype by J. Brown		P. S. Duval & Son
189	Erskine Hazard	photograph		P. S. Duval & Son
190	James S. Henry	daguerreotype		P. S. Duval & Co. Steam Lith. Press
191	James S. Henry (2 variants), *Henry's Polka*	daguerreotype by Richardson		P. S. Duval & Co. Steam Lith. Press for Wm. F. Duffy, Henry McCaffrey, and Wm. Hall & Son
192	J. P. K. Henshaw	from life		P. S. Duval
193	Constantin Hering	daguerreotype by W. & F. Langenheim		
194	The Celebrated Heron Family			P. S. Duval
195	The Misses Heron	daguerreotype by Richards		P. S. Duval & Co.'s Steam Lith. Press
196	Henry Hertz, *Souvenir de Henry Hertz*		1847	P. S. Duval for A. Fiot and William Du Bois
197	Henry Hertz			Lehman & Duval for Fiot, Meignen & Co.

	Subject and Publication	Original Artist	Date	Lithography company/ Publisher
198	Rev. George Higgins, *U.S. Ecclesiastical Portrait Gallery*	from life	c. 1841	P. S. Duval for Thomas S. Wagner
199	Henry Hill, *The Hill Family*		1854	P. S. Duval's Steam Lith. Press
200	Henry Hill	miniature in possession of Charles Moore Morris Esqr.		P. S. Duval & Co.'s Steam Lith. Press
201	Margaret Hill, *The Hill Family*		1854	P. S. Duval & Co.'s Steam Lith. Press
202	Stephen P. Hill	ambrotype		P. S. Duval & Co.
203	James Hoban	daguerreotype by W. J. Corcoran	1846	P. S. Duval for W. J. Corcoran
204	Joseph Hopkinson	J. R. Lambdin	1842	P. S. Duval for J. R. Lambdin
205	Joseph Hopkinson	T. Sully		Childs & Inman
206	Matilde T. Howard		1854	P. S. Duval & Co.
207	Joseph Howell			P. S. Duval & Co.
208	William B. Hubbard, *Mirror & Keystone*			P. S. Duval & Co.'s Steam Lith. Press
209	Hayne Hudjihini, *History of the Indian Tribes*	C. B. King	1833	Childs & Inman for Key & Biddle
210	John Hughes (2 variants)	from life	1841	P. S. Duval for John Kennedy
211	Mr. Huidekoper	J. Neagle		Childs & Inman
212	Mr. Huidekoper	J. Neagle		Childs & Lehman
213	M. Hunt	from life		P. S. Duval
214	R. F. Hunt		c. 1854	P. S. Duval & Co.
215	R. F. Hunt, *The Shepard's Sunday Song*		1854	P. S. Duval & Co. for Lee & Walker
216	Thomas P. Hunt	W. E. Winner		P. S. Duval
217	François Hünten		c. 1839	Lehman & Duval for Fiot, Meignen & Co.
218	George B. Ide, *U.S. Ecclesiastical Portrait Gallery*	from life	c. 1841	P. S. Duval for Thomas S. Wagner
219	Joseph R. Ingersoll (2 variants)	H. Inman		Childs & Inman
220	Samuel D. Ingham, *Cabinet*	Moon	1829	Pendleton, Kearny & Childs
221	Washington Irving		1832	Childs & Inman
222	Andrew Jackson	W. J. Hubard	1830	C. G. Childs
223	Andrew Jackson	Hubard from picture painted for C. G. Childs	1833	Childs & Inman
224	Andrew Jackson	W. J. Hubard	1834	Childs & Lehman
225	Andrew Jackson	W. J. Hubard	1846	P. S. Duval for C. S. Williams

	Subject and Publication	Original Artist	Date	Lithography company/ Publisher
226	Andrew Jackson	W. J. Hubard		Childs & Inman
227	Andrew Jackson (2 variants)			P. S. Duval
228	Jamison as "Macbeth"	daguerreotype by J. J. E. Mayall	1846	P. S. Duval for J. J. E. Mayall
229	Thomas Jefferson		1846	P. S. Duval for C. S. Williams
230	Thomas Jefferson	G. Stuart		Childs & Inman
231	Thomas Jefferson (2 variants)			P. S. Duval
232	Felix Johnson	ambrotype	1858	P. S. Duval & Son for Joseph M. Wilson
233	Richard M. Johnson	H. Inman	1832	Childs & Inman
234	John Johnston	photograph	1858	P. S. Duval & Son for Joseph M. Wilson
235	William F. Johnston	daguerreotype by England & Gunn		P. S. Duval for England & Gunn
236	Walter Jones			
237	Capt. Justin, U.S. Military Magazine	from life	1841	P. S. Duval for Huddy & Duval
238	Kai-Pol-E-Quah	C. B. King	1833	C. G. Childs for Key & Biddle
239	Kai-Pol-E-Quah, History of the Indian Tribes	C. B. King	1833	Childs & Inman for Key & Biddle
240	Kai-Pol-E-Quah	C. B. King	1836	Lehman & Duval for E. C. Biddle
241	Kai-Pol-E-Quah, History of the Indian Tribes	C. B. King		
242	Charles Kean	H. Inman		Childs & Inman
243	William H. Keim	daguerreotype by C. L. Phillippe		P. S. Duval & Co.'s Steam Lith. Press
244	William H. Keim, U.S. Military Magazine			P. S. Duval for Huddy & Duval
245	Fanny Kemble	John Hayter	1832	Childs & Inman
246	Fanny Kemble	T. Lawrence	1832	Childs & Inman & S. M. Stewart
247	Fanny Kemble	J. Neagle	1832	Childs & Inman
248	Fanny Kemble	T. Sully	1833	Childs & Inman
249	Rev. J. Kennaday, U.S. Ecclesiastical Portrait Gallery	from life	c. 1841	P. S. Duval for Thomas S. Wagner
250	Joseph H. Kennard, U.S. Ecclesiastical Portrait Gallery	from life	c. 1841	P. S. Duval for Thomas S. Wagner
251	Henry King			P. S. Duval & Son

Subject and Publication	Original Artist	Date	Lithography company/ Publisher
252 William R. King			
253 Ki-On-Twog-Ky, *History of the Indian Tribes*	C. B. King	1836	Lehman & Duval for E. C. Biddle
254 Kish-Kallo-Wa, *History of the Indian Tribes*	C. B. King	1836	Lehman & Duval for E. C. Biddle
255 James Kitchen, M.D.			P. S. Duval
256 William Kneass	J. Wood	c. 1834	Childs & Lehman
257 Louis Kossuth, *Kossuth: Grand Reception March*		1852	P. S. Duval's Steam Lith. Press for Lee & Walker
258 Louis Kossuth	daguerreotype by N. S. Bennett		P. S. Duval & Co.'s Steam Lith. Press for N. S. Bennett
259 Madame Lafarge, *Memoirs of Madame Lafarge*		1841	P. S. Duval
260 Mary Lamar, *The Hill Family*		1854	P. S. Duval & Co.
261 John Lane			P. S. Duval
262 Capt. Leoser & Dr. Jackson, *U.S. Military Magazine*	from life		P. S. Duval for Huddy & Duval
263 James N. Lewis	R. Peale		P. S. Duval's Steam Lith. Press
264 William D. Lewis	daguerreotype by S. Broadbent	1851	P. S. Duval's Steam Lith. Press
265 Jenny Lind, song sheet			P. S. Duval for Lee & Walker
266 Jenny Lind, *Jenny Lind's Songs*			P. S. Duval for A. Fiot and Du Bois
267 John Lisle	daguerreotype by J. J. E. Mayall		P. S. Duval
268 Margaret Lisle	daguerreotype by J. J. E. Mayall		P. S. Duval
269 Little Crow, *History of the Indian Tribes*	C. B. King	1836	Lehman & Duval for Key & Biddle
270 R. R. Little			P. S. Duval
271 R. R. Little			P. S. Duval's Steam Lith. Press
272 John C. Lowber	J. Wood		Lehman & Duval
273 N. M. Ludlow			Lehman & Duval
274 Charles Lyell	daguerreotype by J. J. E. Mayall	1846	P. S. Duval for J. J. E. Mayall
275 William Maclure	T. Sully		P. S. Duval

	Subject and Publication	Original Artist	Date	Lithography company/ Publisher
276	Major Gen. A. Macomb, *Cabinet*	T. Sully	1829	Pendleton, Kearny & Childs
277	Rev. E. McCurdy			P. S. Duval
278	John McDowell, *U.S. Ecclesiastical Portrait Gallery*	from life	1841	P. S. Duval for Thomas S. Wagner
279	John McDowell			P. S. Duval for G. F. Gordon
280	Charles P. McIlvaine	H. Inman		Lehman & Duval
281	McIntosh, *History of the Indian Tribes*	C. B. King	1836	Lehman & Duval for E. C. Biddle
282	Thomas L. McKenney			P. S. Duval
283	Donald C. McLaren	daguerreotype		P. S. Duval & Son for Joseph M. Wilson
284	John McLean (2 variants)	T. Sully	1831	Childs & Inman for Benjamin Mathias
285	John McLean	T. Sully	1832	Childs & Inman
286	John McLean	T. Sully	1832	Childs & Inman for Benjamin Mathias
287	C[?] S. McRae			P. S. Duval & Son
288	James Madison		1846	P. S. Duval for C. S. Williams
289	James Madison (2 variants)			P. S. Duval
290	John N. Maffitt	miniature by E. Wellmore		
291	Ma-Has-Kah, *History of the Indian Tribes*	C. B. King	1837	Lehman & Duval for E. C. Biddle
292	Young Ma-Has-Kah, *History of the Indian Tribes*	C. B. King	1837	Lehman & Duval for E. C. Biddle
293	Madame Malibran			Lehman & Duval for Fiot, Meignen & Co.
294	Joseph Markle	W. F. Cogswell	1844	P. S. Duval for J. W. Siddall
295	John Markoe			Lehman & Duval
296	John Marshall	H. Inman	1831	Childs & Inman
297	Theobald Mathew		1841	P. S. Duval for John Kenedy
298	Theobald Mathew			P. S. Duval's Steam Lith. Press
299	Aileen Mavoureen, *Ballad*			P. S. Duval for A. Fiot
300	J Gordon Maxwell, *U.S. Ecclesiastical Portrait Gallery*	from life	c.1841	P. S. Duval for Thomas S. Wagner

	Subject and Publication	Original Artist	Date	Lithography company / Publisher
301	Robert Campbell Maywood as "Tam O' Shanter"	T. Sully, Jr.		P. S. Duval
302	Thomas Mellon			P. S. Duval
303	Santiago Mendez de Vigo (2 variants)	A. H. Wallace		P. S. Duval
304	Wright Merrick, *Merrick Lodge I.O.O.F. Quick Step*			P. S. Duval's Steam Lith. Press for Lee & Walker
305	Mrs. Elizabeth Messchert	J. M. de Franca		P. S. Duval
306	H. Messchert	J. M. de Franca		P. S. Duval
307	M. Huizinga Messchert	daguerreotype by M. A. Root		P. S. Duval
308	M. Huizinga Messchert	J. M. de Franca		Childs & Lehman
309	Mary Messchert	J. M. de Franca		P. S. Duval
310	Mrs. Mary Ann Messchert	daguerreotype by M. A. Root		P. S. Duval
311	E. J. P. Messinger			P. S. Duval
312	Meta-Koosega, *History of the Indian Tribes*	C. B. King	1836	Lehman & Duval for King & Biddle
313	Joseph Meyers	daguerreotype by M. A. Root		
314	A[?] Miller			P. S. Duval & Son
315	Mo-Hon-Go & Child, *History of the Indian Tribes*	C. B. King	1834	Lehman & Duval for E. C. Biddle
316	James Monroe			P. S. Duval
317	P. E. Moriarty, *U.S. Ecclesiastical Portrait Gallery*	from life	c. 1841	P. S. Duval for Thomas S. Wagner
318	P. E. Moriarty	from life		P. S. Duval
319	Edward Joy Morris	photograph		P. S. Duval
320	Edward Joy Morris	photograph		P. S. Duval & Son
321	Henry A. Muhlenberg	Schoener		P. S. Duval
322	Simon Murray	J. Kyle		P. S. Duval for Joseph How
323	Napoleon Bonaparte			P. S. Duval
324	Naw-Kaw, *History of the Indian Tribes*	C. B. King	1834	Lehman & Duval for E. C. Biddle
325	John Neagle	T. Sully		C. G. Childs
326	Henry Neill	daguerreotype by W. & F. Langenheim		P. S. Duval

128

	Subject and Publication	Original Artist	Date	Lithography company / Publisher
327	Ne-Son-A-Quoit, *History of the Indian Tribes*	C. B. King	1837	Lehman & Duval for E. C. Biddle
328	Ne-Sou-Aquoit	C. B. King	1837	Lehman & Duval for E. C. Biddle
329	Albert Newsam	from life		
330	Richard Newton	daguerreotype by McClees & Germon	1850	P. S. Duval's Steam Lith. Press for H. C. Howard
331	Ojibwa Mother and Her Child, *History of the Indian Tribes*	C. B. King	1836	Lehman & Duval for E. C. Biddle
332	Okee-Makee-Quid, *History of the Indian Tribes*	C. B. King after J. O. Lewis	1836	Lehman & Duval for E. C. Biddle
333	Ole Bull			P. S. Duval
334	Ole Bull *Souvenir d'Ole Bull*		1844	P. S. Duval for A. Fiot
335	Ong-Pa-Ton-Ga, *History of the Indian Tribes*	C. B. King	1836	Lehman & Duval for E. C. Biddle
336	J. E. Owens as "Jakey"	daguerreotype by McClees & Germon		P. S. Duval
337	William F. Packer	ambrotype by Walter Dinmore		P. S. Duval & Son
338	Gen. Paez			
339	Paganini, *The Parlour Review*		1838	P. S. Duval
340	Paganini, *La Clochette et le Concert—Deux Rondos*			P. S. Duval for A. Fiot & W. Dubois
341	James Page	H. Inman	1830	C. G. Childs
342	James Page, *U.S. Military Magazine*	from life		P. S. Duval
343	Pah-She-Pah-How, *History of the Indian Tribes*	C. B. King		Lehman & Duval for E. C. Biddle
344	B. Frank Palmer, *The Scalpel*	daguerreotype by M. A. Root		P. S. Duval & Co.'s Steam Lith. Press
345	Ely Parry	ambrotype by Gutekunst & Brother		P. S. Duval & Son
346	Mme. Pasta, *The Parlour Review*		1838	P. S. Duval
347	Payta-Kootha, *History of the Indian Tribes*	C. B. King	1836	Lehman & Duval for E. C. Biddle
348	Peah-Mas-Ka, *History of the Indian Tribes*	C. B. King	1837	Lehman & Duval for E. C. Biddle

	Subject and Publication	Original Artist	Date	Lithography company/ Publisher
349	Pedro I			Childs & Inman for S. M. Stewart
350	John Pemberton			P. S. Duval
351	David Pepper	John Neagle		Lehman & Duval
352	Petalesharoo, *History of the Indian Tribes*	C. B. King	1836	Lehman & Duval for E. C. Biddle
353	William Peter	daguerreotype by T. Faris		P. S. Duval & Co.'s Steam Lith. Press
354	Henry M. Phillips	daguerreotype by W. L. Germon		P. S. Duval & Co.
355	Philip Syng Physick	H. Inman	c. 1830	C. G. Childs
356	Philip Syng Physick	H. Inman	1831	Childs & Inman
357	Philip Syng Physick	H. Inman		P. S. Duval
358	A. L. Pickering	Parker		P. S. Duval
359	Franklin Pierce, *President Pierce's March and Quick Step*	daguerreotype by M. A. Root	1853	P. S. Duval & Co.'s Steam Lith. Press for G. Willig Jr.
360	Gen. Pleasanton			
361	J. P. Pleasants			P. S. Duval & Co.'s Steam Lith. Press
362	Pocahontas	T. Sully		P. S. Duval
363	George Poindexter	C. B. King		Lehman & Duval
364	James K. Polk		1846	P. S. Duval for C. S. Williams
365	James K. Polk			P. S. Duval
366	James Pollock			P. S. Duval & Co. for Martin E. Harmstead
367	James Pollock	daguerreotype by James E. McClees		P. S. Duval & Co.
368	? Porter	S. S. Osgood		Childs & Lehman
369	David R. Porter	John F. Francis	1838	P. S. Duval for John F. Francis
370	David R. Porter, *U.S. Military Magazine*	A. Newsam, W. Huddy, and A. Koellner	1841	P. S. Duval for Huddy & Duval
371	D. Powell			P. S. Duval
372	Tyrone Power			
373	Tyrone Power	Merrill		P. S. Duval
374	John T. Pressly	photograph by George W. Taylor	1858	P. S. Duval & Son for Joseph M. Wilson
375	William C. Preston	S. S. Osgood		Childs & Lehman
376	Push-Ma-Ha-Ta, *History of the Indian Tribes*	C. B. King	1833	Lehman & Duval for E. C. Biddle

	Subject and Publication	Original Artist	Date	Lithography company/ Publisher
377	Qua-Ta-Wa-Pea, *History of the Indian Tribes*	C. B. King	1836	Lehman & Duval for E. C. Biddle
378	Patrick Rafferty	photograph by Willard	1859	P. S. Duval for Saint Francis Xavier Literary Institute
379	Robert Ralston			
380	Rant-Che-Wai-Me, *History of the Indian Tribes*	C. B. King	1837	Lehman & Duval for E. C. Biddle
381	William Rawle	H. Inman	1832	Childs & Inman
382	Charles H. Read	daguerreotype	1858	P. S. Duval & Son for Joseph M. Wilson
383	Red Jacket, *History of the Indian Tribes*	C. B. King	1834	Lehman & Duval for E. C. Biddle
384	Gustavus Reichhelm			P. S. Duval
385	Philip Ricketts	G. Freeman		P. S. Duval
386	Joseph Ritner	J. F. Francis	1838	P. S. Duval for J. F. Francis
387	Joseph Ritner	A. T. Lee	1837	Lehman & Duval
388	Charles Roberts	daguerreotype by R. Cornelius		P. S. Duval
389	Joseph Roberts	M. J. de Franca		Lehman & Duval
390	Major Roberts	H. Inman	1830	C. G. Childs
391	Solomon W. Roberts	M. J. de Franca		Lehman & Duval
392	M. B. Roche	B. Otis	1831	Childs & Inman
393	Thomas Cadwalader Rockhill			P. S. Duval & Co.'s Steam Lith. Press
394	Henry Rohbock, *L'Etoile*		1848	P. S. Duval for Lee & Walker
395	Rossini, *The Parlour Review*		1838	P. S. Duval
396	Mme. Sabatier, *Thy Hand*		1846	P. S. Duval for A. Fiot
397	Mme. Sabatier, *Blue Eyes*		1846	P. S. Duval for A. Fiot
398	J. Sanderson	J. Neagle	c. 1830	C. G. Childs
399	John Sargeant	H. Inman		Childs & Inman
400	Thomas Say		1835	Lehman & Duval
401	Robert H. Sayre	ambrotype by H. P. Osborn		P. S. Duval & Son
402	John Schwartz	photograph by C. L. Phillippi		P. S. Duval & Son for Gov. Simon Synder
403	Lewis De Schweinitz			Lehman & Duval
404	Daniel Scott	J. Kyle		P. S. Duval for Joseph How
405	Harriet Scott and Child, *The Hill Family*		1854	P. S. Duval & Co.

	Subject and Publication	Original Artist	Date	Lithography company / Publisher
406	John R. Scott as "St. Pierre"	T. Sully, Jr.		P. S. Duval
407	W. A. Scott		1858	P. S. Duval & Son's for Joseph M. Wilson
408	W. A. Scott	photograph by M. P. Simons		P. S. Duval & Son for Joseph M. Wilson
409	Mr. Sequin, *The Bold Brigand*			P. S. Duval for Fiot, Meignen & Co.
410	Se-Quo-Yah, *History of the Indian Tribes*	C. B. King	1833	Childs & Inman for King & Biddle
411	Shin-Ga-Ba-W'ossin, *History of the Indian Tribes*		1833	Lehman & Duval for E. C. Biddle
412	Francis R. Shunk	T. Sully, Jr.	1844	P. S. Duval
413	Adele Sigoigne	M. Riboni		Lehman & Duval for the Misses Della Costa
414	J. S. Silsbee	daguerreotype		P. S. Duval
415	J. S. Silsbee as "Sam Slick"			P. S. Duval
416	Henry Simmons	J. Kyle	1838	P. S. Duval for Joseph How
417	Sioux Warrior, *American Turf Magazine*	P. Rindisbacher	1829	Pendleton, Kearny & Childs
418	Thomas H. Skinner	T. Sully		Childs & Inman
419	John Smith			Childs & Inman and Peabody & Co.
420	Jonathan Smith	J. Neagle		P. S. Duval
421	Mlle. Sontag		c. 1830	C. G. Childs for R. H. Hobson
422	Jared Sparks	T. Sully	1832	Childs & Inman
423	R. L. Stevens, *Rail Road Polka*		1852	P. S. Duval & Co.'s Steam Lith. Press for I. W. Gougler
424	Charles Stewart, *U.S. Military Magazine*	from life	1841	P. S. Duval for Huddy & Duval
425	Dugald Stewart	H. Raeburn	1830	C. G. Childs
426	Peter Stichter			
427	William and Charles Stoever	daguerreotype by M. A. Root		
428	William Strickland	J. Neagle	c. 1830	C. G. Childs
429	Rev. W. Suddards	G. W. Conarroe		Lehman & Duval
430	Jacob Sulger	daguerreotype by Simons		P. S. Duval & Co.
431	Mrs. Jacob Sulger			P. S. Duval & Co.
432	Harriet Elizabeth Georgiana (Howard) Sutherland	T. Lawrence		Childs & Inman

Subject and Publication	Original Artist	Date	Lithography company / Publisher
433 Mlle. Taglioni			
434 Tah-Chee, *History of the Indian Tribes*		1837	E. C. Biddle
435 Samuel A. Talcott			C. G. Childs
436 Maurice Talleyrand	Joffroy		Childs & Inman
437 Maurice Talleyrand	Joffroy		Childs & Lehman
438 Talma, *The Parlour Review*		1838	P. S. Duval
439 Zachary Taylor		1846	P. S. Duval for C. S. Williams
440 Zachary Taylor		1849	S. Augustus Mitchell, Jr.
441 Zachary Taylor (uniform)	J. Atwood	1847	P. S. Duval for J. Atwood
442 Zachary Taylor (civilian clothes)	J. Atwood	1847	P. S. Duval for J. Atwood
443 Tens-Kwan-Ta-Waw, *History of the Indian Tribes*			Childs & Inman for Key & Biddle
444 Theresa, *The Maid of Athens*	Allason	1832	Childs & Inman
445 Anna Thillon	McClees and Germon		P. S. Duval and Co.
446 Anna Thillon, *Charlie*	McClees and Germon		P. S. Duval & Co.'s Steam Lith. Press for Lee and Walker
447 Anna Thillon, *Dreams of Home*	McClees and Germon		P. S. Duval & Co.'s Steam Lith. Press for Lee and Walker
448 David Thomas			P. S. Duval & Son
449 Jonah Thompson	daguerreotype by Langenheim		P. S. Duval & Co.
450 M. L. P. Thompson	photograph	1858	P. S. Duval & Son for Joseph M. Wilson
451 M. L. P. Thompson	ambrotype	1858	P. S. Duval & Son for Joseph M. Wilson
452 Samuel Thompson	T. Sully		P. S. Duval
453 James Thorne as "Figaro"	Joseph Bushe		P. S. Duval
454 S[?] Tobias			P. S. Duval & Co.'s Steam Lith. Press
455 Elisha Townsend	daguerreotype		P. S. Duval & Co.'s Steam Lith. Press
456 The Twins	T. Sully	1829	Pendleton, Kearny, & Childs
457 John Tyler		1846	P. S. Duval for C. S. Williams
458 John Tyler			P. S. Duval for Daniel Richardson

Subject and Publication	Original Artist	Date	Lithography company / Publisher
459 Stephen H. Tyng, *U.S. Ecclesiastical Portrait Gallery*		c. 1841	P. S. Duval for Thomas S. Wagner
460 Martin Van Buren		1846	P. S. Duval for C. S. Williams
461 Martin Van Buren			P. S. Duval
462 Robert Vaux	H. Inman	c. 1830	Childs & Inman
463 Robert Vaux	H. Inman		P. S. Duval
464 Vezin	miniature by J. H. Brown		P. S. Duval & Co.'s Steam Lith. Press
465 Waa-Pa-Shaw, *History of the Indian Tribes*	C. B. King	1836	Lehman & Duval for E. C. Biddle
466 Wa-Em-Boesh-Kaa, *History of the Indian Tribes*	C. B. King	1836	Lehman & Duval for E. C. Biddle
467 George A. Waggaman	S. S. Osgood		Childs & Lehman
468 James William Wallack (2 variants), *Burton's Gentleman's Magazine*	Wageman		P. S. Duval
469 Robert Walsh, Jr.	T. Sully	c. 1830	C. G. Childs
470 Thomas U. Walter	J. Neagle	1836	Lehman & Duval
471 Reuben H. Walworth	R. Peale	1842	P. S. Duval
472 Wa-Na-Ta, *History of the Indian Tribes*		1837	Lehman & Duval for E. C. Biddle
473 Thomas Wardrope	ambrotype	1858	P. S. Duval for Joseph M. Wilson
474 Thomas Wardrope	ambrotype by Lockwood		P. S. Duval & Son for Joseph M. Wilson
475 George Wasington	G. Stuart	c. 1832	Childs & Inman and Peabody & Company
476 George Washington, *Tomb of Washington at Mount Vernon*	Houdon	1840	P. S. Duval for Carey & Hart
477 George Washington			P. S. Duval
478 George Washington		1846	P. S. Duval for C. S. Williams
479 George Washington	G. Stuart		Childs & Inman
480 John G. Watmough	H. Inman	1831	C. G. Childs
481 Watson	E. Troye		Childs & Inman
482 William H. Watson	John Plumbe, Jr.	c. 1846	John Plumbe, Jr.
483 Thomas Webb			P. S. Duval & Son
484 Daniel Webster			

	Subject and Publication	Original Artist	Date	Lithography company / Publisher
485	Francis C. Wemyss	T. Sully, Jr.		P. S. Duval
486	Francis C. Wemyss	T. Sully, Jr.		Lehman & Duval
487	Wesh-Cubb, *History of the Indian Tribes*	C. B. King	1836	Lehman & Duval for E. C. Biddle
488	Robert Wharton			C. G. Childs
489	Daniel Wheeler		1839	P. S. Duval
490	J. D. White	daguerreotype by McClees & Germon		P. S. Duval & Co.'s Steam Lith. Press
491	Josiah White	ambrotype by J. Brown		P. S. Duval & Son
492	Philip S. White	daguerreotype by T. P. & D. C. Collins		P. S. Duval for T. P. & D. C. Collins
493	William White	silhouette	1838	P. S. Duval for Thomas Latimer
494	William White, *Annual Report... Pa. Institution for the Deaf and Dumb*		1844	P. S. Duval
495	William White, *U.S. Ecclesiastical Portrait Gallery*	H. Inman	c. 1841	P. S. Duval for Thomas S. Wagner
496	Walter Williamson	daguerreotype by John H. Steck	1849	P. S. Duval for John H. Steck
497	George Willig			P. S. Duval
498	John G. Wilson	from life		P. S. Duval
499	Joseph P. Wilson	Waddle		Joseph How
500	Samuel Winchester			
501	William Wirt	A. Dickinson		Childs & Inman
502	William R. De Witt	J. F. Francis		Sunday School Teachers of the Presbyterian Church
503	George Wolf	A. B. Rockey	1833	Childs & Inman
504	George Wolf, *Columbia March*		1850	P. S. Duval's Steam Lith. Press for Lee & Walker
505	Joseph Wolff		1837	Lehman & Duval
506	Mrs. Wood as "Amina"	J. Neagle	1836	Lehman & Duval for James S. Earle
507	Andrew Gifford Wylie	ambrotype	1858	P. S. Duval & Son for Joseph M. Wilson
508	John Young			P. S. Duval & Co.
509	John Young	G. Stuart		P. S. Duval & Co.
510	Lorenzo de Zavala			C. G. Childs

Portrait Prints by
John Sartain

KATHARINE
MARTINEZ

To his contemporaries in the nineteenth century, John Sartain (fig. 1) was the preeminent portrait engraver of Philadelphia. When his name appeared in print, it was usually accompanied by glowing, if exaggerated, claims: the father of mezzotint engraving in America; the first good mezzotint engraver in America; even the only mezzotint engraver in America.[1] As an editor of the *New York Commercial Advertiser* described him at the age of seventy:

> *John Sartain, the engraver, is one of the noted characters of Philadelphia.... He is said to have been the first mezzotint engraver of any repute, and to have produced more works than any living member of his profession.... It is often asserted that he is the youngest artist in feeling and*

---

1 Some publications that promulgated these glowing claims include Clara Erskine Clement and Lawrence Hutton, *Artists of the Nineteenth Century and Their Works* (1885; rept. Saint Louis; Mo., 1969), p. 235; William Spohn Baker, *American Engravers and Their Works* (Philadelphia, 1875), p. 151; *The National Cyclopaedia of American Biography* 6 (1907; rept. Ann Arbor, Mich., 1967): 472; "Sartain the Artist," *Nineteenth Century* 1 (1848): 365; Joseph Jackson, *Encyclopedia of Philadelphia* (Harrisburg, Pa., 1931–33), pp. 1068–69; John Thomas Scharf and Thompson Westcott, *History of Philadelphia, 1609–1884*, 3 vols. (Philadelphia, 1884), 2:1060–61; Charles Morris, *Makers of Philadelphia* (Philadelphia, 1894), p. 132; *Philadelphia and Popular Philadelphians* (Philadelphia, 1891), p. 229; *A Biographical Album of Prominent Pennsylvanians*, 3 vols. (Philadelphia, 1888–90), 2:341–46.

JOHN SARTAIN.

Engraved for the Nineteenth Century.

1

John Sartain, 1808-1897. Mezzotint, circa 1848, by Sartain after daguerreotype by Marcus Aurelius Root, 12.7 × 10.1 cm. From the *Nineteenth Century,* 1(1848). (*Library Company of Philadelphia*)

expectation in all Philadelphia. He has new schemes every day, and to carry half of them out, he would need to live at least 300 years. William Sartain, the well-known New York artist, is his son who frequently regrets that he is so much older than his father.[2]

Sartain's success was unusual for a nineteenth-century engraver and can be attributed mainly to his adaptability as an artist. Although most of his attention was focused on mezzotint engraving, he also turned variously to lithography, etching, bank-note engraving, portrait painting in oils, and photography. He had a wide and varied circle of friends and acquaintances (among them Edgar Allan Poe) and was energetically involved in Philadelphia's artistic and cultural activities. At different points during his long career he was a magazine publisher, a member of the Franklin Institute, a prominent Freemason, a director of the Pennsylvania Academy of the Fine Arts, an officer of the Artists' Fund Society and the Art Union of Philadelphia, a vice-president of the School of Design for Women (the present Moore College of Art), the secretary of the Fine Arts Commission of the Great Central Fair of 1864, and the chief of the Bureau of Art for the Centennial Exhibition in 1876. Held in esteem by the entire art community, he gave advice to many young artists. When Thomas Eakins went to Paris to apply to the Ecole des Beaux Arts, his letter of introduction from Sartain was partially responsible for his acceptance into the private studio classes of Jean-Léon Gérôme.

Sartain's energy was legendary. In response to the great demand for his mezzotint portraits, he produced a prodigious quantity of prints, probably close to fifteen hundred. Inevitably, his ever-increasing production necessitated the reworking of worn plates to print more impressions. In the opinion of one critic, "His mezzotint plates were virtually spoiled by their popularity, being reinforced by sturdier line engraving to make the plates equal to enormous editions."[3] For this reason, twentieth-century art historians have traditionally dismissed Sartain's work: "Many of his plates were printed from so much that the impressions were mere ghosts, and the copper then touched up with burin or roulette in a futile

2   Quoted in A *Biographical Album of Prominent Pennsylvanians*, 2:345.

3   Sophia Antoinette Walker, "The Work of John Sartain," circa 1897, Archives of American Art, roll P28, Smithsonian Institution, Washington, D.C.

effort to restore lost richness; the effect was that of a patch upon a pair of trousers."[4]

These criticisms are based on isolated examples of Sartain's many magazine illustrations. Though the objections may be valid for individual plates, Sartain's work as a whole needs reevaluation. His accomplishments were extraordinary, and his influence was widespread. Three aspects of his career, particularly, are too significant to be dismissed and are the focus of this paper: the mezzotint portrait commissions of the 1830s and 1840s, the reintroduction of mezzotint plates for use in book and magazine illustration, and, finally, his involvement with photography.

When John Sartain arrived in Philadelphia from London in 1830, at the age of twenty-two, he was already a trained mezzotint engraver with substantial professional experience. As an apprentice in 1822, he had been employed by William Young Ottley to complete a series of engravings illustrating a history of early Florentine painting.[5] This association resulted in Sartain's first exposure to the London art world. Ottley had an outstanding personal collection of prints and paintings and moved in the social circles of Sir Thomas Lawrence, Charles R. Leslie, and the poet Samuel Rogers. Gradually Sartain was introduced to the major artistic influences of his day. In *Reminiscences of a Very Old Man,* he recalled his first awareness of the work of William Blake,[6] and a number of his early watercolor sketches show attempts to emulate Blake's style.

Sartain learned the art of mezzotint engraving from Henry Richter, with whom he studied in 1827–28. This type of engraving was considered to be the most prestigious of the printmaking techniques and the most suitable for portraiture. It had been a favorite practice in England since the seventeenth century. William Gilpin, in his *Essay upon Prints*, noted the advantages mezzotint engraving had over other techniques: "The characteristic of mezzotint is softness; which adapts it chiefly to portraits.... Nothing, except paint can express flesh more naturally, or the

---

4   Clipping from Sartain file (probably written by Frank Weitenkampf) in New York Public Library Print Department, Archives of American Art, roll N107, Smithsonian Institution, Washington, D.C.

5   William Young Ottley, *A Series of Plates, Engraved after the Paintings and Sculptures of the Most Eminent Masters of the Early Florentine School* (London, 1826).

6   John Sartain, *Reminiscences of a Very Old Man* (New York, 1899), pp. 108–9.

flowing of hair, or the folds of drapery, or the catching lights of armour." Gilpin also maintained that "mezzotint excells each of the other species of prints in its capacity of receiving the most beautiful effects of light and shade."[7]

In the 1820s, when Sartain was learning the technique, mezzotint engraving still enjoyed its special position in the arts, particularly when, in 1822, the introduction of steel plates to replace softer copper plates allowed for larger editions. As a result of this innovation, mezzotints were increasingly used as book illustrations, in both limited-edition and mass-produced publications. At one end of the spectrum were the handsome landscape mezzotints after J.M.W. Turner that illustrated *Liber Studiorum* (1807–19) and *River Scenery of England* (1823–30), some of which were engraved by Turner himself. Both John Martin and John Constable chose the mezzotint technique for book illustrations in order to represent the dramatic light effects in their paintings. At the other end of the spectrum were the illustrated annuals introduced from Germany by the London publisher and print dealer Rudolph Ackermann. These ornamental literary miscellanies, containing mezzotints and line engravings, were inexpensive and popular and were published in large editions. Aware of the financial benefits of working with a publisher like Ackermann, Sartain engraved illustrations for his most successful giftbook, *The Forget Me Not,* in the late 1820s. Through such publications, Philadelphia engravers and publishers may already have been familiar with Sartain's work when he arrived in the city in 1830.

Sartain decided to emigrate after hearing that there were great opportunities in America for a mezzotint engraver. It was a sensible decision for such an ambitious artist. His association with Ottley, Richter, Ackermann, and other notable painters and printmakers of London must have illustrated to Sartain his own strengths and weaknesses. His early drawings show that he was an adequate draftsman, but his greatest skill was as a mezzotint engraver. As such, he could have spent the rest of his life in London with a moderately successful but insignificant career. Sartain, however, wanted more out of life.

Armed with letters of introduction, he and his wife set sail for America: "At the London docks I chose a ship that sailed for Philadelphia, although my destination was New York, for I found the cabins preferable

7   William Gilpin, *An Essay upon Prints*, 4th ed. (London: 1792), pp. 38–39.

to those on the packets for the other port; and besides, I thought I might as well deliver my Philadelphia letters of introduction on my way through, instead of travelling there for the purpose. . . . Mr. Kennett, the American bookseller in London, had given me a letter to Mr. Henry C. Carey, the [Philadelphia] publisher."[8]

Once Sartain arrived in Philadelphia, he decided to settle there. "I was introduced to Mr. Sully and other artists," he recalled. "Mr. Sully was warm in his commendation of Philadelphia as a place of residence, and advised me by all means to settle in it." Before long, he had made the acquaintance of the local art community: "The first Sunday I was installed, I was visited by so many artists that it looked as if they had come by pre-arrangement, but they said it was not so. The group included Thomas Sully, John Neagle, Jacob Eichholtz, Thomas Doughty, Cephas G. Childs, and Joshua Shaw."[9] Obviously, Sartain's arrival aroused a great deal of interest among Philadelphia's most prominent artists, and commissions came immediately. Henry Carey ordered an engraving after a portrait of a Miss Jackson painted by Thomas Sully in 1808. Sartain also recalled that "Mr. Thomas T. Ash, the publisher, and Mr. Thomas Doughty ordered a plate to be done, in the pure line manner of a deer in the foreground of a landscape,"[10] which appeared as the first plate in Doughty's *Cabinet of Natural History and American Rural Sport,* published in 1830.

Guaranteeing Sartain's success was the immediate attention of two of Philadelphia's leading portrait painters, Thomas Sully and John Neagle, both of whom were keenly aware of the importance of engraved reproduction. "Engravers generally do not understand the masses of a broad painter," Neagle wrote. "They copy the lines and proportions, but they do not share the feelings of the painter. . . . They may give all the details of the picture, and yet lose the pictorial effect by neglecting the strength and breadth of his masses. Engraving is not a copy, but a translation from color to black and white, and in order to make it successful, the engraver should enter into the spirit and feeling of the painter."[11]

8   Sartain, *Reminiscences,* pp. 130, 142.

9   Ibid., pp. 142–43.

10   Ibid., p. 142.

11   Thomas Fitzgerald, "John Neagle, the Artist," *Lippincott's Magazine* 1 (1868): 488.

Engraved by J. Sartain from the Original Picture by Neagle Philadelphia.

2

Patriotism and Age. Mezzotint, circa 1830-31, by Sartain after John Neagle, 22.4 × 18.5 cm. (*Historical Society of Pennsylvania, Philadelphia*)

Sartain seemed to have this sensitivity. Shortly after his arrival, Neagle commissioned him to engrave a plate after his own painting *Patriotism and Age.* The subtle tonal variations that Sartain achieved in his mezzotint (fig. 2) must have surprised and delighted painters and patrons alike. Compared with the stipple engravings that were available at the time, Sartain had quite a different product to offer. His mezzotints, such as *Samuel A. McCoskry,* also after Neagle (fig. 3) or *Robert Gilmor* after Sir Thomas Lawrence (fig. 4), were visually rich images with dramatic contrasts of light and dark.

Sartain believed that an engraver should imitate "the drag and sweep of a painter's brush,"[12] and part of his success lay in his ability to adjust to the mood and style of the original painting. Soon after meeting him, Thomas Sully commissioned a mezzotint of his portrait of the Right Reverend William White (fig. 5).[13] A delicate, sketchlike image, it was

12 John Sartain, *A Brief Sketch of the History and Practice of Engraving* (Philadelphia, 1880), p. 19. John Sartain Papers, Historical Society of Pennsylvania, Philadelphia (hereafter PHi).

13 Sartain, *Reminiscences,* p. 142.

3
Samuel A. McCoskry, 1804-1886.
Mezzotint, circa 1836, by Sartain
after John Neagle, 24.7 × 19.2 cm.
(*Historical Society of Pennsylvania,
Philadelphia*)

engraved in subtle tones of gray rather than the deep, rich blacks usually associated with mezzotint. After this auspicious beginning, Sartain copied many of Sully's portraits of prominent Philadelphians, including two founders of the Pennsylvania Academy of the Fine Arts, Joseph Hopkinson (fig. 6) and Horace Binney.

It was not only the painters who were impressed; sometimes the sitter himself financed an engraving. In 1831 Nicholas Biddle commissioned Sartain to engrave his portrait as soon as Sully had finished painting it. Having already spent seventy-five dollars on the painting, Biddle paid sixty more for the engraving plus seven dollars for the plate. Since the painting was destroyed in the nineteenth century, Sartain's mezzotint (fig. 7) is the only record of this likeness, which was, according to Nicholas Wainwright, the only image to capture "Biddle's well-known exuberance and dash."[14]

14   Nicholas B. Wainwright, "Nicholas Biddle in Portraiture," *Antiques* 108 (Nov. 1975): 961.

ROBERT GILMOR ESQ?

Engraved by John Sartain

From the Original Portrait by Sir T. Lawrence

4

Robert Gilmor, Jr., 1774-1848. Mezzotint, 1830-35, by Sartain after Sir Thomas Lawrence, 22.8 × 19.1 cm. (*Historical Society of Pennsylvania, Philadelphia*)

In 1837 Sartain began work on an important commission, a large, full-length mezzotint of Martin Van Buren (fig. 8), after a painting by Henry Inman which today, as then, hangs in the City Hall of New York. Recalling the circumstances of engraving the plate, he described his working methods: "The city authorities refused to lend the picture so I made a sketch by the eye alone, without the aid of any of the usual appliances. After engraving the plate in my studio in Philadelphia, I took a proof to New York and touched on it with white chalk for corrections, and thus finished my work, having had only four days in all with the original. When I submitted the proof to the painter he was very much pleased with it, and had no suggestion to offer for its further improvement."[15] Nearly thirty years later, Sartain altered the face and background of the plate and published it as a portrait of Abraham Lincoln.[16] Although the body looks

15   Sartain, *Reminiscences*, p. 233.

16   Milton Kaplan, "Heads of State," *Winterthur Portfolio* 6 (1970): 135–36.

5

William White, 1748-1836. Mezzotint, circa 1830-31, by Sartain after
Thomas Sully, 28.4 × 24.4 cm. (*National Portrait Gallery, Smithsonian
Institution*)

Jos. Hopkinson

6

Joseph Hopkinson, 1770-1842. Mezzotint, circa 1832-35, by Sartain after Thomas Sully, 16 × 13.1 cm. (*Historical Society of Pennsylvania, Philadelphia*)

7

Nicholas Biddle, 1786-1844. Mezzotint, 1831, by Sartain after Thomas Sully, 19.4 × 16.4 cm. (*Historical Society of Pennsylvania, Philadelphia*)

MARTIN VAN BUREN.

President of the United States

8

Martin Van Búren, 1782-1862. Mezzotint with line engraving and etching, 1837-41, by Sartain after Henry Inman, 51.3 × 35.6 cm. (*National Portrait Gallery, Smithsonian Institution*)

Henry Clay, 1777-1852. Mezzotint with line engraving and etching, 1843,
by Sartain after John Neagle, 51 × 37.8 cm. (*Library of Congress*)

nothing like Lincoln's tall and lanky figure, a full-length mezzotint by Sartain was impressive enough as an image to compensate for the inaccuracies.

Another of Sartain's full-length engravings was his mezzotint of Henry Clay (fig. 9). A group of Philadelphia Whigs known as the Clay Club sent John Neagle down to Ashland to paint Henry Clay's portrait in 1842. Neagle wrote to Sartain from Kentucky, giving him a progress report, which leads one to assume that the painting and its mezzotint copy were commissioned simultaneously.[17]

Assured of sales, printsellers and publishers frequently financed portraits from Sartain. In 1837 James S. Earle published Sartain's mezzotint portrait of the minister Albert Barnes, who was then deeply involved in the divisive controversy between Old and New Schools of American Presbyterianism. Two years later, he published Sartain's mezzotint of David Paul Brown (fig. 10), a lawyer active in the early development of Philadelphia's Artists' Fund Society.

Another important acquaintance for Sartain was Cephas G. Childs, print publisher, engraver, and lithographer. Some of Sartain's first American mezzotints have Childs's name cited as printer in the inscription. The *United States Gazette* for January 20, 1832, noted that "Messrs. Childs and Inman have published an engraved likeness of Sir Thomas Lawrence. . . . The picture is a mezzotint by Sartain and is creditable to the artist, the head especially." Although Childs was actively engaged in the early 1830s in setting up Philadelphia's first important lithography firm, he was still selling and printing engravings, including his own views of Philadelphia (1827–30). Selling Sartain's mezzotints supplemented rather than competed with his lithography business. He believed that there was a market for fine, expensive engraved portraits as well as the less costly lithographic likenesses that he was promoting.

Three other significant works either were printed by Childs in the early 1830s or were orders that Sartain received through Childs's influence. The large mezzotint of William Penn (fig. 11) was commissioned between 1834 and 1835 by the Penn Society of Philadelphia. Unable to raise sufficient funds to erect a commemorative monument, the society decided to commission a painted portrait. Sartain recorded the cir-

17   John Neagle to John Sartain, Nov. 15, 1842, Filson Club, Louisville, Ky.

10

David Paul Brown, 1795-1872. Mezzotint, 1839, by Sartain after John Neagle, 23.1 × 19 cm. (*Historical Society of Pennsylvania, Philadelphia*)

William Penn, 1644-1718. Mezzotint, 1834-35, by Sartain after Henry Inman, 52.5 × 40.2 cm. (*Pennsylvania Academy of the Fine Arts*)

12
Andrew Jackson, 1767-1845. Mezzotint, 1832, by Sartain after William J. Hubard, 16.8 × 12.7 cm. (*Historical Society of Pennsylvania, Philadelphia*)

cumstances with a tinge of sarcasm: "It was quite natural that this commission should go to the leading artist of the city, who of course could be no other than Sully. He showed me the colour study he had prepared for the composition. The formal contract for the picture had not been consummated, but what could seem more sure?" Cephas Childs, however, succeeded in diverting the commission from Sully to his partner, Henry Inman. Then, Sartain recalled, "as soon as Inman had completed the painting of William Penn, the Society determined to commission me to engrave a large plate from it, and opened a subscription list for the impressions. But they failed to obtain enough to pay for it, so I volunteered to assume the risk and publish the engraving myself, but it was never remunerative."[18] It is curious that Childs did not choose to finance the publication of the print, since he had diverted the commission away from Sully to his partner. In any event, Sartain later sold the plate to James S. Earle, who at the time was exhibiting and selling paintings and prints in his Philadelphia framing shop.

Sartain took full advantage of his connections with Childs. One of his small prints, *Andrew Jackson* (fig. 12), probably made as a book illustration,

18 Sartain, *Reminiscences*, pp. 161–62.

was copied either from the original painting by William James Hubard, which had been commissioned by Childs, or from the lithograph after it by Albert Newsam. Since the painting is now lost, it is difficult to know which portrait Sartain copied. His version is somewhat different from the lithograph, with noticeable changes in the rug pattern and the picture frame.

At some point during their association, Childs must have convinced Sartain to try his hand at lithography. The Pennsylvania Academy of the Fine Arts has a lithograph of Napoleon II (fig. 13), copied from a French print of 1831. The pencil inscription at the bottom, in Sartain's handwriting, reads: "On stone by John Sartain, 1832, for Joseph Bonaparte of Bordentown." Apparently, however, it was just an experiment, for no other lithographs by him are known.

Despite his successes, Sartain remembered the early years in Philadelphia as difficult. The printing of his plates caused him particular frustration. In London, trained, experienced printers, the most modern presses, and the appropriate inks were taken for granted. But Philadelphia was not London. "The most serious difficulty with which I had to contend at the beginning," he remembered later, "was the inferior quality of the plate printing. Frankfort black ink was an article unknown, and yet it is the one sole material suitable for the production of first-class mezzotint work. Accordingly I took steps to import from Paris a barrel of the proper black, and also waited on Mr. Mathias Baldwin with a drawing of a press to ascertain the cost."[19] Mathias Baldwin, best known as an early manufacturer of American railway locomotives, was making engravers' tools and printing presses in the early 1830s.

Sartain's major problem at that time, he remembered, was finding a skilled printer: "Isaac Sansom was my first plate printer, a mechanic from Birmingham, England, whom I taught because I could not get the regular printers out of their old rut; they were unteachable."[20] Sartain's complaints about printers were not unique. In 1823 John Trumbull had to import a copperplate printer from England to print Asher B. Durand's engraving of his *Declaration of Independence*, "there being no one in the country qual-

---

19 Ibid., pp. 159–60.

20 John Sartain to James Monaghan, April 28, 1895, John Sartain Papers, PHi.

ified to do that class of work."[21] By 1835 Durand himself was grappling with the challenge of finding a skilled printer for his engraving of Ariadne, since most of the impressions pulled from the plate had had to be rejected. Another Philadelphia printmaker, James B. Longacre, also had difficulty getting his large plates properly printed; he had to send some of them to New York City for the Mavericks to print.[22]

Perhaps the combined problems of printers, presses, and inks proved overwhelming for a brief period in 1835 and 1836, during which time Sartain attempted to paint in oils. In 1837, however, with a newly trained printer, Isaac Sansom, he returned to engraving. Proper printing must have improved the appearance of his mezzotints, for in 1838 he won the silver medal, the highest prize awarded, at the Franklin Institute's exhibit of "Domestic Manufactures."

Unfortunately for Sartain, the Panic of 1837 disrupted artistic life; and Philadelphia, as the nation's economic headquarters, was especially affected. With a growing family to support, Sartain needed a steady income. Soon after arriving in Philadelphia, he had done some mezzotints for the annual *Pearl,* and now he turned again to magazine and book illustration to supplement his income. Though illustrations were engraved in mezzotint in England, the technique was not commonly used in America. Having revived it for separately published prints, Sartain proceeded to introduce the rich mezzotint plate for mass-produced book illustration.

Philadelphia was already an important center for book and magazine publishing. By the 1840s it had become the capital of the illustrated women's magazine, the widest-circulating being *Godey's Lady's Book.* Eventually, the editors of distinguished literary magazines, such as *Graham's Magazine* and the *Eclectic,* began to concentrate on high artistic, as well as literary, standards. By mid-century, a magazine produced in Philadelphia that did not contain illustrations was unlikely to sell. Although plates were expensive, the leading local magazines contained at least two engravings or colored fashion plates in every issue. *Graham's*

---

21   John Durand, *The Life and Times of A. B. Durand* (New York, 1894), p. 26.

22   Information on Longacre provided by Gordon Marshall, Library Company of Philadelphia.

Magazine often spent two thousand dollars on the illustrations for a single issue.[23]

The publisher of this magazine, George Graham, employed John Sartain from 1840 to 1848 to engrave the illustrations. Graham had made a significant innovation when he decided to have a fresh plate engraved for each issue instead of the usual practice of using old, worn plates purchased from other publishers. Sartain commented that

> *the boldness of the enterprise, astonished me, yet I did not give expression to my surprise, or thought I did not, but after two or three months of extraordinary success Graham told me that he could see that I had wondered, and he explained what led him to adopt such a measure. He said that before deciding on the details of his plans he consulted all he could reach whose experience with periodical literature might assist his judgement. Principal among these was Israel Post, of New York. Post's advice was "Go to John Sartain and get a new plate for every number and I guarantee success. I sold three thousand of that number of Burton's* Gentleman's Magazine *that had his plate of 'The Pets' in it."*[24]

Sartain noted that the circulation of *Graham's Magazine* grew rapidly: by the end of the second year, forty thousand copies of each issue were printed, and he had to engrave four steel plates of each subject to meet the increased demand.

In addition to his work for *Graham's Magazine*, Sartain was making one portrait illustration per issue for the *Eclectic Magazine* between 1844 and 1862. For the May 1861 issue, he engraved a self-portrait based on an ambrotype by his son Henry. Another of his subjects was Washington Irving (fig. 14), about whom he recalled:

> *I myself met Irving in 1856 when I spent a most delightful afternoon with him in his library at Sunnyside on the Hudson. I went with Mr. W. H. Bidwell of New York, proprietor and editor of* The Eclectic Magazine. *He wanted Irving to sit for a portrait to be engraved for his periodical, but Irving said that he had so often declined to pose that he feared he would give*

23 Frank Luther Mott, A *History of American Magazines, 1741–1850*, 5 vols. (1930; rept. Cambridge, Mass., 1966–68), 1:521.

24 Sartain, *Reminiscences*, p. 198.

156

WASHINGTON IRVING

Washington Irving

14
Washington Irving, 1783-1859. Mezzotint with line engraving and etching, 856-58, by Sartain from life, 17.5 × 13.2 cm. From the *Eclectic Magazine* 45 (Oct. 1858). (*National Portrait Gallery, Smithsonian Institution*)

too much offense by consenting now. However, he seemed to divine my purpose of attempting a portrait from memory. I observed him closely as I sat in a favorable point of view, studying his habitual position and characteristic expressions. I made a drawing entirely from memory that was pronounced so good a likeness that it was ordered to be engraved, and was published in The Eclectic *in the number for October, 1858.*[25]

During the 1840s and 1850s other magazines in addition to *Graham's* and the *Eclectic* were also presenting portrait prints to the exclusion of other subjects. The *U.S. Democratic Review, American Quarterly Register,* and *American Whig Review* included small, uninspired engravings done in line and stipple. By comparison, Sartain's portrait prints are more elegant and highly finished. He worked in a rich combination of etching, mezzotint, and line engraving and chose as his subjects the great names of literature, science, politics, and the arts, such as Jenny Lind (fig. 15), Louis Agassiz, Henry Wadsworth Longfellow, and Samuel F. B. Morse. Sartain had a good eye for liveliness in a subject, and his portraits exhibit a characteristic dynamic quality in both poses and facial expressions.

25 Ibid., pp. 185–86.

15

Jenny Lind, 1820-1887. Mezzotint with line engraving and etching, 1857,
by Sartain after daguerreotype by Frederick Dubourg Richards, 15.9 ×
12.7 cm. from the *Eclectic Magazine* 41 (June 1857). (*Library of Congress*)

Although some of the vast number of these illustrations might be faulted today for overt sentimentality, occasional sloppiness of technique resulting from hurried execution, and overprinting of the plates, Sartain's work at its best was technically unexcelled. His rich and vibrant technique generally upgraded the quality of book and magazine illustration, and the popularity of his plates indicated a growing sophistication in the public attitude toward the pictorial arts.

As his career progressed, John Sartain became increasingly interested in photography. He often worked from photographs of paintings rather than from the original works and copied daguerreotypes of individuals for his portrait prints. His enthusiasm for the early forms of this new medium indicates that he was not troubled, as were some artists and critics, by photography's challenge to the pictorial arts as the chief interpreter of the visual world. A city like Philadelphia, with its long history of scientific and technological innovations, provided a ripe environment for the energetic Sartain to experiment with the new science of photography, especially in its application to art.

Sartain's papers are filled with examples of his use of photography. Artists such as George Caleb Bingham, Christian Schussele, and Peter Rothermel sent him photographs of their work for his use in preparing engravings. Sartain himself was familiar with the techniques and procedures of photographic processes; his commonplace book included an entry describing how a daguerreotype was made. In 1879, while visiting a photographer friend in England, he wrote to his daughter, Emily, requesting that she send his friend the recipe for the collotype process that he had previously recorded in a notebook.[26] In another letter, he discussed with her the prices of solar enlargements.[27] Although no portrait photographs actually taken by Sartain are known, he was probably an active participant in amateur photography circles in Philadelphia. In 1891 he was made an honorary member of the Photographic Society, a group of artists who held regular exhibitions.

Sartain's interest in photography may have been stimulated by his acquaintance with Marcus Aurelius Root, a major figure in American

26   John Sartain to Emily Sartain, July 3, 1879, John Sartain Papers, PHi.

27   John Sartain to Emily Sartain, July 3, 1875, John Sartain Papers, PHi.

16

John Sartain, 1808-1897. Mezzotint
with line engraving and etching,
1861, by Sartain after daguerreotype
by Marcus Aurelius Root, 11.5 × 9.4
cm. From Marcus Aurelius Root,
The Camera and The Pencil (Philadelphia, 1864). (*National Portrait
Gallery, Smithsonian Institution*)

photography. In 1848 Sartain engraved a self-portrait (see fig. 1) after
Root's daguerreotype for the magazine *Nineteenth Century*. Sartain himself
may have chosen the elegant and somewhat unusual pose for this portrait.
In 1864 Root published *The Camera and the Pencil,* one of the first books on
the history and aesthetics of photography. Most of the illustrations are
portrait prints by Sartain. His mezzotint of Daniel Webster, after a
daguerreotype by John Whipple, was expressly included in the book as an
example of what the author considered bad portrait photography. The
other portraits were after Root's own daguerreotypes. Images of William
Draper and Samuel F. B. Morse, both pioneer daguerreotypists, were
illustrated, as well as an image of Sartain himself (fig. 16). That Sartain
was included among this illustrious group was an indication of Root's
respect for him and for his ideas.

Sartain's interest in the use of photography in his printmaking and his
familiarity with its technical aspects demonstrate not only curiosity and
flexibility but his concern with making art more accessible to the public.
He probably would have agreed with Rembrandt Peale, who wrote that
photography, "far from being a rival, is in truth a most important auxiliary
to the resources of the artist." Although "photography can never assume a
higher rank than engraving," Peale stated, its advantage was nonetheless

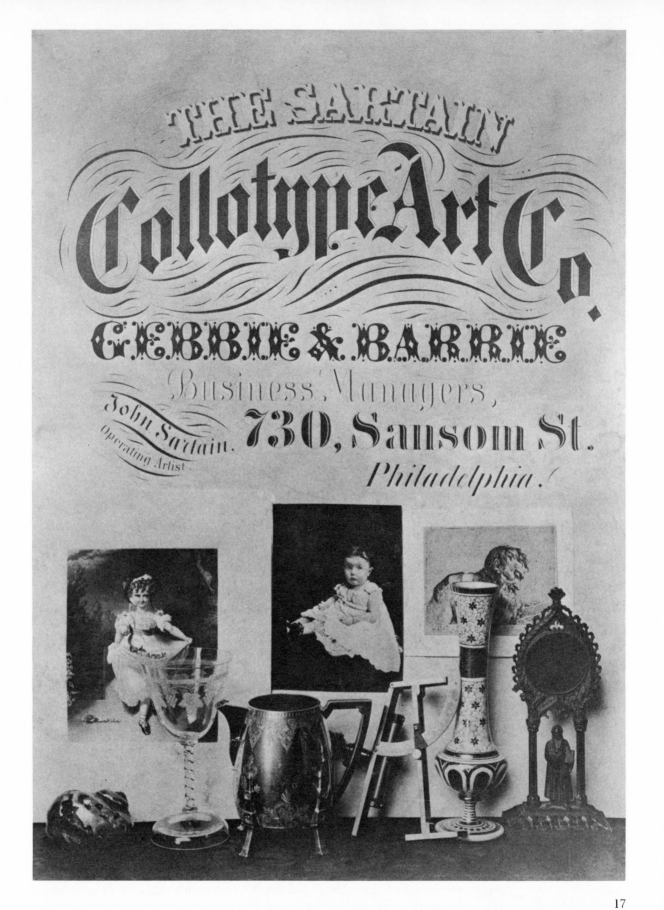

The Sartain Collotype Art Co. Collotype advertisement, circa 1873-80, 23.1 × 16.5 cm. (*Library Company of Philadelphia*)

in its cheapness, which would increase the taste for portraiture and thus improve the situation for artists in America.[28]

A final evidence of Sartain's involvement with the early development of photography is an advertisement for "The Sartain Collotype Art Co. (fig. 17). The advertisement is itself a collotype, illustrating an assortment of bric-a-brac that one might find in a photographer's studio. The company's location is given as 730 Sansom Street, next door to Sartain's residence at 728 Sansom. The proprietors, Gebbie and Barrie, undoubtedly met Sartain when they published *The Illustrated Catalogue of the Masterpieces of the International Exhibition,* which described the exhibits at the Philadelphia Centennial of 1876, for which Sartain was the chief of the Bureau of Art. According to this advertisement, Sartain was the operating artist of the company, which probably meant that he supervised the choice of subject matter. Certainly the use of his name would have added to the prestige of Gebbie and Barrie's business venture.

In the final analysis, Sartain was a successful businessman who happened to be an artist. In Philadelphia he was given the most important portrait commissions; he worked for the most successful magazines; he was on the most prestigious art committees. Contemporaries, such as Gebbie and Barrie, equated his name with success. Arriving in America two years after the death of Gilbert Stuart in 1828 and dying in 1897, John Sartain had an energetic career that spanned almost the entire nineteenth century and encompassed many of the changes and developments in American visual arts.

28 Rembrandt Peale, "Photography," *Crayon* 1, no. 11 (March 1855): 170.

David Claypoole Johnston's Theatrical Portraits

DAVID
TATHAM

A successful theatrical portrait is the outcome of the interaction of three persons: the player whose likeness we see; the character whose role the player acts; and the artist who, in telling us about the player and character—about how each is transformed by the other—tells us also about himself. The best portraits in character depict far more than the likeness of a costumed player; they embody the power of transformation that lies at the heart of the arts of the theater.

American masters of this kind of portraiture have been few. The first was Charles Willson Peale, whose splendid painting, of 1771, of Nancy Hallam as Imogen in Shakespeare's *Cymbeline* (Colonial Williamsburg) is a masterpiece of its age. Not until the early decades of the nineteenth century, when the American theater began its first sustained growth, did other American artists make memorable portraits of players in character. The best-known theatrical portraitists of this generation are the painters Thomas Sully and John Neagle. The least known, perhaps, but by no

Among the many persons who aided the development of this paper, Georgia Bumgardner, Curator of Graphic Arts at the American Antiquarian Society, Jeanne Newlin, Curator of the Harvard University Theatre Collection, and John S. Mayfield, Curator Emeritus of Rare Books and Manuscripts at Syracuse University, merit special thanks for their assistance, good counsel, and encouragement over several years. The Syracuse University Office of Research furthered the progress of this study by covering some of the costs of photographic work.

means the least interesting, is the printmaker David Claypoole Johnston (1798–1865).[1]

Johnston's theatrical portraits, of which twenty-eight have so far been located, are the products of an artist who was also an actor. Between 1821 and 1826 Johnston was a member of two of the leading stock companies in the United States. For the most part, his theatrical portraits depict the actors and actresses with whom he worked. In most, if not all, cases he seems to have begun with a quick watercolor sketch of his subject in character, using this as the basis for a print. He sometimes also painted a version in oils. It is not clear to what extent his portraits were products of commissions by their subjects, but Johnston surely made the print versions not only from a desire to record the likenesses of friends but also from a hope that he could market them profitably to a public which was as enamored of the stage as he was. Even during his years as an actor, Johnston's primary occupation was that of a graphic artist. He was well known for his book and periodical illustrations and for his satirical prints and caricatures. His caricatures sometimes touch on the theater,[2] but his theatrical portraits are not satirical. They are, despite their amiability, serious likenesses.

Of the twenty-eight known portraits, twenty-three were separately published, four were designed to be plates in books, and one was made to embellish the title page of a published song. Johnston made these likenesses between 1821 and about 1837. With one exception (Appendix, no. 8), they are from life, and they constitute the first substantial body of

1 The essential literature concerning Johnston and his work includes Clarence Brigham, "David Claypoole Johnston," *Proceedings of the American Antiquarian Society* 50 (April 1940): 98–110; Malcolm Johnson, *David Claypool* [sic] *Johnston* (Boston and Worcester, 1970); David Tatham, "A Note about David Claypoole Johnston and a Check List of His Book Illustrations," *Courier* 34 (Spring 1970): 11–17, and 35 (Summer 1970): 26–31; and David Tatham, "D. C. Johnston's Satiric Views of Art in Boston, 1825–1850," *Art & Commerce: American Prints of the Nineteenth Century* (Charlottesville, Va., 1978), pp. 9–24. The question of whether Johnston used a final "e" in his middle name remains unresolved.

2 Johnston's most elaborate theater-based caricatures are found in his *Outlines Illustrative of the Journal of F****** A*** K****** (Boston, 1835)—eight etchings in wrappers, all satirizing Fanny Kemble's *Journal*, and through it her first tour of America as a star actress.

original portrait prints of actors and actresses in America.[3]

It at first seems odd that this important, interesting, and attractive group of original portraits is so little known, but the reasons are not hard to find. As prints, Johnston's portraits have suffered the neglect of scholars that, until recently, was the fate of nearly all American art other than painting. Further, the prints are rare. They evidently were made in small editions and sold locally only in Philadelphia and Boston. The few impressions that have survived are widely scattered and rarely exhibited. For the most part, Johnston's subjects are unfamiliar names even to specialists in the history of the American theater (though playbills, newspapers of the era, and contemporary memoirs make it clear that nearly all were figures of consequence in their own time). Moreover, the most frequently reproduced of Johnston's portraits, in the twentieth century, has been that of the noted tragedian Edwin Forrest, which, though it is a well-made print, is in some ways the least characteristic of the lot. For these and other reasons, Johnston's portraits have remained largely unnoticed.

They deserve to be better known. They are important documents of the development in America of a democratic theater which was expected at once to entertain and to enlighten, to diminish class distinctions while it elevated the level of national culture. The portraits are evidence of the first strong stirrings of nationalism in native drama, of an era when the British actors and plays that had dominated the American stage began to give way to homebred substitutes. Some of Johnston's portrait prints are unique records of faces, figures, costumes, and scenery otherwise pictorially undocumented. The portraits also significantly illuminate the progress of style in the graphic arts in America, at first reflecting Regency elegance and wit but soon showing a robust naturalism more in keeping with the democratic individualism of Jacksonian America. And not the least of their values is the evidence they give us of the mind and hand of one of the most interesting and entertaining artists in antebellum America.

D. C. Johnston—he consistently used only the initials of his first two

---

3 Several of Johnston's contemporaries, including Edward W. Clay, made portrait prints of players in character, but none of them seems to have been as active or able as Johnston in this genre. The engraved frontispiece portraits in Mathias Lopez and Francis C. Wemyss, eds., *Acting American Theatre*, 4 vols. (Philadelphia, 1826–27), are after paintings and consequently do not qualify as original portrait prints.

names—was born in Philadelphia in 1798 to a family steeped in the theater.[4] His father was for many years bookkeeper and box-office manager for the Chestnut Street Theatre. His mother had been an actress. An aunt and uncle were both important performers in the 1790s. The aunt, Susannah Haswell Rowson, was already well known for her novel *Charlotte Temple* when she took to the stage in 1793 as actress and playwright. She and her husband, the actor-musician William Rowson, moved in 1796 to the Federal Street Theatre in Boston, prefiguring a move their nephew would make nearly thirty years later.

In 1815 Johnston was apprenticed to the Philadelphia engraver Francis Kearny, and in 1819 he entered the trade on his own. Among his first original prints were a number of caricatures, some signed in the plate with ludicrous pseudonyms.[5] The caricatures proved more controversial than Johnston had expected. Some years later, in a letter to the artist, playwright, and historian William Dunlap, he explained how these prints had led to a career on the stage.

> *Dandies and exquisites held it not honest to have their follies thus set down and exposed at shop windows; and valiant militia colonels and majors, in overhanging epaulets, breathed naught but blood and thunder; my customers, the print and book sellers, being threatened with libel suits on one hand and extermination on the other, chose rather to avoid such difficulties than to continue the sale of my productions. This unexpected turn of tide rendered it necessary for me to look about for employment in some way that would enable me to provide [myself with] food and clothing. . .and at the same time allow me a portion of leisure to devote to my pencil. I was at this time fond of the theatre and had acquired no inconsiderable reputation among my acquaintance as a mimic not only of actors but of many individuals in private life, and was reckoned good at a comic song, and altogether a nice man for a small party. These* wonderful accomplishments *induced me to try my fortune on the boards. . . . I made application to the manager, Mr. [William] Wood, who selected me for the part of Henry*

4 Biographical information concerning Johnston is drawn from the sources cited in note 1 except as otherwise specified.

5 Among Johnston's pseudonyms was "Gebolibus Crackfardi," used on at least three prints between 1819 and 1824. In 1819 he also used "Drawn by Busybody—Engraved by Nobody." Johnson, pp. 22–38.

in Speed the Plow, *in which character I . . . made my debut. . . . The first appearance of a novice has been compared to the state of a person who has just been shot at and missed, but . . . I must have looked more like a person hit than missed, the shot having carried away the words of my author.*[6]

Finding himself, on his first night (March 10, 1821), unable to recall Henry's lines, he improvised an elaborate and protracted solo dance, though it had little to do with the dramatic action. The audience was amazed, as were his fellow actors. When he had danced himself out, the audience applauded warmly, and Johnston found himself a success. Explaining this to Dunlap, he said, "Instead of asking myself where could Henry have learned to dance? I merely asked, like a sensible actor, what can I do to get applause?"[7]

Johnston spent three-and-a-half seasons with the Chestnut Street Theatre company, from March 1821 through the spring of 1824. His roles included Backbite in *The School for Scandal*, Fenton in *The Merry Wives of Windsor*, Lennox in *Macbeth*, and the drunken servant in *She Stoops to Conquer*.[8] Though these were lesser roles, he played them with the leading figures of the American and British stage. In his letter to Dunlap, Johnston wrote, "During my actorship [in Philadelphia] I occasionally put forth something in a print way, sometimes a political caricature and now and then a theatrical star."[9] Six of his known portrait prints of actors and actresses come from his years in Philadelphia.

The earliest of the six is Johnston's portrait of the tempestuous English tragedian Edmund Kean as Richard III (fig. 1), a role in which he was widely admired. Kean's four-week engagement in Philadelphia began in January 1821. Johnston's stipple engraving, unsigned but unquestionably his work, was probably made and published during this time.

---

6   Johnston's letter is printed in William Dunlap, *History of the Rise and Progress of the Arts of Design in the United States*, 2 vols. (New York, 1834), 2:327–32. The passage quoted appears on pp. 329–30.

7   Ibid., 2:331.

8   Playbills for the Chestnut Street Theatre and Walnut Street Theatre, Philadelphia, in the Harvard Theatre Collection, Harvard University.

9   Dunlap, 2:332.

1

Mr. Kean as Richard, Duke of Gloster.
Stipple engraving, 1821, by Johnston,
11.8 × 11.5 cm. (*Harvard Theatre
Collection*)

Except in details of costume, none of the many other British and American
portrait prints of Kean as Richard corresponds to this print, either in
pictorial image or in characterization. Few artists in any medium captured
so well as did Johnston the animalism of Kean's Richard. Kean's tour of
America in 1820 and 1821 began as a brilliant success but ended in
shambles in Boston, where he offended much of the populace by refusing
to act to a small house. When Kean returned to Boston four years later, a
long-smouldering residue of hostility toward him, fueled by reports in the
press of his intemperance and alleged adultery, flared into a riot at the
Boston Theatre as he was about to appear in *Richard III.* The play was
hooted from the stage before it could begin; the theater was vandalized;
Kean fled from town; and Johnston, who was in the cast, must surely have
counted the evening as among his most memorable.[10]

10   The portrait of Kean as Richard III is ascribed to Johnston on grounds of style. The
     Harvard Theatre Collection impression was obtained from a descendent of the artist
     who believed it to be his work. It could scarcely be by anyone else. For an account of
     Kean's appearances in Boston, see William Clapp, *Record of the Boston Stage*
     (Boston, 1853), pp. 180–93, 226–38.

MᴿᴹATHEWS AS MONSIEUR MORBLEU

Fip—The Seasons;my old favourite Thomson

Mor—Diable! Tonson come again!

2

Mr. Mathews as Monsieur Morbleu.
Stipple engraving, 1823, by Johnston,
12.5 × 11.5 cm. (*Harvard Theatre*
Collection)

In 1823 Johnston made three portraits of the English actor Charles Mathews, who first toured America in the season of 1822–23. Though he was an able repertory actor, Mathews's fame rested on his one-man entertainments. These consisted of a series of sketches and songs in which he imitated and gently satirized a wide range of human types, inventing, in all, some four hundred characters. He concluded many of his entertainments with a short play in which, through rapid changes of costume and voice, he played all the parts. Though he intended to limit his American tour to his one-man show, problems of transport repeatedly delayed the arrival of his costumes, and so he turned to conventional comedies and farces for the first evenings of his engagement in each city. In Philadelphia he opened in a double bill of Holcroft's *The Road to Ruin* and Moncrieff's *Monsieur Tonson*. In the latter, Johnston played Jack Ardourly to Mathews's Morbleu, and it is in this role that we see the English actor in Johnston's stipple engraving (fig. 2). Morbleu, an émigré from the French Revolution living in London, is beset, he thinks, by a mysterious and omnipresent Mr. Thompson, whom he calls Tonson. At the moment Johnston has portrayed him, he is astounded to find (wrongly) that his

3

Characters in The Polly Packet *as Represented by Mr. Mathews*. Stipple engraving, 1823, by Johnston, 16.2 × 22 cm. (*Harvard Theatre Collection*)

tormentor is the author, James Thomson, of that then-ubiquitous book of verse, *The Seasons*.[11]

Johnston's second portrait of Mathews shows him in the several roles he assumed in *The Polly Packet*, one of the costumed short plays that concluded his entertainments (fig. 3). We are shown the cabin of a channel packet, the *Polly*, whose passengers include such varied caricatures of humanity as Major Longbow, a fabricator of astonishing exploits; M. Jeu-Singe, the proprietor of the troupe of dancing dogs whom he tries to feed while struggling with his own seasickness; and Theophilus Tulip, a mollycoddled young man traveling with his imperious mother.

11 An early edition of the script of Moncrieff's *Monsieur Tonson* (Philadelphia, 1824) lists, on the *Dramatis Personae* page, Mathews as Morbleu, Johnston as Ardourly, and Joseph Jefferson as Fip, a character referred to but not shown in Johnston's print. For Mathews's tour and descriptions of his entertainments, see Anne Jackson Mathews, *Memoirs of Charles Mathews, Comedian*, 4 vols. (London, 1839), 3:52–62, 301–407.

4

Mr. Mathews at Home in The Diligence. Stipple engraving, 1823, by Johnston, 19.5 × 24.3 cm. (*Harvard Theatre Collection*)

The visual appeal of Mathews's characterizations spawned well over a hundred portrait prints in the course of a quarter of a century.[12] Most of them are the sorry products of unskilled draftsmen. A few of the more competent attempted to integrate a selection of Mathews's characters into a unified design, and none did this better than Johnston in his third portrait of the actor (fig. 4), in which he shows the characters of the short play *La Diligence*. They are grouped in a composition which is centered on the paunch of Hezekiah Hulk, an attorney. In other guises, Mathews is shown as Evelina Evergreen, a spinster; Samuel Starch, a dandy; and, among others, M. Peremtoire, whose name explains him well enough. By any measure, this print is one of the finest accomplishments in the graphic arts in America through the first quarter of the nineteenth century. In drawing, composition, execution, and characterization, it marks a major advance in Johnston's development.

12   Lillian Arvilla Hall, *Catalogue of the Dramatic Portraits in the Theatre Collection of the Harvard College Library*, 4 vols. (Cambridge, Mass., 1930), 3:168–77

In the legend of this stipple engraving, as well as in that of *The Polly Packet*, Johnston has inscribed "Sketched, (from memory)," to acknowledge, probably, that Mathews did not sit to him. Similar statements appear on other portraits by Johnston. In these cases Johnston, in the quiet of his studio, seems to have reenacted in his mind the playing of Mathews and other subjects, identifying with them as only a fellow actor can, aided by his recollections of performances and probably also by a few quick sketches taken in the theater. It is likely that the portraits of Mathews were published during, or not long after, the actor's first Philadelphia engagement in 1823, but it is certain that they were out well before the publication in June 1824 of *The Cat-Fight* by Ebenezer Mack. This book states on its title page that it is "illustrated by D. C. Johnston of Philadelphia, Author from Recollection of 'Mathews at Home in La Diligence,' 'Polly Packet,' etc."[13]

The fifth of the Philadelphia portraits is *Mr. J. Wallack as Dick Dashall* (fig. 5), in the farce *My Aunt.* James William Wallack was an English actor who played Dashall for the first time in Philadelphia in January 1823. He had a long and prosperous career in America as an actor and manager.

Wallack, Mathews, and Kean were touring stars. The only portrait by Johnston (located so far) of a member of the Chestnut Street Theatre's stock company is that of Joseph Jefferson I, whose grandson and namesake later in the century would become a major luminary of the American stage. Johnston shows the elder Jefferson in full-length profile as Bob Logic in *Tom and Jerry*, Moncrieff's popular adaptation of Pierce Egan's *Life in London*, a loosely constructed novel of high and low life in Regency England.

In 1824, perhaps in New York, Johnston etched a portrait of a Scottish actor newly arrived in America, James Roberts, for the title page of the comic song "Massa Georgee and General La Fayette," a piece inspired by Lafayette's visit to America in that year.[14] Johnston's vignette has long been regarded as the first depiction in America of a black person

---

13 Ebenezer Mack, *The Cat-Fight* (New York, 1824).

14 Words and music by Micah Hawkins. Hawkins, an uncle of the painter William Sidney Mount, was the author of another work illustrated by Johnston: *Mynhieur*

5

Mr. J. Wallack as Dick Dashall. Stipple engraving, 1823, by Johnston, 13 × 10 cm. (*Harvard Theatre Collection*)

on American printed music, and also, since Roberts was not black, as the first representation in America of a white actor in blackface. To a greater extent than in his other portraits, Johnston here leaned toward caricature, as was appropriate for Roberts's own caricaturelike stage portrayal.

In his autobiographical letter to Dunlap, Johnston told of his departure from Philadelphia for Boston.

Between my salary, my pencil, and my graver, I lived rather comfortably; but as I never was positively stage-struck, I kept a sharp look out for an opportunity to bid adieu to . . . carrotty wigs and poisoned goblets. To facilitate this object I engaged with Boston managers for the season of 1825. My motive for making this move was owing to a more extensive sale of my graphic productions in that city than in my native place. A short residence in

---

Herrick von Heimelman, the Dancing-Master; and the Big Red Nose (New York, 1824). Johnston's title-page portrait of Roberts is reproduced in my *Lure of the Striped Pig* (Barre, Mass., 1973), p. 37.

MR. KILNER as CAPT COP
In *CHARLES* the *SECOND*.

"*In the time of the Rump*
When old admiral Trump &c.

Sketd. from memory Engd. & published by Throop & Johnston.
Boston 1825

6

Mr. Kilner as Capt. Cop. Etching,
1825, by Johnston, 10.9 × 6.6 cm.
(*Harvard Theatre Collection*)

Boston convinced me that by applying myself to cut copper, I should soon be
enabled to cut the boards.[15]

In fact, Johnston had settled in Boston some months before the
opening of the season. By March 1825 he had established a short-lived
partnership with another engraver. John V. N. Throop. Of the few prints
bearing the imprint of Throop & Johnston, two are theater portraits—
those of Thomas Kilner and Henry J. Finn, the last of which is dated
March 1825 in the plate. Kilner and Finn had been members of the
resident company of the Boston Theatre (also known as the Federal Street
Theatre) since the early 1820s. They became co-managers beginning with
the 1825–26 season, and they hired Johnston. They were among the best
comic actors in America.

Johnston shows *Mr. Kilner as Capt. Cop* (fig. 6) in the play *Charles the*

15   Dunlap, 2:332.

174

7

*"Doctor Logic"...as Represented by
Mr. Finn.* Etching, 1825, by John-
ston, 11.2 × 7 cm. (*Harvard Theatre
Collection*)

Second by John Howard Payne, and Finn as *Doctor Logic* (fig. 7) in *Tom and
Jerry*, a role in which Johnston had depicted Joseph Jefferson, also in
profile, a year or two earlier. Johnston's watercolor study of Finn as Logic
is owned by the American Antiquarian Society; a different watercolor of
the same subject is owned by the Harvard Theatre Collection. Though
both engraved portraits are unquestionably by Johnston, the cursive script
is probably by Throop, who specialized in such work. The Throop and
Johnston partnership was dissolved before the end of 1825.

Johnston's debut at the Boston Theatre was as Hastings in Oliver
Goldsmith's *She Stoops to Conquer* on September 19, 1825. A review in the
Boston Galaxy was noncommittal:

> *Never having seen him on the stage until this evening, we cannot speak in
> reference to dramatic talent, for the character [of Hastings] admits of the
> display of very little energy or talent. Mr. Johnson [sic] is favorably known
> to the public as a painter and engraver, several of his productions, especially
> the Picture of the Great Elm on the common[location unknown] and the
> characteristic engravings of Finn in Bob Logic and Kilner as Capt. Copp,*

Mᴿ HAMBLIN

8

*Mr. Hamblin of the Theatre Royal
Drury-Lane.* Lithograph, 1826, by
Johnston after Henry J. Finn, 14.2 ×
13.1 cm. (*American Antiquarian
Society*)

*having attracted the notice of amateurs in the arts; and we hope he will be
equally successful in living dramatic personations.*[16]

In fact, Johnston did not meet with equal success on the stage. From all
accounts, he was a competent actor but not one of distinction. As in
Philadelphia, he played minor roles with the major actors and actresses of
his day, in the most demanding dramatic works acted in America; but, now
in Boston, he turned his energies increasingly to the graphic arts.

Four portraits record plays and players of Johnston's first (and only)
season at the Boston Theatre. They are all lithographs, as would be most of
his likenesses from this point on. The new medium had been introduced to
Boston in the fall of 1825; Johnston quickly mastered it.

The first of these four portraits is that of the English actor Thomas
Hamblin, who made his debut in Boston as Hamlet, the role in which
Johnston shows him, in January 1826 (fig. 8). His career thereafter was in
America, first as an actor and then as a manager. The print's legend states
that the portrait is on stone by Johnston after a drawing by Finn. Finn may
have sketched the actor in New York while arranging his Boston engagement, so that Johnston might have impressions of the print ready for
Hamblin's opening night. There is an introspective somberness in the
portrayal, appropriate to the character of Hamlet though rather foreign to
Johnston's temperament, and to his prints. To the extent that this portrait
reveals something of Hamblin to us, it is Finn's work.

The second portrait from Johnston's acting season in Boston is *Mrs.*

16 *Boston Galaxy*, Sept. 23, 1825.

176

MRS. PELBY AS CHERRY

9

Mrs. Pelby as Cherry. Lithograph, 1826, by Johnston, 17 × 15 cm. (Hoblitzelle Theatre Arts Collection, Humanities Research Center, the University of Texas at Austin)

Pelby as Cherry (fig. 9), shown in the extravaganza *Cherry and Fair Star, or The Childen of Cyprus,* first performed in February 1826. Rosalie French Pelby was for many years a great favorite in Boston. An oil painting of her is owned by the Bostonian Society. The two other portrait prints show the actor John Barnes in comic roles: Johnny Atkins in *Mogul Tale* by Mrs. Inchbald and Delph in the farce *Family Jars,* both performed in March 1826.

Related to Johnston's season of 1825–26, though a product of late 1826, is a double portrait of the company's co-managers, Finn and Kilner, whose earlier engraved separate likenesses have already been mentioned. The two actors are now shown as *Paul Pry and Col. Hardy* (fig. 10) in the farce *Paul Pry* by John Poole, which was first played in Boston in December

PAUL PRY AND COL HARDY.

AS REPRESENTED BY

Mʀ FINN AND Mʀ KILNER.

10
Paul Pry and Col. Hardy as Represented by Mr. Finn and Mr. Kilner. Lithograph, 1826, by Johnston, 14.2 × 12.9 cm. (*American Antiquarian Society*)

1826. Paul Pry was one of Finn's most popular parts. Johnston shows him in the costume described by the playwright as "striped unmentionables and bob-tail coat." An oil painting of this subject by Johnston is in a private collection.

Finn and Johnston were friends for many years and collaborated on at least one book.[17] Finn, in addition to being an actor of uncommon ability, was a skilled artist, playwright, and wit. Born in Nova Scotia and educated in the United States, including at Princeton, Finn began his acting career in London and settled in Boston in 1822. A contemporary of his recalled that "he invariably kept the public in a continual roar by his mirth-

17 Henry J. Finn, ed., *American Comic Annual* (Boston, 1831).

11

Mr. Reed as Roderick Dhu. Lithograph, 1826, by Johnston, 15.5 × 8 cm. (*Private collection*)

provoking sallies, but in private he was very sedate; and to see him quietly seated in the [Boston] Athenaeum, his favorite place of resort, no one would imagine that the spare man with eyes so intent upon some foreign review was he who at night...would keep the audience 'laughing in tiers.' "[18] Finn perished in the burning of the steamer *Lexington* in Long Island Sound in January 1840, a disaster whose depiction by American lithographers holds an important place in the history of popular prints in America.[19]

Though no longer a member of the company after the spring of 1826, Johnston remained close to the Boston Theatre and continued to make portraits of its players. It is significant that both in Philadelphia and Boston he depicted only performers in the legitimate theater. He ignored tumblers, fire-eaters, ropewalkers, singing families, and myriad other entertainers, except in caricature. He took the theater, comic and tragic, very seriously.

18 Clapp, p. 207.

19 The significance of the *Lexington* print in the development of illustrated newspapers, the disaster-view genre, and the retailing of popular prints is briefly discussed in Harry T. Peters, *Currier & Ives*, 2 vols. (Garden City, N.Y., 1929), 1:38–40; and in Peters's later work with the same title but a substantially different text (Garden City, N.Y., 1942), pp. 1–2. The print was not universally well received when it appeared, however. The *Boston Atlas* of Jan. 20, 1840, with Finn among others in mind, said: "We were sorry to see . . . displayed at the window of a respectable bookstore a picture purporting to represent the burning of the steamer Lexington. One would suppose it was enough to mourn the loss of dear friends without having . . . one's feelings lacerated by an attempt to picture the means of their death."

12
Mr. Wilson as Bertram. Lithograph, circa 1828, by Johnston, 22.4 × 16.6 cm. (*American Antiquarian Society*)

Late in 1826 or early in 1827, Johnston portrayed Daniel Reed as the Highland chieftain Roderick Dhu (fig. 11) in a dramatization of Walter Scott's *Lady of the Lake*. In the fall of 1827, he portrayed George Andrews, new to the company, as Luke in the melodrama *Luke the Laborer, or The Lost Son*. In time, Andrews became manager of a theater company formed in Boston by the merging of Kilner and Finn's old troupe with a rival company which had been assembled in 1827 and for whom the Tremont Theatre had been built.[20]

The touring star Alexander Wilson, an adherent of the eye-rolling school of tragic acting to judge from Johnston's portraits of him, appeared at the Boston Theatre as Pierre, in January 1828, in Otway's *Venice Preserved* and later as Count Bertram in Charles Maturin's *Bertram, or The Castle of Aldobrand* (fig. 12). In a more cheerful mood—one always more congenial to Johnston—is John Sloman, shown singing the comic song "Jerry Smart's Trip in Search of Sweet Kitty Clover." Sloman first played Boston in January 1828, a month after his arrival from England.

Four portraits from 1828 to 1830 merit closer examination, each for a different reason. From 1828, though probably begun in 1827, is Johnston's engraving of Mrs. Owen Morris (fig. 13), of which at least three states exist, in one of which her name is misspelled "Moris." She is shown in character—her costume is of the eighteenth century—but her role is not clear. The engraving was meant to be the frontispiece for one of the plays edited by Mathias Lopez, prompter at the Chestnut Street Theatre, and Francis Wemyss, actor in (and later manager of) that company, and published in Philadelphia in 1826 and 1827 by A. R. Poole under the series

20 Clapp, pp. 248–54, 274–76, 375.

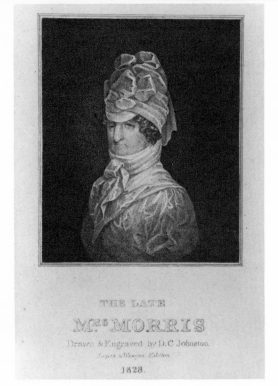

13

The Late Mrs. Morris. Stipple engraving, 1828, by Johnston, 8.8 × 7.2
cm. (*Hoblitzelle Theatre Arts Collection, Humanities Research Center,
the University of Texas at Austin*)

title *Acting American Theatre.* Each play was graced with a portrait of a
player in character, most of them engraved by Asher B. Durand or James
B. Longacre after painted portraits by John Neagle. The series ceased
publication prematurely in 1828 before the portrait of Mrs. Morris could
be used. Johnston seems to have published it separately.[21]

Elizabeth Morris, who was born in 1753, made her debut at An-
napolis in 1772. After a long career on the stage, she died in Philadelphia in
1826. She was a link between Johnston's generation and many of the
earliest significant figures of the early American theater, including Lewis
Hallam, with whom she acted, and his company. Johnston's engraving is
based on a small watercolor sketch (now at the American Antiquarian
Society), which he made from life or recollection. It is the only recorded
likeness of Mrs. Morris, and it no doubt explains why Johnston, in Boston,
was asked to supply a portrait for a series otherwise produced in Philadelphia. To be consistent with Durand's and Longacre's work, he executed the portrait as a deep-toned stipple engraving.

In a lithograph drawn in November 1828, Johnston portrayed Louisa
Lane, then about eight years old, as all of the five characters she played in
the farce *Twelve Precisely, or A Night at Dover* (fig. 14). Miss Lane was one
of a number of child stars who made a specialty of Mathews-like virtuosity,
acting multiple roles through changes of costume and voice. Like most of

21   In one state, the engraving's legend reads: "The Late / Mrs. Morris / Drawn and
Engraved by D. C. Johnston. / Lopez & Wemyss Edition / 1828." Other states
carry other legends, none of which mentions Lopez & Wemyss.

MISS LANE.

[EIGHT YEARS OF AGE]

IN THE FIVE CHARACTERS IN "TWELVE PRECISELY"

Boston Nov 5 1828

14

*Miss Lane . . . in the Five Characters in
"Twelve Precisely."* Lithograph, 1828,
by Johnston, 13.5 × 18.5 cm. (*Hoblitzelle Theatre Arts Collection, Humanities Research Center, the University of Texas at Austin*)

the juvenile performers of her day, and like Dickens's "Infant Phenom-
enon" of *Nicholas Nickleby* a decade later, Miss Lane was not quite as
young as her advertisements made her out to be; she was probably nine or
ten. But, unlike most other juvenile performers, she went on to a long and
rewarding life in the theater.

Born in England to a family that had been associated with the stage
since Elizabethan times, she came to America with her mother in 1827. In
an autobiographical sketch written late in life and published after her
death in 1897, she recalled: "Mother, being ambitious for me, accepted an
engagement at Boston . . . where we jointly received a salary of $16 per
week. . . . At the corner of Bowdoin Square . . . we had a large room on the
second story, a trundle bed, a large closet in which we kept a barrel of ale
and all our dresses, and [we] passed a very happy two seasons."[22]

22 Louisa Lane Drew, *Memoirs of Mrs. John Drew* (New York, 1899), pp. 65–66.

182

15

Goldfinch as Represented...by A. J. Allen, the American Costumer. Lithograph, circa 1828, by Johnston, 15.2 × 9 cm. (*Hoblitzelle Theatre Arts Collection, Humanities Research Center, the University of Texas at Austin*)

Her powers as an actress developed rapidly, and she toured extensively. She married for the first time at age sixteen and for the third and last time in 1850 at age thirty, to the actor John Drew, from which time she was known professionally as Mrs. Drew. She was a major figure of the American stage during the last half of the century, both as an actress and as a manager. Her three children were distinguished performers in their own right, and her grandchildren, Lionel, Ethel, and John Barrymore, carried on the traditions of a great acting family. Johnston's portrait was noted and praised in the Boston press less than two weeks following her first performance. Mrs. Drew preserved an impression of the print throughout her life.[23]

23 Reproduced, ibid., facing p. 30.

Probably in 1829, Johnston drew Andrew Jackson Allen (fig. 15), actor, manager, costumer, restaurateur, impresario of balloon ascensions, and, to quote a charitable assessment of him, "a very eccentric person."[24] Andrew Allen, to give him his original name—he took "Jackson" as a middle name in 1815 out of admiration for the hero of the Battle of New Orleans—was born in New York about 1786. He first acted professionally as a child. In later life he adjusted the year of his birth by a decade or so to the more notable year of 1776, claimed to be the oldest living native-born actor in America, and thereafter referred to himself, until his death in 1853, as "The Father of the American Stage."[25]

As an actor, Allen operated under two handicaps. First, he was hard of hearing and depended on lipreading to keep pace with the dialogue. Second, he was incapable of properly enunciating most consonants, *m* and *n* in particular, with the result that he sounded, to quote another contemporary, "as though he was always laboring under the effects of a bad cold in his head without a pocket handkerchief to help himself with."[26] He pronounced his name "Addrew Jacksod Alled," and his lines similarly.

There were few subtleties in his performances. A fellow actor recalled him in one role as "an extremely savage-looking confidential servant to a villainous usurper. . . and it was his particular province to attempt all the assassinations; to be most unmercifully beaten by men with clubs and other rescuers of innocence; and to cry, 'Confusion! Foiled again!' and rush off, shaking his dagger at his audience. . . with a look at his intended victim which indicated, as plainly as looks *can* indicate, that it wouldn't be well. . . to let him catch her alone again. . . . He made a great impression on me."[27]

---

24 Thomas Allston Brown, *History of the American Stage* (New York, 1870), p. 9. Important anecdotal sketches of Allen include Laurence Hutton, *Curiosities of the American Stage* (New York, 1868), pp. 138–40; Henry Dickinson Stone, *Personal Recollections of the Drama* (Albany, 1873), pp. 177–80; and Henry P. Phelps, *Players of a Century* (Albany, 1880), pp. 227–32.

25 Following Allen's death on Oct. 30, 1853, the New York *Post* (Nov. 3) gave his age at decease as sixty-five years. He was probably born in the 1780s.

26 Solomon Smith, *Theatrical Management in the West and South for Thirty Years* (New York, 1868), p. 139.

27 Ibid., p. 138.

Despite his handicaps, Allen succeeded on the stage after a fashion. He was admired as Caleb Quotem in *The Review* by Colman the younger and especially as Goldfinch in Holcroft's *The Road to Ruin,* the role in which Johnston has portrayed him. Johnston captures some of the man's insistent vitality and emphasizes the dandified costume specified by Holcroft for Goldfinch, a costume not much different from Allen's usual dress.[28] On one impression of the print, perhaps colored by Allen himself (now in the Harvard Theatre Collection), he scribbled a note to Samuel Maverick in New York, which reads, in part: "So, you are again to turn manager. Well, I wish you success. If you want me I should be happy to serve under your banner. Jackson to the backbone."

Allen's success as a restaurateur in Albany, and later in New York, was notable, though his cookery was no less eccentric than his acting. He was renowned for two fancy dishes, Calapash and Calapee. To quote one who savored them, "Calapash was made of old cheese, codfish, onions, mustard, rum, and wine. Calapee was the same, with the addition of cabbage."[29] He advertised his specialties with a theatrical flair. His turtle soup, served once a week or so, was "conspicuously advertised the day previous by the doomed turtle . . . who was allowed to promenade at the end of a long string up and down the sidewalk in front of the restaurant. . . . After a time it was noticed that while the soup was uniformly good, the turtles were uniform also"[30]—and it was at last comprehended that the soup was mock and that the turtle seemed assured of a long life.

In 1830 Johnston drew the American tragedian Edwin Forrest, then twenty-three years old, in the character of Metamora (fig. 16). The drama *Metamora, or The Last of the Wampanoags,* by John Augustus Stone, had won the first of the competitions Forrest sponsored to encourage the writing of serious plays on American subjects, a competition whose panel of judges was chaired by William Cullen Bryant. The play *Metamora* dealt with the tragic consequences of the clash between English and aboriginal

28   Thomas Holcroft, *The Road to Ruin* (Lincoln, Neb., 1968), p. 40. Holcroft's description reads: "Enter Goldfinch in a high-collared coat, several under-waistcoats, buckskin breeches covering his calves, short boots, long spurs, high crowned hat, hair in the extreme, etc."

29   Stone, pp. 179–80.

30   Phelps, pp. 230–31.

Mr. E. FORREST as METAMORA

IN Mr STONE'S NEW PRIZE TRAGEDY

16
Mr. E. Forrest as Metamora. Lithograph, 1830, by Johnston, 24.9 × 20
cm. (*Hoblitzelle Theatre Arts Collection, Humanities Research Center,
the University of Texas at Austin*)

cultures in colonial America. It embodied the well-established notion of
the American Indian as noble savage, a notion which by 1830 had been
reinforced by the first three of Cooper's "Leatherstocking" tales. The play
also seemed pertinent to the controversial Indian-removal policies of the
Jackson administration.

In 1860 the actor George Vandenhoff recalled Forrest as Metamora,
using similes of nature that were as appropriate to Forrest's romantic
playing of the role as to the setting of the play in the American wilderness.
Vandenhoff's often-quoted description reads, in part: "For power of
destructive energy, I never heard anything on the stage so tremendous in
its sustained *crescendo* swell and crashing force of utterance as his defiance
of the Council in that play. His voice surged and roared like the angry sea,
lashed into fury by a storm, till as it reached its boiling, seething cli-
max. . . it was like the falls of Niagara in its tremendous down-sweeping

cadence. It was a whirlwind, a tornado, a cataract of illimitable rage."[31]

Johnston's portrait conveys none of this. It shows a mild-mannered Metamora, placidly exotic rather than noble or tragic or wild. Instead of a sense of identification with his subject, Johnston here conveys distance and a lack of empathy that is fatal to a satisfactory portrait in character. Johnston's talents as a theatrical portraitist were genuine but limited to the narrow range of comic roles to which he was temperamentally suited. He was out of his element in tragedy, both as an actor and as an artist. In relation to this portrait of Metamora, that limitation is a pity, since of all Johnston's subjects, Forrest has proved to be the most important as a historical figure. At least Johnston's print has the merit of documenting the appearance of the young Forrest; it is among the earliest likenesses of the actor.

Forrest's career touched nearly everyone associated with the American stage. As a young man, he acted with Jefferson, Kilner, Finn, Mrs. Pelby, and the nine-year-old Louisa Lane. In the early 1830s he hired Andrew Jackson Allen as his costumer. Allen attached himself securely to Forrest for many years and claimed much of the credit for Forrest's triumphs at home and abroad, a claim so patently preposterous that it bothered no one, least of all Forrest. Allen's skills as a costumer were considerable; he designed, constructed, maintained, and transported Forrest's extensive wardrobe. On one occasion, traveling alone across upstate New York, Allen exhibited in a local hotel a selection of costumes from several historical plays with an abundance of helmets, halberds, swords, shields, and battle-axes. Instead of explaining them as theatrical artifacts, he circulated throughout the village a brief and entirely untrue account of his capture by a fierce tribe of Eskimos, his forced participation in their wars throughout the Arctic, his ingenious escape with a splendid collection of their war dresses and arms, and his happiness in now having the privilege of showing the collection to the populace for a modest fee of admission.[32] He was an amiable and inventive fraud whom Forrest, and Johnston, must have found amusing. The contemplation of the ludicrous is an intellectual pursuit of distinguished lineage; it informs the work of

31 George Vandenhoff, *Leaves from an Actor's Note Book* (New York, 1860), pp. 200–201.

32 Phelps, p. 230.

MR. JOHNSON AS CRACK.

"Now I'm a kind of Bond-street man of fashion."

Turnpike gate. Ac.1.Sc.2

[D. C. Johnston, del]

17
Mr. Johnson as Crack. Lithograph, circa 1830-37, by Johnston, 22 × 15.8 cm. (*Private collection*)

Hogarth, Rowlandson, Gillray, Cruikshank, and their successor in America, Johnston. A comic subject need not result in caricature or satire, nor does it in Johnston's portrait of the ludicrous Allen.

Two other individual portraits date from the 1830s. One of these is a stipple engraving of the English actress Ellen Tree, later Mrs. Charles Kean, as Julia in John Sheridan Knowles's *The Hunchback*. It probably dates from Miss Tree's Boston debut in 1837. It is not a complete success. Though apparently taken from life, it is rather lifeless, as if Johnston had little personal knowledge of his subject, which was probably the case. Far more vivid is the lithograph, probably dating from between 1830 and 1837, titled *Mr. Johnson as Crack* (fig. 17). It is full of life, but it presents two puzzles: the identity of the actor and the reasons for the comic signature that appears on one state of the print. Most probably, the actor is William F. Johnson (d. 1859), who played leading comic roles in Boston throughout the 1830s, but about whom little is known.[33] In one of its two states, the print is signed "Drawn on stone by Mr. Raphaelle Cocking from a sketch by Tintoretto Mavrikadarti, Esqr.," a jibe perhaps at the artist names of some of the sons of Charles Willson Peale, sons whom Johnston is likely to have known, and perhaps also at one or another of the Maverick family of engravers in New York.[34] The signature marks a return to the kind of facetious pseudonyms Johnston used in some of his early caricatures in Philadelphia, though why he should use such a signature on this print is unclear. The portrait is very well drawn, and the characterization is full of intense vitality.

The last three of the twenty-eight prints are etched group portraits, each about two by four inches in image size, and of great historical importance. Two of the groups were issued as frontispieces in the two-volume *Galaxy of Wit*, a book first published in Boston in 1826. The two groups constitute a miniature pictorial summary of great moments on the Boston stage from 1821 through 1826, Johnston's last season on the boards. He had acted with most, if not all, of the players he shows, even—at least in rehearsal for the ill-fated *Richard III* of 1825—with Kean. Johnston portrayed an important and deeply felt part of his life in these two little groups: they are autobiographical. It is possible that a self-portrait exists among the unidentified background figures, for Johnston, like his idol in these years, George Cruikshank, occasionally depicted himself in his work, but no close likeness is apparent. The third group was published in 1831 as a frontispiece in the book *The Aurora Borealis, or Flashes of Wit*. It summarizes the final years of the decade.[35] Like its predecessors, it is an

33 Clapp, pp. 282, 350. Another actor, Samuel D. Johnson, played in Boston in the 1840s. Playbills for the Tremont Theatre in the 1830s record W. F. Johnson's presence in major comic roles during most of that decade.

34 As a young artist in Philadelphia in the years between 1815 and 1824, Johnston surely knew of the Peales, though he may not have known them personally. He doubtless was acquainted with Rembrandt Peale in Boston in 1825 and 1826, when both were associated with the Pendletons' lithographic press.

35 *The Galaxy of Wit, or Laughing Philosopher*, 2 vols. (Boston, 1826); and *The Aurora Borealis, or Flashes of Wit; Calculated to Drown Out Care and Eradicate the Blue Devils* (Boston, 1831). The *Aurora Borealis* etching and one of the two (Appendix no. 27) in *The Galaxy of Wit* are reproduced in William Murrell, *A History of American Graphic Humor* (New York, 1933), 1:106.

important document of the attitudes, gestures, and costumes of a number of the leading actors of the day.

Among the figures in each of the groups are some, such as Forrest and Barnes, whom Johnston had previously portrayed on a larger scale in different roles, and others, such as the British tragedian William Macready and the juvenile actor William Blake ("The Irish Roscius"), whom Johnston apparently portrayed only in these groups. There are some notable absences, including all actresses and Andrew Jackson Allen.

Though Johnston's career as a graphic artist continued successfully into the 1860s in Boston, he seems to have made no theatrical portraits after 1837. Even in the 1830s he portrayed none of the actors—of whom the best known were James Hackett and George Handel Hill—who, in that decade, richly developed the first specifically American comic characters widely accepted here and abroad: Solomon Swap, Industrious Doolittle, Nimrod Wildfire, Jedediah Homebred, and others of their sort whose humor was consonant with Johnston's own.[36] Johnston's important contribution to the development of popular national characters of this kind occurred offstage, chiefly in the form of his original illustrations for Seba Smith's humorous and influential book *The Life and Writings of Major Jack Downing,* published in 1833.[37]

Johnston's theatrical portraits hold a special place in his life's work. Many of them are among his finest prints, carefully executed and aesthetically pleasing in ways that few other American prints of the era can match. As portraits, most of them are strongly realized characterizations, successful in summarizing the essential transformations that have occurred in players and their roles. The best of them glow with Johnston's admiration for his subject. Though they are governed by an intellect most comfortable in the realm of wit and humor, these portraits are from the heart; the genuineness of Johnston's feeling endows them with a power quite out of proportion to their size. It is not the least of the merits of this body of prints that they reveal Johnston as an artist of even more substance, skill, and seriousness of purpose than his better-known caricatures and genre subjects have shown.

36 For an account of the rise of national character types in the 1830s, see Francis Hodge, *Yankee Theatre* (Austin, Tex., 1964).

37 Seba Smith, *The Life and Writings of Major Jack Downing of Downingville* (Boston, 1833).

APPENDIX   Checklist of Johnston's Theatrical Portraits

Dimensions, in centimeters, are given height before width for the image only. Inscriptions are in italics. The locations of impressions of Johnston's portraits are given in abbreviated form, as used in the *National Union Catalogue;* the full names are listed below:

CSmH   Henry E. Huntington Library, San Marino, Calif.

DFo   Folger Shakespeare Library, Washington, D.C.

MB   Boston Public Library, Boston.

MBAt   Boston Athenaeum, Boston.

MH   Harvard University, Cambridge, Mass.

MHi   Massachusetts Historical Society, Boston.

MWA   American Antiquarian Society, Worcester, Mass.

NHi   New-York Historical Society, New York.

TxU   University of Texas, Austin.

INDIVIDUALS   1   Andrew Jackson Allen (circa 1786-1853)
Allen as Charles Goldfinch in *The Road to Ruin* by Thomas Holcroft
Goldfinch as Represented in the Principal Southern Theatres by A. J. Allen. The American Costumer. How you stare! a'nt I a genus? that's your sort
Lithograph, 15.2 × 9 cm., circa 1828
Signed *D. C. J. del   Pendleton's Lith.*   MH, MWA, TxU

2   George H. Andrews (1798-1866)
Andrews as Luke in *Luke the Laborer, or The Lost Son*
Mr. Andrews as Luke the Laborer. My wife fell stone dead down at my feet—I stood looking on her white face for near an hour and didn't move from the spot— Act 1st Sc 2nd
Lithograph, 14.6 × 13.4 cm., 1827
Signed *D. C. Johnston del   Lith of Pendleton*   MWA, TxU

3   John Barnes (1781-1841)
Barnes as Johnny Atkins in *Mogul Tale, or The Descent of a Balloon* by Elizabeth Inchbald
Mr. Barnes as Johnny Atkins. Mogul Tale
Lithograph, 14.5 × 10 cm., 1826
Signed *D. C. Johnston delt   Pendleton's Lith*   MH, MWA

A watercolor drawing of this subject by Johnston is owned by the Hoblitzelle Theatre Arts Library, Humanities Research Center, University of Texas.

4   John Barnes (1781-1841)
Barnes as Delph in *Family Jars*
Mr. Barnes as Delph in Family Jars. "A captain's da'ghter—thousand pounds—"
Lithograph, 13.8 × 10 cm., 1826
Signed *D. C. Johnston del   Lith of Pendleton*   MH, MWA

5   Henry James Finn (1785-1840)
Finn as Bob Logic in *Tom and Jerry, or Life in London* by William Moncrieff
"Doctor Logic" ("Ladies and Gentlemen") As represented by Mr. Finn
Stipple engraving, 11.2 × 7 cm., 1825
Signed *D. C. Johnston del. Sketcd. from memory. Engd. & Published by Throop & Johnston. Boston March 4th. 1825*   CSmH, MH, MHi

A watercolor sketch of Finn as Logic by Johnston is owned by the American Antiquarian Society. A different and more fully articulated watercolor of Finn in the same role is owned by the Harvard Theatre Collection.

6   Henry James Finn (1785-1840) and Thomas Kilner (1777-1862)
    Finn as Paul Pry and Kilner as Colonel Hardy in *Paul Pry* by John Poole
    Paul Pry and Col Hardy as represented by Mr. Finn and Mr. Kilner
    Lithograph, 14.2 × 12.9 cm., 1826
    Signed *D C Johnston del   Lith of Pendleton*   MH, MWA
    A lithographic copy of this print, limited to fifty impressions, was made in 1872 by T. H.
    Morrell (Hall, *Catalogue,* 2:26). An oil painting of the same subject is in a private collection.

7   Edwin Forrest (1806-1872)
    Forrest as Metamora in *Metamora, or The Last of the Wampanoags* by John Augustus Stone
    Mr. E. Forrest as Metamora. In Mr. Stone's New Prize Tragedy
    Lithograph, 24.9 × 20 cm., 1830
    Signed *Drawn on stone by D. C. Johnston*
    Lith of Pendleton. Boston   CSmH, MH, MWA, TxU

8   Thomas S. Hamblin (1800-1853)
    Hamblin as Hamlet in *Hamlet* by William Shakespeare
    Mr. Hamblin of the Theatre Royal Drury-Lane
    Lithograph, 14.2 × 13.1 cm., 1826
    Signed *H. J. Finn del.   Drawn on stone by D. C. Johnston*
    Lithog of J. Pendleton   MWA, TxU

9   Joseph Jefferson I (1774-1832)
    Jefferson as Bob Logic in *Tom and Jerry, or Life in London* by William Moncrieff
    Mr.Jefferson as Logic. Tom & Jerry
    Stipple engraving, 13.7 × 7.8 cm., circa 1823-24
    Signed *Sketched & Engd by D. C. Johnston*   MH

10 William F. Johnson? (d. 1859)
    Johnson as Crack in *Turnpike Gate* by Thomas Knight
    Mr. Johnson as Crack in Knight's "The Turnpike Gate." "Now I'm a kind of Bond-street man of
    fashion." Turnpike gate, Ac. 1 Sc. 2
    Lithograph, 22 × 15.8 cm., circa 1830-37
    Signed *Drawn on stone by Mr. Raphaelle Cocking, from a Sketch by Tintoretto Mavrikadarti*
    Esqr.   MH, MWA, MB

11 Edmund Kean (1787-1833)
    Kean as Richard in *Richard III* by William Shakespeare
    Mr. Kean as Richard, Duke of Gloster. Why I can smile & smile & murder when I smile
    Stipple engraving, 11.8 × 11.5 cm., 1821
    Unsigned   MH

12 Thomas Kilner (1776-1862)
    Kilner as Captain Copp in *Charles the Second, or The Merry Monarch* by John Howard Payne
    Mr. Kilner as Capt. Cop in Charles the Second. "In the time of the Rump When old admiral Trump
    &c."
    Stipple engraving, 10.9 × 6.6 cm., 1825
    Signed *Sketcd. (from memory) Engd. & Published by Throop & Johnston.*
    Boston 1825   MBAt, MH
    See also no. 6.

13 Louisa Lane (later Mrs. John Drew) (1818-1897)
    Miss Lane as characters in *Twelve Precisely, or A Night at Dover*
    Miss Lane (Eight Years of Age) in the Five Characters in "Twelve Precisely." Boston Nov 3 1828
    Lithograph, 13.5 × 18.5 cm., 1828
    Signed *Drawn on stone by D. C Johnston   Lith of Pendleton*   DFo, MH, MWA, TxU

14 Charles Mathews (1776-1835)
Mathews as Morbleu in *Monsieur Tonson* by William Moncrieff
Mr. Mathews as Monsieur Morbleu. Fip—The Seasons: my old favourite Thomson   Mor—Diable!
Tonson come again!
Stipple engraving, 12.5 × 11.5 cm., 1823
Signed *Sketched & Engd by D. C. Johnston*   MH, TxU

15 Charles Mathews (1776-1835)
Mathews as Theophilus Tulip, Major Longbow, Dan'l O'Rourke, Isaac Tabinett, Mrs. Tulip,
and Mons Jeu-Singe in *The Polly Packet* by R. B. Peake
Characters in the Polly Packet as Represented by Mr. Mathews
Stipple engraving, 16.2 × 22 cm., 1823
Signed *Sketched, (from memory) Engraved, & Published by D. C. Johnston*   MH, TxU

16 Charles Mathews (1776-1835)
Mathews as Mons Poudre Meneur, Mons Peremtoire, Miss Evergreen, Hezekiah Hulk, Sam'l
Starch, and Jemmy in *La Diligence* by James Smith
Mr. Mathews at Home in the Diligence
Stipple engraving, 19.5 × 24.3 cm., 1823
Signed *Sketched, (from memory) Engraved & Published by D. C. Johnston* MH, MWA, TxU

17 Elizabeth (Mrs. Owen) Morris (1753-1826)
Mrs. Morris in an unspecified role
The Late Mrs. Morris
Engraving, 8.8 × 7.2 cm., 1828
Signed *Drawn & Engraved by D. C Johnston*   MH, MWA, NHi, TxU
This was apparently intended as a frontispiece for a play in the series *Acting American Theatre*,
edited by Mathias Lopez and Francis Wemyss and published in Philadelphia by A. R. Poole in
1826 and 1827. The series seems to have been discontinued in 1828 before Johnston's portrait
could be used. Johnston may have published it as a separate print. At least three states exist,
with variations in titles as follows: (1) *The Late Mrs. Morris / Lopez & Wemyss Edition / 1828;*
(2) *Mrs. Moris* [sic]; (3) *Mrs. Morris.* A watercolor sketch of Mrs. Morris by Johnston is
owned by the American Antiquarian Society and is presumably the basis for the engraved
portrait.

18 Rosalie French Pelby (1793-1857)
Mrs. Pelby as Cherry in *Cherry and Fair Star, or The Children of Cyprus*
Mrs. Pelby as Cherry   act 1st scene 4th
Lithograph, 17 × 15 cm., 1826
Signed *D. C. Johnston del   Lith of Pendleton*   MH, TxU
An oil painting of the same subject is owned by the Bostonian Society.

19 Daniel Reed (d. 1836)
Reed as Roderick Dhu in an adaptation of Walter Scott's *Lady of the Lake*
Mr Reed as Roderick Dhu   Act 2d Sc 4th   FitzJ   What deem ye of my path way-laid my life meanly
beset by cowardly surprise? Rod.   As of a punishment to rashness due.
Lithograph, 15.5 × 8 cm., 1826 or 1827
Signed *D. C. Johnston del   Lith of Pendleton*   Private collection

20 James Roberts (1799-1833)
Roberts as a fictitious black officer of the Continental army
Massa Georgee Washington and General La Fayette
Etched title page vignette, 9.5 × 12.7 cm., 1824
Signed *D. C. Johnston del't et sc't*   MWA, MH
For the song by Micah Hawkins, published by E. Riley, New York

21 John Sloman (1794-1873)
Sloman performing the comic song "Jerry Smart's Trip in Search of Sweet Kitty Clover"
Mr. Sloman. "Sweet Kitty Clover she bothers me so. Oh, oh, oh, oh!"
Lithograph, 12 × 10.7 cm., 1828
Signed *D. C. Johnston del   Lith of Pendleton*   MBAt, MH, MWA, TxU

22 Ellen Tree (Mrs. Charles Kean) (1805-1880)
Miss Tree as Julia in *The Hunchback* by John Sheridan Knowles
Miss E. Tree as Julia. "I have wronged him. He can't be happy, does not look it, is not. The Hunchback Ac 4 Sc 2
Stipple engraving, 14 × 12.4 cm., circa 1837
Signed *Sketched & eng by D. C. Johnston*   MWA

23 James William Wallack (1795-1864)
Wallack as Dashall in *My Aunt* by John Galt
Mr. J. Wallack as Dick Dashall, in the Farce of My Aunt. "I beg your pardon ma'am."
Stipple engraving, 13 × 10 cm., 1823
Signed *Sketched & Engd by D C Johnston*   MH, TxU

24 Alexander Wilson (?-1854)
Wilson as Bertram in *Bertram, or The Castle of Aldobrand* by Charles Maturin
Mr. Wilson as Bertram. I come to do the deed that must be done!
Lithograph, 22.4 × 16.6 cm., circa, 1828
Signed *D C Johnston del   Pendletons Lith*   MWA

25 Alexander Wilson (?-1854)
Wilson as Pierre in *Venice Preserved* by Thomas Otway
Mr. Wilson as Pierre. Are these the wreaths of triumph ye bestow, on those that bring you conquest home and honours?
Lithograph, 12.5 × 11 cm., 1828
Signed *D. C. Johnston del   Lith of Pendleton*   MH

Groups 26 William Francis (circa 1756-1826) as Sir Anthony Absolute in *The Rivals* by R. B. Sheridan; Henry Wallack (1791-1870) as Goldfinch in *The Road to Ruin* by Thomas Holcroft; William Pelby (1793-1850) as Brutus in *Brutus* by John Howard Payne; William Warren (1767-1832) as Falstaff in *The Merry Wives of Windsor* by William Shakespeare; Thomas Burke (d.1825) as Dr. Panglos in *The Heir at Law* by George Colman the younger; William B. Wood (1779-1861) as Glenalvon in *Douglas* by John Home; Thomas Hilson (1784-1834) as Paul Pry in *Paul Pry* by John Poole
Sir. A. Absolute / Mr. Francis Goldfinch / H. Wallack Brutus / Pelby Falstaff / Warren Dr. Panglos / Burke Glenalvon / Wood Paul Pry / Hilson
Etching, 5.5 × 10.8 cm., 1826
Signed *D. C. Johnston del Boston*
Plate in *The Galaxy of Wit*, 2 vols. (Boston, 1826)   DFo, MH, MWA, TxU

27 Edmund Kean (1787-1833) as Richard in *Richard III* by William Shakespeare; John Barnes (1781-1841) as Crack in *Turnpike Gate* by Thomas Knight; John Mills Brown (1782-1859) as Jerry in *Tom and Jerry* by William T. Moncrieff; Henry James Finn (1785-1840) as Logic in *Tom and Jerry* by William T. Moncrieff; Thomas Kilner (1777-1862) as Captain Copp in *Charles the Second* by John Howard Payne; Joseph Jefferson I (1774-1832) as Nipperkin in *Springs of Laurel* by John O'Keeffe; Charles Mathews (1776-1835) as Monsieur Morbleu in *Monsieur Tonson* by William T. Moncrieff
Richard Third / Kean Crack / Barnes Jerry / Brown Logic / Finn Capt Copp / Kilner Nipperkin / Jefferson Mon Morbleu / Mathews
Etching, 5.8 ×10.5 cm., 1826
Signed *D. C. Johnston del Boston*
Plate in *The Galaxy of Wit*, 2 vols. (Boston, 1826)   MH, MWA

28 George Andrews (1798-1866); Edwin Forrest (1806-1872); William Charles Macready (1793-1873); George Holland (1791-1870); Thomas A. Cooper (1776-1849); John Sloman (1794-1873); Francis Blissett (1773-1850); and Joseph Burke (b. 1818) in unspecified roles
Andrews Forrest Macready Holland Cooper Sloman Blissett Mast Burke
Etching, 5.6 × 10.5 cm., 1831
Signed *D. C. Johnston sc.*
Plate in *The Aurora Borealis, or Flashes of Wit* (Boston, 1831)   MH, MWA

Daguerreotypes onto Stone

*The Life
and Work of
Francis D'Avignon*

WILLIAM
F.
STAPP

Francis D'Avignon is remembered primarily as the lithographer and printer of the portrait plates in Mathew Brady's *Gallery of Illustrious Americans*.[1] This publication appeared in 1850 and is regarded today as the most ambitious attempt—in terms of quality and expense—to publish lithographic reproductions of daguerreotype portraits of prominent Americans. The venture was a financial disaster but an artistic success: D'Avignon's lithographs were not only remarkably faithful to the original daguerreotypes; they were also aesthetically excellent, some of the best domestic portrait prints of the period. Photographic historians, who have paid more attention to *The Gallery of Illustrious Americans* than anyone else, typically give Brady, the daguerreotypist, the credit.[2] In doing so, they minimize D'Avignon's rather impressive achievement of translating the daguerreotype images into lithographs with remarkable fidelity and simultaneously investing the lithographs with their own aesthetic integrity. This narrow point of view not only denigrates D'Avignon's skill as a lithographer; it also obscures the fact that he had an extensive career in this country, to which a considerable number of surviving lithographs bear witness. These prints carry the imprints of some of the more important printers and publishers of the time. Many of them are after now-lost

---

1 D'Avignon's name was frequently but inconsistently anglicized as Davignon. For the sake of uniformity, I have adopted the French spelling.

2 See, for example, Robert Taft, *Photography and the American Scene* (New York, 1978), pp. 59–60.

194

daguerreotypes and provide the best visual record we have of those plates and the studios that produced them. It is worthwhile, therefore, to take a closer look at Francis D'Avignon and to discuss the full course of his career.

Unfortunately, the details of D'Avignon's life are sketchy.[3] He was born in France in 1813 but grew up in Saint Petersburg, Russia, where his father had been employed by the czar "to promote polytechnic education and the fine arts." He was educated at the Russian military academy and passed the examinations in military engineering in 1828, although he did not accept his commission. He went instead on a Grand Tour of the Continent (1828-31). On this trip, "a visit to the great galleries, the studios of distinguished artists, and the scenes where art had achieved its noblest triumphs, weaned him entirely from the pursuit for which he had been educated." He decided to become a painter and went on to study under Horace Vernet and "the best artists of Paris." D'Avignon returned to Saint Petersburg in 1834 and opened a studio. He was active there until 1840, when he left for a twelve-month tour of Great Britain. He never returned to Russia; instead he established himself in Hamburg, Germany, and opened a new studio, "where he gathered his collection of paintings, drawings, engravings, and books, and settled down to pursue his profession." His timing was unfortunate: a few months after his arrival, Hamburg was almost totally destroyed by the great fire that swept the city in May 1842. D'Avignon, who lost everything, "at once determined to come to America to repair his fortunes." He set sail on the S.S. *Stephani* and arrived at the port of New York on July 26, 1842.[4]

3   The two contemporary accounts of D'Avignon's life are both by Charles Edwards Lester, the editor of *The Gallery of Illustrious Americans*. The first is a short article that appeared in the *Fly Leaf of Art and Criticism*, no. 2 (Jan. 15, 1850) (see Appendix 2). The *Fly Leaf* was printed on the cover sheet of each issue of *The Gallery of Illustrious Americans*. Because these wrappers were usually separated from the plates, it is an extremely rare publication: only one complete set is known. Lester's second account comprises one long paragraph in *Glances at the Metropolis* (New York, 1854), p. 178 (see Appendix 3). The *Fly Leaf* article is probably more accurate, since certain details (D'Avignon's place and date of birth and his departure from Hamburg) can be verified in American archival sources. Unless otherwise noted, this section on D'Avignon's biography is synopsized from these two articles, and the quotations also derive from them.

4   Index to Passenger Lists Arriving at New York, 1820–96, microcopy 261, roll 22, and Passenger Lists of Vessels Arriving New York, 1820–97 (June 1–July 30, 1842),

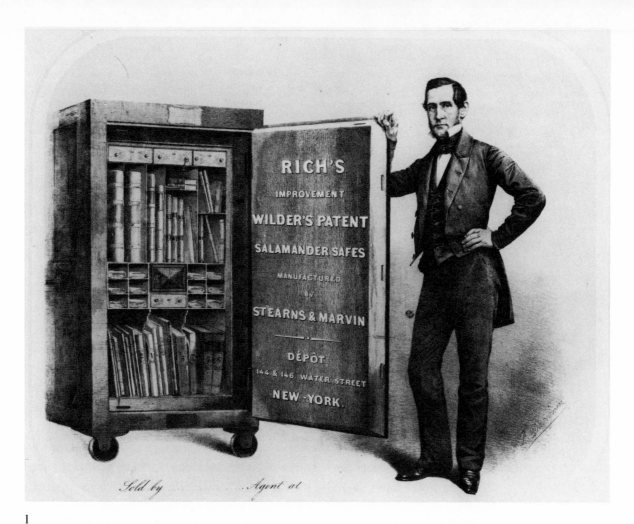

1

Rich's Improvement, Wilder's Patent Salamander Safes. Lithograph, circa 1853, by D'Avignon, 39.4 × 47.3 cm. (*The New-York Historical Society, New York City*)

Perhaps because of the Hamburg fire, virtually nothing is known of D'Avignon's European oeuvre. There is some suggestion that he was a student at, if not a member of, the Saint Petersburg Academy of Fine Arts,[5] but there is no way to document this or even trace its influence in his work.[6] The one picture from this period cited in the literature that may be attributed to D'Avignon is, interestingly enough, a portrait lithograph of the Russian actor N. O. Dürr; unfortunately, the print is now unlocated

microcopy M-237, roll 49, National Archives and Records Service. I am indebted to Ms. Laurie Baty, now at the Maryland Historical Society, who researched federal archival records on D'Avignon. Her assistance was crucial to this paper.

5 His first American print, the portrait of John Endecott, was imprinted "F. D'Avignon, R.I.A." The initials possibly stand for "Russian Imperial Academy." He never used them again.

6 See University Gallery, University of Minnesota, *The Art of Russia, 1800–1850* (Minneapolis, 1978), pp. 14–18, 22–37, for discussions of the Saint Petersburg Academy of Fine Arts and its aesthetic standards.

and therefore cannot be used to indicate the evolution of his lithographic technique.[7]

Francis D'Avignon's career as an American portrait lithographer spans the years 1843 to 1860, the dates of the earliest and latest prints he is known to have made in this country. Some two hundred lithographs, ranging from small book illustrations, sheet-music covers, and miscellaneous subjects (fig. 1) to the large portrait prints for which he is best known, document his career. He worked primarily in New York City—and changed addresses there frequently—but he also spent time in Philadelphia (1845-46) and Hartford (1849), and finally settled permanently in the Boston area in 1859.[8] Although the reasons for his frequent moves (at least fourteen in seventeen years) can only be guessed at, the various addresses provide a convenient and fairly precise way to date many of the prints. Since the majority of these prints are portraits, most of them copied from other images and photographic likenesses that are now lost, they also provide important dated visual references to the works of some significant photographers—including figures like Mathew Brady, Philip Haas, and Samuel Root.

It seems to have taken D'Avignon almost seven years (1842-49) to establish himself in this country. The prints of this period indicated two short-lived partnerships, with Joseph Vollmering from 1847 to 1848 (see Appendix 1, nos. 17, 121, 205) and with Abram J. Hoffmann in 1849 (App. 1, nos. 9, 53, 96, and 171). He seems to have particularly influenced Hoffman, whose full-length lithograph *Frank Pierce,* published by Tappan and Bradford, is drawn in a similar style. By the end of the period D'Avignon had established his artistic independence, joining in partnerships occasionally with publishers but rarely with other lithographic

---

7 This print is cited in Ulrich Thieme and Felix Becker, *Allgemeines Lexikon der Bildender Künstler* (Leipzig, 1913), 8:471, with reference to a Russian catalogue by Dmitrii Aleksandrovich Rovinskii, presumably his *Podrobnyi slovár russkikh gravironvanykh portretov* (1886). Thieme and Becker tentatively attribute the print to one François Jean Davignon, a porcelain worker from Sèvres, employed at the Imperial Porcelain works at Saint Petersburg in the early nineteenth century. Though this attribution is erroneous, it raises the intriguing possibility that Lester's account of D'Avignon's origins was falsified, perhaps by D'Avignon himself.

8 See the city directories for New York, Philadelphia, Hartford, and Boston for these years. The city directory entries are the most precise means of dating D'Avignon's activities.

2

James Harper, 1795-1869. Lithograph, circa 1844-45, by D'Avignon from life, 29.4 × 29.3 cm. (*National Portrait Gallery, Smithsonian Institution*)

artists. From the beginning, D'Avignon worked primarily as a copyist, and only a single portrait—*James Harper,* mayor of New York (fig. 2)—is known to be drawn from life. Throughout this first period, there is an inconsistency in the style and draftsmanship of his lithographs, although the variations seem to relate more to the quality of the originals being copied and to the characteristic style or standards of the publisher who commissioned them than to D'Avignon's own hand. Thus, his first known American print, a portrait of *John Endecott*, printed and published by George and William Endicott in 1843, is stiff and wooden, reflecting quite faithfully the qualities of the original seventeenth-century portrait.

Similarly, it is difficult to attribute the crude outline drawing of Henry Clay in Epes Sargeant's *The Life and Public Services of Henry Clay* (1844) to the same hand that drew the magnificent Clay portrait printed and published by the Endicotts that same year (fig. 3). The substantial qualitative difference in the two prints was clearly dictated by the publishers' requirements: an inexpensive, quickly printed book illustration vis-à-vis a large, finely detailed framing print copied from an excellent daguerreotype likeness by one of the best studios of the time, Anthony, Edwards and Company. The large *Henry Clay* portrait is the earliest major print to show clearly D'Avignon's own characteristic lithographic technique of rubbing the crayon on the stone to obtain continuous variations in

Henry Clay, 1777-1852. Lithograph, 1844, by D'Avignon after Anthony,
Edwards and Co., 47.4 × 37.6 cm. (*National Portrait Gallery, Smithsonian Institution*)

200

4

Mandarin Esing. Lithograph, 1847, by D'Avignon after Philip Haas, 26 × 26 cm. (*Prints Division, the New York Public Library, Astor, Lenox and Tilden Foundations*)

tones (Weitenkampf's "lineless sauce of crayon tint")[9] rather than using lines to differentiate tonalities. It was a drawing technique perfectly suited for reproducing the continuous tones of photographic images, and it was undoubtedly precisely because of this that prominent daguerreotypists like Anthony, Brady, Haas, the Meade Brothers, and Root commissioned him directly to make large copies of their daguerreotypes. Apparently, however, it was extremely difficult to print D'Avignon's stones. Indeed, the Endicott company, his major printer and publisher through 1846, eventually made him pull his own prints.[10]

The difficulty of printing his stones properly may be reflected in the flat, low-contrast inking that typifies many of D'Avignon's lithographs

9 Frank Weitenkampf, *American Graphic Art* (New York, 1912), p. 188.

10 "The drawings of D'Avignon, owing to his peculiar method of picking and scraping were difficult to print. . . . To insure success, he undertook to etch his own drawings and wished the regular prover to roll them up. That the prover declined—preferring to let D'Avignon take all the responsibility which he did" (Charles Hart, "Lithography: Its Theory and Practice. Including a Series of Short Sketches of the Earliest Lithographic Artists, Engravers, and Printers of New York," unpublished manuscript [1902], New York Public Library, p. 177). Hart was an apprentice printer for the Endicotts in the early 1840s and was personally acquainted with the difficulties of printing D'Avignon's stones, having printed his 1844 *Henry Clay* on an "Old Star wheel French press." I am indebted to Mrs. Wendy Wick Reaves for bringing this reference to my attention.

5
Samuel Houston, 1793-1863. Litho-
graph, 1848, by D'Avignon after
Bartlett and Fuller, 39 × 30.7 cm.
(*Library of Congress*)

from the 1840s, with the very notable exception of those printed by Louis
Nagel. Nagel, like D'Avignon himself, was European born and trained. [11]
He worked for the Endicotts in the early 1840s, and D'Avignon undoubtedly met him there. [12] He was the only printer who could realize the
full potential of these stones. It is certain that D'Avignon employed him
whenever he wanted maximum print quality. Nagel printed the 1847
Mandarin Esing after a daguerreotype by Haas (fig. 4). This image was
D'Avignon's first lithograph to emulate perfectly the presence of a daguerreotype likeness. He also pulled the 1848 *Samuel Houston* after a
daguerreotype by Bartlett and Fuller of Hartford (fig. 5) and the 1856
Henry Clay after an unidentified daguerreotypist (fig. 6); these are perhaps
the most outstanding lithographs ever done by D'Avignon. Finally, Nagel
was the printer of the 1849 *President Taylor and His Cabinet* (fig. 7) for
Mathew Brady, the piece which seems to have inspired Brady's partnership with D'Avignon.

Late in 1849 Francis D'Avignon founded his own press at 323
Broadway. This event seems to have inaugurated a period of prosperity for
him, since he remained there through 1853 (the longest stay at one address
in his career), producing more large-format portrait prints than at any

11 George C. Groce and David H. Wallace, *The New-York Historical Society's Dictionary of Artists in America* (New Haven and London, 1957), p. 464.

12 Hart, pp. 113–15.

Henry Clay, 1777-1852. Lithograph, 1856, by D'Avignon after unidentified, 75 × 52 cm. (*Library of Congress*)

Zachary Taylor, 1784-1850, and his cabinet. Lithograph, 1849, by D'Avignon and Abram J. Hoffman(n) after Mathew Brady, 43.5 × 64.1 cm. (*National Portrait Gallery, Smithsonian Institution*)

other time. These years were dominated by *The Gallery of Illustrious Americans* and his partnership with Mathew Brady. D'Avignon supposedly received $100 for each stone and, presumably, a share of the profits, which could not have been substantial since publication ceased after only twelve of the proposed twenty-four issues appeared. In spite of its failure, *The Gallery* was a monumental concept, and enough examples of it have survived to make its plates of famous Americans, such as *John J. Audubon* (fig. 8), the best known of D'Avignon's lithographs. Although Brady, D'Avignon and Company did not survive the year, the partnership produced one of the great moments in the history of American portrait prints and, ironically, American photography.

8

John James Audubon, 1785-1851.
Lithograph, 1850, by D'Avignon after
Mathew Brady, 28 × 24.3 cm. From
Mathew Brady, *Gallery of Illustrious
Americans* (New York, 1850).
(*National Portrait Gallery, Smithsonian
Institution*)

In spite of the attention given to *The Gallery of Illustrious Americans*,
most of the work D'Avignon did between 1849 and 1853 was for other
daguerreotypists. Of these prints, those after likenesses by Philip Haas are
perhaps the most consistently interesting as portraits; they are also the
most comprehensive record we have of this early and important photographer's later work. A large number of them are theatrical portraits, the
most notable being the lithograph of James Hudson (fig. 9), a dramatic
image because it is of a full, freestanding figure in a dynamic stage pose.
The print is an outstanding example of D'Avignon's lithographic
virtuosity: the delicate and subtle modeling of the figure together with the
impeccable rendition of detail impart an almost photographic visual presence to the image, and the effect is enhanced by the contrasts of black and
white unencumbered by tintstone shading. D'Avignon was sufficiently
pleased with this print to have inscribed and signed the one known example
of it in pencil.

Among the pictures he did for other daguerreotypists, the portrait of
Louis Kossuth (fig. 10), after a daguerreotype by Samuel Root, stands out

9

James Hudson, 1811-1879. Lithograph, circa 1849-53, by D'Avignon after Philip Haas, 46 × 32.1 cm. (*Harvard Theatre Collection*)

as an impressive example of D'Avignon's extraordinary skill with the lithographic crayon. Within a tightly composed portrait, he carefully reproduces and differentiates between five similar but substantially different textures: cloth, fur, hair, plush, and feathers are all distinctly delineated in this beautifully drawn and printed work. D'Avignon's lithographs for the Meade Brothers, on the other hand, seem more softly drawn than his other prints of this period. His lithograph of Daguerre (fig. 11) reproduces their single most popular portrait—they were the only Americans to daguerreotype the inventor of the process. He also lithographed the Meade brothers themselves (fig. 12), apparently combining the images of two separate daguerreotypes to produce a double portrait. There is visual evidence in this print that D'Avignon had some difficulty with freehand composition: the very awkward foreshortening of the legs and arms of the figure on the right contrasts markedly with the excellent perspective of the figure on the left, suggesting that the image was composed from separate portraits, one a full seated figure, the other a vignetted bust.

After 1853 D'Avignon's fortunes began to wane. Over the next seven

10

Louis Kossuth, 1802-1894. Lithograph, 1851, by D'Avignon after Root
and Company, 21.5 × 21.4 cm. (*Library of Congress*)

11

Louis Jacques Mandé Daguerre,
1787-1851. Lithograph, 1849, by
D'Avignon and Abram J. Hoffman(n)
after Meade Brothers, 21.4 × 22.5
cm. (*National Portrait Gallery, Smithsonian Institution*)

12

Meade Brothers (Charles R. Meade, 1827–1858, and Henry W. M. Meade, circa 1823-1865). Lithograph, circa 1852, D'Avignon after Meade Brothers, 36.3 × 36.3 cm. (*National Portrait Gallery, Smithsonian Institution*)

years, he moved five times, the last time to Boston. His commissions declined in importance: between 1854 and 1858 he did only one large political portrait (*Edward Everett,* after a daguerreotype by Whitehurst), some sheet-music covers, several large theatrical portraits—one of them exceptional—and a number of small portraits of Dartmouth College students for class albums. The most outstanding piece of this period was

A PHYSICIAN FOR EVERY HOUSE.

BEING USEFUL DIRECTIONS for the RELIEF of WOUNDED PERSONS, with SUGGESTIONS of PROMPT and EFFECTUAL REMEDIES for ORDINARY ACCIDENTS of ALL KINDS.

DENTIST.

DISEASES of the EYE.

ITCH.

SUFFOCATION from INHALING NOXIOUS GASES.

DROWNING, ASPHYXIA from SUBMERSION.

DISLOCATIONS, SPRAINS, &c.

BLOWS on the HEAD, FALLS, &c.

SEA SICKNESS.

GOUT.

CUTS and EXCORIATIONS.

HEMORRHAGE, DISCHARGES of BLOOD.

CRUSHED FINGERS, HANDS or FEET.

EAR-WIGS, INSECTS in the EAR.

POISONING.

STINGS AND BITES of INSECTS.

CORNS, WARTS, EXCRESCENCES on the SKIN.

FOOT-ACHE.

CHILBLAINS, CHAPPED HANDS, CHAPES, &c.

BURNS.

WOUNDS by NEEDLES, SPLINTERS, &c.

FELLON or WHITLOW.

INDIGESTION.

SAND, &c. IN THE EYE.

PINS or NEEDLES in the THROAT.

HYDROPHOBIA, or BITE of a MAD DOG.

BEEF-TEA.

GUM-SYRUP.

SOOTHING DRINK.

LEMONADE, &c.

CLARIFIED WHEY.

SEVENTH WINE.

WINE of BARK.

EMOLLIENT POULTICE.

MUSTARD PLASTER.

CLOTHES THAT HAVE TAKEN FIRE.

VACCINATION.

POISONING.

BLEEDING.

A. PONCHON & Co. Publishers, No 1, & 3, Amity Street.
NEW-YORK.

the large lithograph of Henry Clay (see fig. 6), which D'Avignon published himself in 1856 on Clay's birthday. Highly detailed, beautifully modeled, and richly printed (by Nagel, rather than D'Avignon himself), it was a masterpiece of draftsmanship and a lithographic tour de force clearly meant to revitalize his reputation and his business. This print epitomized the abilities of Francis D'Avignon: it climaxed his career, even though he continued to receive commissions into 1860.

Of his later works, *A Physician for Every House* (1857) (fig. 13) is the most charming, if the least artistically accomplished. This piece, a large poster, illustrates a variety of common ailments and injuries (everything from hydrophobia to warts to indigestion to drowning) in a series of small, cartoonlike vignettes and describes the accepted remedies. The drawings are surprisingly naive, and are difficult to associate with the familiar hand of Francis D'Avignon the portraitist, but this could reflect a conscious stylistic decision by the publisher as much as the skill of the draftsman. The print itself is easily the most amusing thing that D'Avignon ever did.

The final chapter of Francis D'Avignon's artistic career began in 1858, when Charles Brainard, the Boston publisher, commissioned him to lithograph a daguerreotype portrait of Stephen A. Douglas. The following year they formed a partnership, and D'Avignon moved to Medford, a Boston suburb. Brainard envisioned a new publication patterned on *The Gallery of Illustrious Americans* and issued at least two portraits—*Rufus Choate* and *Henry W. Longfellow* (figs. 14 and 15)—which were qualitatively equal to, if not actually better than, the prints in the Brady-D'Avignon publication. This venture collapsed even more quickly than its predecessor: only prints of Douglas, Longfellow, Choate, and Horace Mann from the series are known to exist, while unlocated portraits of John A. Bingham, John Sherman, and Andrew Johnson are referred to in contemporary sources.[13] These were D'Avignon's last significant prints.

13 See the notice from the Boston *Transcript* quoted in Leroy F. Graf and Ralph W. Haskins, eds., *The Papers of Andrew Johnson,* 3 (Knoxville, Tenn., 1972): 273.

The same volume prints correspondence between Andrew Johnson and Charles Brainard concerning D'Avignon's lithograph of Johnson, pp. 271–73. In a later letter to Brainard, now in the collection of the Massachusetts Historical Society, Johnson rejects the portrait, commenting that it was a "good picture but no likeness" and that the face "was entirely too smoothe and youthful in appearance." I am grateful to Ms. Sally Pierce of the Boston Athenaeum for bringing these references to my attention.

14
Henry Wadsworth Longfellow,
1807-1882. Lithograph, 1859, by
D'Avignon after John A. Whipple,
39.8 × 29.4 cm. (*National Portrait
Gallery, Smithsonian Institution*)

15
Henry Wadsworth Longfellow,
1807-1882. Daguerreotype, circa
1850, by John A. Whipple, 10.7 ×
8.1 cm. (*The Museum of Modern Art,
New York, Gift of A. Conger
Goodyear*)

Yours truly, A. Lincoln

16
Abraham Lincoln, 1809-1865. Lithograph, circa 1860, by D'Avignon after Thomas Murphy Johnston, 32 × 28 cm. (*Essex Institute, Salem, Mass.*)

Although he produced four final prints in 1860, including one of Abraham Lincoln (fig. 16), his career really ended with the failure of Brainard's scheme only months after it had begun.

When the Civil War broke out, D'Avignon lied about his age and enlisted as a corporal in Company I, Second Massachusetts Volunteers.[14] His military career was brief and inglorious: he was demoted to private for losing his canteen, and he went AWOL for three weeks at Winchester, Virginia, on the first anniversary of his enlistment. In September 1862 he was transferred to the Headquarters of the Defenses of Washington as clerk to General Nathaniel Banks. In November he was detailed on extra duty as a draftsman for the Banks Expedition to Louisiana. In December, Banks personally engineered D'Avignon's discharge from the army and had it made retroactively effective from May 11, 1862. Saying that D'Avignon

14 D'Avignon's General Service Record, available through the National Archives and Records Service.

was "too old and infirm for service as a private, but has excellent qualities as an artist," Banks then hired him as a topographical assistant at four dollars a day, a substantial salary for the time.[15] D'Avignon spent the remainder of the war as a civilian draftsman employed by the United States Army. Several small manuscript maps and some large lithographed ones document this period: the last map, dated 1865, is the last known product of Francis D'Avignon's hand.[16]

D'Avignon returned to Medford after the war, but what finally became of him is not known. The only contemporary reference to him after 1865 is in the 1870 census,[17] where he was listed as a laborer. There are no records of his death or burial in Massachusetts, even though he had children living there into the late 1870s.[18] What finally happened to one of America's foremost lithographic draftsmen during a golden age of portraiture may never be known.

15 General Nathaniel P. Banks to Brigadier General George Thomas, May 11, 1862, with covering letter dated Dec. 22, 1862, Record Group 94, 11569-A-1875, National Archives and Records Service. The date on Banks's original shows clear signs of having been fraudulently altered. See also Adjutant General's Office, Memo for Establishing Final Record 1859.B.76 (Dec. 19, 1874), Record Group 94, 11569A. A.G.O. (E.B.) 75, National Archives and Records Service.

16 Cartographic Records, Record Group 77, M 105–109, M123, US 250, and Z 293, National Archives and Records Service.

17 1870 Census, Middlesex County, MF no. 629, p. 124, for Medford, National Archives and Records Service.

18 Joseph, D'Avignon's eldest son by his second wife, died in 1879 at the age of twenty-six (Death Book, 1879, vol. 311, p. 125, Bureau of Vital Statistics, Massachusetts State Archives). There were four younger children, who presumably outlived their brother.

The prints in this checklist were all drawn on stone by Francis D'Avignon. The information in each entry derives from inscriptions on the prints examined. (Other states of the prints may have different inscriptions.) Information in brackets is supplied by the author on the basis of his research. The terms "lithographed by" or "Lith. of" which often appear in the inscriptions are sometimes ambiguous, but they generally refer to the lithography company that produced, printed and/or published the image. D'Avignon himself at times owned a press and fulfilled these functions, as well as drawing the image on the stone.

Location Abbreviations	DLC	Library of Congress, Prints and Photographs Division
	DNA	National Archives and Records Service
	NMAH(SI)	National Museum of American History, Smithsonian Institution
	NPG(SI)	National Portrait Gallery, Smithsonian Institution
	MB	Boston Public Library
	MH(TC)	Harvard University Theatre Collection
	MSaE	Essex Institute
	MWA	American Antiquarian Society
	MWA(D)	American Antiquarian Society, Dartmouth 1857 Album
	MdBH	Maryland Historical Society
	NCNY	Museum of the City of New York
	NHi	New-York Historical Society, Print Collection
	NN	New York Public Library, Print Collection
	NN(TC)	New York Public Library, Theater Collection
	PPL	Library Company of Philadelphia

1   Alexander, F.
    Printed by L. Nagel
    After a daguerreotype by Phillip Haas
    Cited in Harry T. Peters, *America on Stone: The Other Printmakers to the American People* (1931; rept. New York, 1976), p. 291.

2   Audubon, John James
    Printed by D'Avignon's Lithographic Press, 323 Broadway
    Published by Brady, D'Avignon & Co., 323 Broadway
    Published in *The Gallery of Illustrious Americans,* no. 7
    After a daguerreotype by Mathew B. Brady
    1850   NPG(SI)

    Arditi, Luigi. See Bottesini

3   Avezzana, General Giuseppe
    Lithographed by F. D'Avignon, 323 Broadway
    Published by Goupil, Vibert & Co.
    After a daguerreotype by Philip Haas
    [circa 1849]   MB

4   Bangs, Nathan
    Lithographed by D'Avignon, 132 Nassau Street
    After a painting by Paradise
    [1847]   MWA

5   Bangs, Mrs. Nathan
    Lithographed by F. D'Avignon, 132 Nassau Street
    After a painting by Frothingham
    [1847]   MWA

6 Barili, Clotilda, "Rôle de Marie de Rohan"
   1854   MH(TC)

7 Bates, Edward
   Printed by J. H. Daniels, Boston
   Published by J. Spore & Co., St. Louis
   After a painting by W. Cogswell
   1860   DLC

8 Beck, J. B.
   Lithographed by D'Avignon, 323 Broadway
   [circa 1849-53]   NN

9 Benedetti, Sesto
   Lithographed by F. Davignon & Hoffman, 323 Broadway
   Printed by Nagel & Weingaertner
   [circa 1849]   MH(TC)

10 Benedict, Sir Julius
   Published by William Hall & Co.
   After a daguerreotype by Root
   1850   MH(TC)

11 Beneventano, G. F.
   Printed by L. Nagel
   After a daguerreotype by Philip Haas
   [circa 1847]   MH(TC)

12 Bennett
   Lithographed by D'Avignon, 80 Leonard St.
   [1855]   MWA(D)

13 [Bingham, John A.]
   [Lithographed and published by C. H. Brainard]
   [1859]
   Known from a notice in the *Boston Evening Transcript* included in a letter of Brainard to Andrew
   Johnson, April 27, 1859, Graf and Haskins, *The Papers of Andrew Johnson* 3: 273

14 Bishop, Anna
   Printed by Charles Currier
   Published by Firth, Hall & Pond
   1847   MWA
   Sheet-music cover of "The Songs of Madame Anna Bishop" from the same stone   MWA

15 Bissell, E. C.
   Lithographed by D'Avignon, 80 Leonard St.
   [1855]   MWA(D)

16 Blangy, Hermine
   On the stone by D'Avignon & [Gustavus] Pfau
   Printed by L. Nagel
   After a print by "Cauchie" [*sic*]
   [circa 1848]   MH(TC)

17 Blangy, Hermine
   On the stone by D'Avignon & [Joseph] Vollmering
   [circa 1848]   MH(TC)

18 Bottesini, Giovanni, and Luigi Arditi
   Printed by Charles Currier
   After a daguerreotype by Philip Haas
   [circa 1847]   NN(TC)

19 Bouchelle, Mdme Wallace
    Published by Samuel C. Jollie, New York
    After a daguerreotype by Philip Haas
    [circa 1851]   MH(TC)
    Sheet-music cover printed from the same stone   MH(TC)

20 Boucicault, Dion
    1855   MH(TC)

21 Bradstreet, Governor
    Lithographed by F. D'Avignon, 323 Broadway
    Published in Nehemiah Cleaveland, *Address Delivered at Topsfield in Massachusetts, August
    28, 1850* (New York, 1851)   MWA

22 Brady, Mathew B.
    Published in *Photographic Art Journal* (Jan. 1851)

23 Bridges, Eloise
    Lithographed by D'Avignon
    1854   MH(TC)

24 Broadus, Marie
    1859   MH(TC)

25 Brown, Francis F.
    Lithographed by F. D'Avignon, 80 Leonard St.
    [1855]   MWA(D)

26 Brown, S. Edward
    Lithographed by F. D'Avignon, 80 Leonard St.
    [1855]   MWA(D)

27 Bryant, Dan, "The Essence of Old Virginny"
    Lithographed by D'Avignon
    Published by F. D'Avignon
    After a photograph by the Meade Brothers   MH(TC)

28 Bryant, Jerry
    Published by F. D'Avignon
    After a photograph by the Meade Brothers   MH(TC)

29 Bryant, Neil
    Lithographed by F. D'Avignon, 61 Franklin St.
    After a daguerreotype by the Meade Brothers
    1857   MWA

30 Buck, Charles W.
    Lithographed by F. D'Avignon, 80 Leonard Street
    [1855]   MWA, MWA(D)

31 Butler, Benjamin F.
    Lithographed by Endicott
    Published in *Democratic Review* 14 (1844): 221
    After a daguerreotype
    1844   NPG(SI)

32 Caldwell, John C.
    Lithographed by F. D'Avignon, 80 Leonard St.
    1855   MWA(D)

33 Calhoun, John C.
    Lithographed by D'Avignon's Lithographic Press, 323 Broadway
    Published by Brady, D'Avignon, & Co.
    Published in *The Gallery of Illustrious Americans*, no. 2
    After a daguerreotype by Mathew B. Brady
    1850   NPG(SI)

34 Carson, Alfred
    Sheet-music cover: "The Fireman's Polka"
    Lithographed by F. D'Avignon
    Published by William Hall & Sons
    After a daguerreotype by the Meade Brothers
    1851   MWA, NCNY

35 Cass, Lewis
    Printed by D'Avignon's Press, 323 Broadway
    Published by Brady, D'Avignon & Co.
    Published in *The Gallery of Illustrious Americans,* no. 12
    From a daguerreotype by Mathew B. Brady
    1850   NPG(SI)

36 Chandler, Adniram
    Lithographed by F. D'Avignon
    After a daguerreotype by M. M. Lawrence   NN

37 Channing, William Ellery
    Printed by F. D'Avignon's Press, 323 Broadway
    Published by Brady, D'Avignon & Co.
    Published in *The Gallery of Illustrious Americans,* no. 11
    From a painting by Spiridione Gambardella
    1850   NPG(SI)

38 Choate, Rufus
    Lithographed by D'Avignon & Brainard
    Published by C. H. Brainard and Elliot White, Boston
    1859   MWA, NN

39 Choate, Rufus
    Lithographed by F. D'Avignon, 80 Leonard St.
    [1855]   MWA(D)

40 Clark, [Lot?]
    Lithographed by F. D'Avignon, 323 Broadway
    After a daguerreotype by Philip Haas
    [circa 1849-53]   DLC

41 Clay, Henry
    Printed by Greeley & McElrath, Tribune Building, New York
    Published in Epes Sargeant, *The Life and Public Services of Henry Clay*
    (New York, 1844)   DLC

42 Clay, Henry
    Lithographed and published by George Endicott
    After a daguerreotype by Anthony, Edwards and Company
    1844   NPG(SI)

43 Clay, Henry
    Lithographed by D'Avignon's Press, 323 Broadway
    Published by Brady, D'Avignon & Co.
    Published in *The Gallery of Illustrious Americans,* no. 5
    After a daguerreotype by Mathew B. Brady
    1850   NPG(SI)

44 Clay, Henry
    Lithographed by F. D'Avignon
    Printed by L. Nagel
    Published by F. D'Avignon, New York
    1856   DLC
    One of D'Avignon's greatest portraits, this was published on the eightieth anniversary of
    Clay's birth.

45 Cleaveland, Nehemiah
    Lithographed by F. D'Avignon
    Printed by F. D'Avignon's Press, 323 Broadway
    Published in Cleaveland, *Address*
    After a painting by Thomas Cole   MWA

46 Cobb, Howell
    Lithographed by D'Avignon, 323 Broadway
    Published by Casimir Bohn, Washington, D.C.
    [circa 1851-53]   NPG(SI)

47 Colton, John Jay
    Lithographed by F. D'Avignon, 80 Leonard St.
    [1855]   MWA(D)

48 Cone, S. H.
    Lithographed by F. D'Avignon
    From a daguerreotype, possibly by M. M. Lawrence   NN

49 Cook, George S.
    Lithographed by F. D'Avignon
    Published in *Photographic Art Journal* (May 1851)

50 Crolius, Clarkson
    Lithographed by F. D'Avignon
    Published by the American Institute
    After a painting by Ezra Ames   NN

51 Crosby, Frances Jane
    Lithographed by Endicott
    After a daguerreotype by August Morand
    [circa 1844]   MWA

52 Daguerre, Louis Jacques Mandé
    Lithographed by F. D'Avignon & Hoffmann, 323 Broadway
    Printed by Nagel & Weingaertner
    Published by the Meade Brothers
    After a daguerreotype by the Meade Brothers
    1849   NPG(SI), MWA

53 Daguerre, Louis Jacques Mandé
    Lithographed by F. D'Avignon, 323 Broadway
    After a daguerreotype by the Meade Brothers
    [circa 1849-53]   NN
    Printed from the same stone as no. 52, with a different imprint, this possibly was published by
    D'Avignon in 1851 to commemorate Daguerre's death.

54 Davie, D. D. T.
    Lithographed by F. D'Avignon
    Published in *Photographic Art Journal* (September 1851)

55 Dean, Julia
    Lithographed by F. D'Avignon   MH(TC)

56 Dean, Julia
    Lithographed by F. D'Avignon
    After a daguerreotype by Root   MH(TC)
    A different, seemingly later, pose than no. 55

57 Delille, Octavia
    After a daguerreotype by Root   MH(TC)

58 Denin, Susan
    Known from a photomechanical reproduction   MH(TC)

59 Denison, George
Lithographed by F. D'Avignon, 80 Leonard Street
[1855]   MWA(D)

60 De Vries, Rosa
After a daguerreotype by Mathew B. Brady
[circa 1853]   MH(TC)

61 Dirkinson, William E.
Lithographed by F. D'Avignon, 362 Broadway
[1854]   MWA(D)

62 Doctorf, Louisa, & F. Edward
Lithographed by F. D'Avignon Lith., 323 Broadway
[1849-53]   NN

63 Douglas, Stephen A.
Printed by Bufford, Boston
Published by Charles Brainard, Boston
After a daguerreotype by Fassett & Cook
1858   MWA
Reproduced in Lloyd Ostendorf and Bruce Duncan, "The Photographic Portraits of Stephen
A. Douglas," *Journal of the Illinois State Historical Society* 67, no. 1 (Feb. 1974): 44

64 Douglas, Stephen A.
Lithographed by Bufford
Published by C. H. Brainard
After a photograph by McClees & Vannerson, Washington, D.C.
1859
Known from a reproduction in Ostendorf and Duncan, pp. 50-51. A vintage print of the
McClees and Vannerson photograph from which the lithograph was copied is in the collection
of the National Portrait Gallery (NPG.77.262).

65 Drake, Dan
Lithographed by F. D'Avignon, 323 Broadway
After a daguerreotype by Philip Haas
[circa 1849-53]   DLC

66 Dunlap, G. E.
Lithographed by F. D'Avignon, 80 Leonard St.
1855   MWA(D)

67 Dwight, D. W.
Lithographed by F. D'Avignon N.Y.
Printed by L. Nagel
After a daguerreotype by M. M. Lawrence   DLC

68 Eddy, Edward
After a daguerreotype by P. Haas
1857   MH(TC)

69 Endecott, John
F. D'Avignon, R.I.A. del.ᵗ
Lithographed by G. Endicott
Published by George and William Endicott
After an unidentified painting
1843   NPG(SI)
This is the earliest American print by D'Avignon yet identified.

70 Esing, Mandarin
Printed by L. Nagel
Copyrighted by D'Avignon
After a daguerreotype by Philip Haas
1847   NN

71 Espinosa, Leon
    After a daguerreotype by Jeremiah Gurney
    1857   MH(TC)

72 Everett, Edward
    Lithographed by F. D'Avignon
    Published by R. Van Dien, Washington, D.C.
    After a daguerreotype by Jesse Whitehurst
    1854   NPG(SI)

73 Farman, E. E.
    Lithographed by F. D'Avignon, 80 Leonard St.
    [1855]   MWA(D)

74 Fillmore, Millard
    Printed by D'Avignon's Press, 323 Broadway
    Published by Brady, D'Avignon & Co.
    Published in *The Gallery of Illustrious Americans*, no. 10
    After a daguerreotype by Mathew B. Brady
    1850   NPG(SI)

75 Fitch, A. H.
    Lithographed by F. D'Avignon, 80 Leonard St.
    [1855]   MWA(D)

76 Florence, Malvina (Mrs. William J.)
    Lithographed by F. D'Avignon, 327 Broadway
    After a daguerreotype by the Meade Brothers
    1857   NPG(SI)

77 Florence, William J.
    After a daguerreotype by "Burney" [*sic*]
    1855   MH(TC)

78 Florence, William J.
    After a daguerreotype by the Meade Brothers
    1857   NPG(SI)

79 Frelinghuysen, Theodore
    Lithographed by George Endicott
    Published by [August] Morand
    After a daguerreotype by Morand
    1844   MWA

80 Frémont, John C.
    Printed by F. D'Avignon's Press, 323 Broadway
    Published by Brady, D'Avignon & Co.
    Published in *The Gallery of Illustrious Americans*, no. 6
    After a daguerreotype by Brady
    1850   NPG(SI)

81 Frezzolini, Erminia Nencini
    After a photograph by the Meade Brothers
    1857   MH(TC)

82 Gilmer, Thomas
    Printed by Endicott
    Published by Anthony, Edwards & Chilton
    After a daguerreotype by Anthony, Edwards & Chilton
    1844   DLC, NMAH(SI)

83 Gockel, August   NN

84 Goldsmith, J. B.
    Lithographed by Endicott
    After a daguerreotype by Jeremiah Gurney
    1845   MWA

85 Gougenheim, Adelaide   MH(TC)

86 Gougenheim, Josephine   MH(TC)

87 Hale, Luther Holman
    Lithographed by F. D'Avignon
    Published in *Photographic Art Journal* (June 1851)

88 Hardon, Charles
    Lithographed by F. D'Avignon, 362 Broadway
    [1854]   MWA(D)

89 Harper, James
    From life and on stone by F. Davignon
    Lithographed by Lewis & Brown
    Published in *Metropolitan and American Review*
    [circa 1844-45]   NN

90 Harper, James
    F. Davignon Pinxt. & Lith.
    Printed & Publ. by Michelin & Cuipers
    1844   NPG(SI)

91 Harris, E. P.
    Lithographed by F. D'Avignon, 80 Leonard Street
    [1855]   MWA(D)

92 Hart, N. Coleman
    Lithographed by F. D'Avignon, 362 Broadway
    [1854]   MWA(D)

93 Hartwell, John
    Lithographed by F. D'Avignon, 80 Leonard St.
    [1855]   MWA(D)

94 Hedding, Bishop
    Lithographed by F. D'Avignon, New York
    After a daguerreotype by S. L. Walker
    1852   MWA

95 Heron, Matilda
    Lithographed by F. D'Avignon
    Printed by G. W. Lewis
    Published by William Hall & Son
    1856   MH(TC)

96 Herz, Henri
    Lithographed by F. D'Avignon & Hoffmann, 323 Broadway
    Printed by Nagel and Weingaertner
    Published by Firth, Pond & Co.
    After a daguerreotype by Philip Haas
    [circa 1849-53]   DLC

97 Houston, Samuel
    Drawn on stone by F. Davignon N.Y.
    Printed by L. Nagel
    After a daguerreotype by Bartlett & Fuller
    1848   DLC

98 Howard, M. S.
    Lithographed by F. D'Avignon, 362 Broadway
    [1854]   MWA(D)

99 Hoyt, Dixi C.
    Lithographed by F. D'Avignon, 80 Leonard St.
    [1855]   MWA(D)

100   Hudson, Henry, "The celebrated and unfortunate Navigator, abandoned by his Crew in Hudson's Bay the 11th of June, 1610"
Lithographed by Lewis & Brown, 37 John St.
[circa 1844]   NN, DLC
Inscribed "Presented Gratuitously to the Visitors of the Original Painting"

101   Hudson, James, "As the Knight of Arva"
Lithographed by F. D'Avignon, 323 Broadway
After a daguerreotype by Philip Haas
[circa 1849-53]   MH(TC)

102   Hughitt, William Edgar
Lithographed by F. D'Avignon, 80 Leonard St.
[1855]   MWA(D)

103   Humboldt, Alexander Von
Lithographed by F. D'Avignon
Published by J. H. Kleefisch
After a painting by E. G. Richards
1858   NN

104   Huntington, Mrs. Alethea
Lithographed by F. D'Avignon, 323 Broadway
After a miniature by G. Freeman
Published in Cleaveland, *Address*   MWA

105   Hutchinson, John W.
After a daguerreotype by (Nathan G.) Burgess   MH(TC)

106   Hutton, Rev. Mancius, D. D.
Lithographed by George & William Endicott
Published by William Archer
[circa 1844-45]   MWA

107   Jay, William L.
Lithographed by F. D'Avignon, 362 Broadway
[1854]   MWA(D)

108   Jefferds, C. D.
Lithographed by F. D'Avignon, 362 Broadway
1854   MWA(D)

109   Jennings, Samuel K., "Aetat 76"
Lithographed by F. Davignon
Printed by Rochler
[1847]   MdBH

110   Jessup, Hon. William, L. L. D.
Lithographed by F. D'Avignon
After a daguerreotype by Jeremiah Gurney   NN

111   Jocelyn, Dana
Lithographed by F. D'Avignon, 80 Leonard St.
[1855]   MWA(D)

112   [Johnson, Andrew]
[Published by C. H. Brainard, Boston]
[After photographs by McClees and Vannerson, Washington, D.C.]
[1859]
Documented in correspondence between Johnson and Brainard. May not have been published, since Johnson did not approve the likeness; cf. Massachusetts Historical Society, *Proceedings* 47 (1913-14): 477-78; Graf and Haskins, *The Papers of Andrew Johnson*, 3: 271-73.

113   Johnson, Gen. Jeremiah
Lithographed by F. D'Avignon
After a daguerreotype by Stansbury   NN, MWA

114 Judson, Adoniram
     Lithographed by George and William Endicott
     Published by J. R. Bigelow & Co.
     1846   DLC

115 Keene, Laura
     After an ambrotype by Mathew B. Brady
     1854   MH(TC)

116 Kelsey, T. H.
     Lithographed by F. D'Avignon, 362 Broadway
     [1854]   MWA(D)

117 Kennedy, John A.
     Lithographed by F. D'Avignon, 323 Broadway
     Published by S. Skinner, Brooklyn
     After a daguerreotype by Mathew B. Brady
     [1849-53]   NN, NPG(SI)

118 Kossuth, Louis
     Lithographed by F. D'Avignon, 323 Broadway
     Published by Root & Co.
     After a daguerreotype by Root & Co.
     1851   DLC

119 Lee, Miss Mary Ann, "as Beatrix in la Jolie fille de Gaude"
     Painted from life and on stone by F. D'Avignon
     Lithographed by P. S. Duval, Philadelphia
     [circa 1845]
     Known from the reproduction in Peters, pl. 42 and pp. 152, 166

120 Lewis, Morgan
     Lithographed by Endicott
     Published by Henry G. Langley
     Published in *Democratic Review* 14 (1844): 445
     After a daguerreotype by Howard Chilton   NN

121 Lincoln, Abraham
     Drawn from life by T. M. Johnston
     Drawn on stone by F. D'Avignon
     [circa 1860]   MSaE

122 Lind, Jenny
     Drawn on stone by Davignon and Vollmering
     Printed by L. Nagel
     Published by J. F. Atwill
     1847   MH(TC)

123 Lind, Jenny
     Lithographed by F. D'Avignon
     Published by M. B. Brady and F. D'Avignon
     1850   DLC

124 Longfellow, Henry W.
     Lithographed by F. D'Avignon & Brainard
     Published by C. H. Brainard, Boston
     From a daguerreotype by Whipple and Black
     1859   NN, NPG(SI)
     The original daguerreotype is in the collection of the Museum of Modern Art.

125 Lord, J. Brown
     Lithographed by F. D'Avignon, 362 Broadway
     [1854]   MWA(D)

126 Lorini, Domenico
     After a daguerreotype by Philip Haas
     [circa 1849]   MH(TC)

127 McClung, Mathew
     Lithographed by F. D'Avignon, 362 Broadway
     [1854]   MWA(D)

128 MacDonald, James
     Lithographed by F. D'Avignon, 323 Broadway
     1852   DLC

129 Mann, Horace
     Lithographed by D'Avignon & Brainard
     Published by Elliot & White, 322 Washington St., Boston
     After a daguerreotype
     1859   NPG(SI)

130 Manzini, Constanza   MH(TC)

131 Maretzek, Max
     Lithographed by F. D'Avignon, 323 Broadway
     After a daguerreotype by Mathew B. Brady
     [circa 1849-53]   NN(TC)

132 Marini, Ignazio
     Lithographed and Published by F. D'Avignon, 323 Broadway
     After a daguerreotype by Mathew B. Brady
     [circa 1849-53]   MH(TC)

133 May, Charles Augustus
     Drawn on stone by F. Davignon
     Lithographed and published by James Ackerman
     [circa 1846]   DLC, MWA

134 Meade Brothers [Charles R. and Henry M.]
     Lithographed by D'Avignon, 323 Broadway
     [circa 1849-53]   NPG(SI)

135 Montagni, William L.
     Lithographed by F. D'Avignon, 362 Broadway
     [1854]   MWA(D)

136 Morand, August
     Lithographed by F. D'Avignon, 323 Broadway
     Published in *Photographic Art Journal* (April 1851)

137 Murdoch, James E.
     From a daguerreotype by McClees and Germon, Philadelphia   MH(TC)

138 Murdoch, James E., as Hamlet
     Published by McClees and Germon
     After a daguerreotype by McClees and Germon
     [circa 1845]   MH(TC), NN(TC)

139 Northall, Julia
     Lithographed by George and William Endicott
     Published by Firth, Hall and Pond
     After a daguerreotype by L. L. Bishop
     1846   MH(TC), MWA
     Sheet-music cover

140 Orne, John, Jr.
     Lithographed by F. D'Avignon, 80 Leonard St.
     [1855]   MWA(D)

141   Orr, James L.
Published by Casimir Bohn, Washington, D.C.
After a photograph by Mathew B. Brady
1858   NPG(SI)

142   Packard, Levi P.
Lithographed by F. D'Avignon, 362 Broadway
[1854]   MWA, MWA(D)

143   Parodi, Teresa
Lithographed by F. D'Avignon
After an ambrotype by Mathew B. Brady
1855   NN(TC), MH(TC)

144   Parsons, James C.
Lithographed by F. D'Avignon, 362 Broadway
[1854]   MWA(D)

145   Patti, Adelina
Sheet-music cover: "To the American Ladies"
Published by J. Sage and Son
1855   MH(TC)

146   Perelli, Natale
After a daguerreotype by Philip Haas   NN

147   Piccolomini, Maria
After a photograph by Silsbee, Case & Co.   MH(TC)

148   Pico, Rosina
Printed by L. Nagel
Published by Louis L. Bishop
1845   MH(TC)

149   Pitt, Charles Dibdin
After a daguerreotype by the Meade Brothers   MH(TC)

150   Porter, P. Chester
Lithographed by F. D'Avignon, 80 Leonard St.
[1855]   MWA(D)

151   Porter, William Trotter
Lithographed and published by F. D'Avignon
After a photograph by the Meade Brothers
1858   MWA

152   Prentice, E. L.
Lithographed by F. D'Avignon, 80 Leonard St.
[1855]   MWA(D)

153   Prescott, William Hickling
Lithographed by F. D'Avignon's Press, 323 Broadway
Published by Brady, D'Avignon & Co.
Published in *The Gallery of Illustrious Americans,* no. 8
After a daguerreotype by Mathew B. Brady
1850   NPG(SI)

154   Rand, A. J., M.D.
Lithographed by F. D'Avignon
After a painting by [John Goffe] Rand   MWA

155   Raphall, J. K., D.D.
Lithographed by F. D'Avignon, 323 Broadway
Published by Philip Haas
After a daguerreotype by Philip Haas
1850   DLC

156 Ravel, Gabriel
     After an ambrotype by Mathew B. Brady
     1855   MH(TC)

157 Richardson, Henry P.
     Lithographed by F. D'Avignon, 80 Leonard St.
     [1855]   MWA(D)

158 Saracco
     Printed by L. Nagel
     Published by William Hall and Son
     After a daguerreotype by Philip Haas   MWA

159 Schmidt, William F.
     Lithographed by F. D'Avignon, N. York
     After a daguerreotype by Mathew B. Brady
     1854   DLC

160 Scott, Winfield
     Printed by D'Avignon's Press, 323 Broadway
     Published by Brady, D'Avignon & Co.
     Published in *The Gallery of Illustrious Americans,* no. 9
     After a daguerreotype by Mathew B. Brady
     1850   NPG(SI)

161 Seabury, Rt. Rev. Samuel
     Printed by W. C. Alden
     Published by C. Kuchel, Hartford, Connecticut
     After a painting
     [circa 1849]   DLC

162 Seward, William H.
     Lithographed by F. D'Avignon
     Published by R. Van Dien, Washington, D.C.
     After a daguerreotype by Jeremiah Gurney
     1855   NPG(SI)

163 [Sherman, Hon. John]
     [Lithographed and published by C. H. Brainard]
     [1859]
     Known from a notice in the *Boston Evening Transcript* included in a letter of Brainard to
     Andrew Johnson, April 27, 1859, Graf and Haskins, *The Papers of Andrew Johnson* 3:273

164 Skinner, Thomas H.
     Lithographed by F. D'Avignon, 323 Broadway
     [circa 1849-53]   MWA, MdBH

165 Snow, Col. Ephraim L.
     Lithographed by Charles Currier
     [circa 1840s]   MWA, NPG(SI)

166 Stanley, Emma
     Printed by G. W. Lewis
     Published by William Hall & Son   MH(TC)

167 Stow, Baron
     Lithographed by J. H. Bufford, Boston
     1859   NN

168 Strakosch, Maurice
     Printed by L. Nagel
     Published by William Hall & Son
     After a daguerreotype by Philip Haas
     [circa 1848]   NN, MWA

169   Strong, Edmund A.
Lithographed by F. D'Avignon, 362 Broadway
[1854]   MWA(D)

170   Stuart, Charles and Alexander
Printed by L. Nagel   MH(TC)

171   Tallmadge, James
Lithographed by George and William Endicott
After a daguerreotype by Anthony, Edwards and Company   NN

172   Taylor, Zachary, and his cabinet
Drawn on stone by D'Avignon & Hoffmann
Printed by Nagel & Weingaertner
Published by Mathew B. Brady
After a daguerreotype by Mathew B. Brady
1849   NPG(SI), DLC, MWA

173   Taylor, Zachary
Lithographed by D'Avignon, 323 Broadway
Published by Brady, D'Avignon & Co.
Published in *The Gallery of Illustrious Americans*, no. 1
After a daguerreotype by Mathew B. Brady
1849   NPG(SI)
Two examples of this lithograph, printed by Nagel and Weingaertner but with the *Gallery of Illustrious Americans* imprint, are known (MB and private collection).

174   Tedesco, Fortunata
Published by Joseph F. Atwill
After a daguerreotype by Philip Haas
1847   MWA, MH(TC)

175   Thomas, C. B.
Lithographed by F. D'Avignon, 362 Broadway
[1854]   MWA(D)

176   [Tyler, John, and his cabinet]
[Printed by L. Nagel]
Mentioned in Peters, p. 106. The print is unlocated.

177   [Vieuxtemps, Henri]
Mentioned in Hart, p. 175. The print is unlocated

178   Wakeman, F. B.
Lithographed by F. D'Avignon, 323 Broadway
Published in *Transactions of the American Institute of the City of New York for the year 1850*
(Albany, 1851)   NN

179   Wallace, William Vincent
Printed by Endicott   MH(TC)

180   Wallace, William Vincent
Lithographed by F. D'Avignon
Published by William Hall & Son
1850   MH(TC)

181   Waltone, Charles H.
Lithographed by F. D'Avignon, 80 Leonard St.
[1855]   MWA(D)

182   Washburn, George
Lithographed by F. D'Avignon, 362 Broadway
[1854]   MWA(D)

183 Washington, George
     Lithographed by J. Bufford, Boston
     Published by Elliot & White, Boston
     After the Athenaeum portrait by Gilbert Stuart
     1860   NMAH(SI)

184 Washington, Martha
     Lithographed by J. Bufford, Boston
     Published by Elliot & White, Boston
     After the Athenaeum portrait by Gilbert Stuart
     1860   MWA

185 Webster, Daniel
     Printed by D'Avignon's Press, 323 Broadway
     Published by Brady, D'Avignon & Co.
     Published in *The Gallery of Illustrious Americans*, no. 3
     After a daguerreotype by Mathew B. Brady
     1850   NPG(SI)

186 Wheeler, John
     Lithographed by D'Avignon, 362 Broadway
     After a daguerreotype by Mathew B. Brady
     [1854]   DLC, PPL

187 Wilson, J. Loren
     Lithographed by F. D'Avignon, 80 Leonard St.
     [1855]   MWA(D)

188 Whipple, John A.
     Lithographed by F. D'Avignon, 323 Broadway
     Published in *Photographic Art Journal* (August 1851)

189 White, Charles   MH(TC)

190 Williams, Barney
     After a daguerreotype by Brinkerhoff & Co.   MH(TC)

191 Wood, James Rushmore
     Printed by L. Nagel
     After a ambrotype by Mathew B. Brady
     [circa 1856]   MB

192 Wright, Silas
     Printed by D'Avignon's Press, 323 Broadway
     Published by Brady, D'Avignon & Co.
     Published in *The Gallery of Illustrious Americans*, no. 4
     After a daguerreotype by Mathew B. Brady
     1850   NPG(SI)

193 Faculty of the College of Physicians and Surgeons of the University of New York
     Portraits on Stone by F. Davignon
     Lithographed by G. & W. Endicott
     Published by S. W. Wood
     After daguerreotypes by John Plumbe
     1846   DLC

194 "The Yankee Song Bobbin' Around" (sheet-music cover)
     Lithographed by F. D'Avignon, 80 Leonard Street.
     Published by Samuel C. Jollie
     1855   MWA

195 "Kaliszanka Polka" (sheet-music cover)
     Lithographed by Lewis & Brown
     Published by F. Riley
     [1844]   MWA

196 "Spring" (sheet-music cover)
Lithographed by Sarony and Major
Published by Firth & Hall   MWA

197 "Summer" (sheet-music cover)
Lithographed by Sarony and Major   MWA

198 "Autumn" (sheet-music cover)
Lithographed by Sarony & Major
Published by Firth, Hall & Pond   MWA
A second cover, printed from the same stone, without the Sarony and Major imprint, was
published by William Hall and Son in 1850   MWA

199 "Winter" (sheet-music cover)
Lithographed by Sarony and Major
Published by Firth, Hall & Pond   MWA

200 Girl with Neck Tumor

201 Boy with Neck Tumor
Items 200 and 201, printed from the same stone but with some alterations in details, were
published in *New York Journal of Medicine* 7, no. 1 (July 1851.)

202 Camp Onondaga
Known from a color reproduction published in *American Heritage* 7, no. 5 (Aug. 1956): 18-19

203 "Distribution of the American Art Union Prizes, at the Tabernacle. Broadway, New York;
24th Dec. 1847"
Lithographed by Sarony & Major
Published by John P. Ridner
After a painting by T. H. Matteson
1848   NCNY, NMAH(SI)

204 "A Physician for Every House. Beeing Useful Directions for the Relief of Wounded Persons,
with Suggestions of Prompt and Effectual Remdies for Ordinary Accidents of All Kinds"
Lithographed by F. D'Avignon, 61 Franklin St.
Published by A. Ponchon & Co., New York
1857   DLC

205 "Rich's Improvement, Wilder's Patent Salamander Safes"
Lithographed by F. D'Avignon
[circa 1853]   NHi

206 "Cemetery, Pittsfield, Mass"
Lithographed by F. D'Avignon, 323 Broadway
After a design by H. Stone   NN

207 "The Landing of the Naval Expedition. Against Tabasco. Com⁑d M.C. Perry in Command"
Drawn on stone by D'Avignon & Volmering
Lithographed and published by Sarony & Major
Published in U.S. National Archives, *The Old Navy, 1776-1860* (Washington, D.C., 1962),
pp. 52-53
After a painting by Henry Walke in H. Walke, *Naval Portfolio: Naval Scenes in the Mexican
War* (1848), no. 6

208 Baton Rouge and Vicinity
Drawn by F. D'Avignon   DNA

209 Profiles of Enemy's Works, Port Hudson
Drawn by D'Avignon and B. von Reizenstein   DNA

210 Battlefield of Five Forks, "Map No. 4 Engineers Office, Military Division of the Gulf"
Drawn for stone by F. D'Avignon
July 1865   DNA

211 Mil. Approaches to New Orleans, "Department of the Gulf. Map No. 10"
B. von Reizenstein [and] F. D'Avignon, delineators
1863
Reproduced in *Military Images*, 4, no. 2 (Sept.-Oct. 1982): 17-18

212   Mobile and Vicinity, "Department of the Gulf. Map no. 11"
      N. F. Hyer, C. E., F. D'Avignon, [and] B. von Reizenstein, delineators   DLC

APPENDIX 2:   Biographical Article by Charles Lester from *Fly Leaf of Art and Criticism*, no. 2 (Jan. 15, 1850)

Francis D'Avignon, the artist from whose accomplished hand we transmit the beautiful portraits of this Gallery to the public, was born near Paris, in 1813. His earliest tastes were for artistic pursuits. He studied four years and passed his examination for admission as a military engineer in the army of the Emperor, at the school of St. Petersburg. His studies being completed in 1828, he travelled three years over the continent with his father. A visit to the great galleries, the studios of distinguished artists, and the scenes where art had achieved its noblest triumphs, weaned him entirely from the pursuit for which he had been educated, and on his return to St. Petersburg, in 1834, he began his career as an artist. His education in the military school had made him, of necessity, familiar with the principles of artistic delineation, and during his travels on the continent, Horace Vernet and other artists of eminence he met with, encouraged his half-formed purpose of becoming a Painter.

He remained in St. Petersburg till 1840, and left for England, having acquired an enviable reputation. After a visit of twelve months to the British islands, he returned to the continent and opened his studio in Hamburg, where he gathered his collection of paintings, drawings, engravings, and books, and settled down to pursue his profession. But he was soon overwhelmed with an irreparable misfortune. In the great fire of Hamburg his studio was burned, and the labors and collections of twelve years lost in a night.

He looked on the ruin, and at once determined to come to America to repair his fortunes. Within thirty days he embarked for New York, where he has won for himself a reputation in many departments of art—Portraits and Cabinet Pictures, Drawings on wood and stone, &c. In the latter field, particularly, he has few equals, even in Europe. With such specimens of his skill and genius as the public are furnished with in this Gallery, it is unnecessary to add any thing further. In the pursuit of art, Mr. D'Avignon has not been insensible to the pleasures of literature. He made many curious researches in the system of encaustic painting, practised by the ancient Greeks. He has also cultivated extensively, many of the modern languages.

APPENDIX 3:   Biographical Article by Charles Lester from *Glances at the Metropolis* (New York, 1854), p. 178

The art of Lithography has in no portion of the world been brought to greater perfection than in New York. This we owe entirely to FRANCIS D'AVIGNON, who has executed the most impressive, beautiful, bold, and artistic works, that have ever been produced by this process; and he is the only artist who has achieved a high reputation in Lithography in this country. His father was a French officer of Rank, who, on being taken prisoner during the wars of Napoleon, was carried to St. Petersburg, where the Emperor Alexander, when he learned his genius offered him his liberty and munificent patronage, if he would enter his service to promote polytechnic education and the fine arts. Young D'Avignon, born with the same enthusiasm for art as his father, enjoyed the very highest facilities for study and practice in St. Petersburg, where, after graduating, he returned to France, studied with Horace Vernet, and the best artists of Paris, and established himself in Hamburg, where he was working in various departments of art with great success, when the great fire of that city ruined him. He was one of the earliest artists in Europe to reach eminence in Lithography. From Hamburg he went to London, where he established himself and remained several years. About ten years ago, he came to New York, where he has executed more fine work in Lithography, especially in large portraits, than has been done by any other living artist. To the common eye, perhaps, the smooth and almost polished surface of the French lithographs may be more taking, but the great artists of Europe have universally acknowledged that in depth, striking contrasts of light and shade, nature, truth, distinctness, boldness and power, with freedom of execution, he has outstripped every rival. He has made a hundred un-successful attempts to procure artists and to teach scholars his style of Lithography; but he has failed in every case. With the exception of the plain portions of his work, he is obliged to execute it all himself. But his power and rapidity of execution are almost incredible. During ten years, he has thrown off, with his own hand, upwards of one thousand different portraits—the twelve published in the Gallery of Illustrious Americans, being the finest series that has ever been executed in Lithography. He is now at his studio, 362 Broadway, making lithographic portraits, from twenty to two hundred dollars each, printing them all himself.

APPENDIX 4:   D'Avignon Chronology

1813	Paris	Born near Paris
1828	Saint Petersburg	Graduated, Saint Petersburg military academy
1828-31	Continent	Grand Tour of Continent:
1831-34	Paris	Studied with Vernet
1834-40	Saint Petersburg	Active as an artist in Saint Petersburg
1840	Great Britain	Twelve-month visit to Great Britain
circa 1841	Hamburg	Opened studio in Hamburg, Germany
May 1842		Hamburg studio destroyed in the Great Fire, with total loss
July 22, 1842	New York	Arrived on the S.S. *Stephani* out of Hamburg
1843		281 Broadway: artist
1844-45		235 Broadway: artist
Nov. 27, 1845	Philadelphia	Son Alexander born

1846		64½ Walnut: portrait painter
1847	New York	33 Spruce and then 132 Nassau St.: artist
1848		289 Broadway: portrait painter, lithographer
May 1, 1849	Hartford, Conn.	Wadsworth St.: artist
1849	New York	323 Broadway: portrait painter
1850		323 Broadway: D'Avignon & Hoffman
1850		323 Broadway: lithographer
1851		325 [sic] Broadway: lithographer
1852		323 Broadway: lithographer
1853		341 Broadway: lithographer
1854		362 Broadway: lithographer
1855		80 Leonard: lithographer
1856		[no business address listed]: painter
1857		327 Broadway: lithographer
1857		[61 Franklin St., given on a dated print]
1858		346 Broadway: lithographer
1859		346 Broadway: lithographer
1860	Boston	134 Washington: lithographic artist
1861		134 Washington: lithographic artist (resident of Medford)
May 25, 1861	Medford	Enlisted Co. I, Second Mass. Infantry as corporal
July 3		Reduced to private
May 25, 1862		Reported missing in action, Winchester, Virginia
June 12		Returned to unit
Sept. 26		Detailed to Headquarters, Defenses of Washington
Nov. 17		Detailed on extra duty as draftsman to Banks Expedition
Dec. 22		Letter from General Banks requesting retroactive discharge for D'Avignon to May 11, 1862
1863-65		Civilian draftsman for U.S. Army
July 1865		Map, Battlefield of Five Forks
1870	Medford	Recorded in census as laborer
	No further record	

American Portrait Etching
of the
Late Nineteenth Century

DARYL
R.
RUBENSTEIN

In 1881 Sylvester Rosa Koehler, known today for his championing of the American etching revival, organized the first important and influential exhibition of American etching at the Museum of Fine Arts in Boston.[1] An artist, collector, and print scholar, Koehler was then the managing editor of the short-lived *American Art Review* (1880–81). This periodical published works by American etchers who were involved in the newly inspired movement that had grown out of the European etching "revival" of the 1850s and 1860s. Though Koehler's exhibition was comprised mainly of landscape views in the romantic, European tradition, it did include more than thirty portraits out of the 549 American works catalogued and was the first visible statement on portrait etching. From an analysis of this and other etching exhibitions and the artists they presented, the development of nineteenth-century American portrait etching may be studied.

Etching did not play a major role in the American portrait tradition for several reasons. First, the technique itself was not commonly known to American artists before 1870, except as an auxiliary to engravers who used etching in the initial preparation of an intaglio plate.

In the second place, portraits were executed in other graphic media that satisfied commercial demand and public taste. Many likenesses were closely worked stipple or line engravings printed from steel plates. The repetitive lozenge-and-dot syntax of these prints, a common stylistic formula that descended from earlier European portrait engraving, became

---

1 Sylvester Koehler, *Exhibition of American Etchings, April 11 to May 9, 1881* (Boston, 1881).

dry and static through slavish copying and the use of mechanical tools, and it precluded individualized rendering of form. Nevertheless, these formal compositions, generally copied from photographs, were the accepted mode for the commercial market. Wood engraving was also used for reproductive work, especially for the fast production of newspaper, book, and periodical illustrations. Skilled technicians transferred the image to the block, priding themselves on meticulous accuracy. This type of graphic work was considered only a tool for disseminating copies in other media. Its chief appeal was the celebrity of the subject, and it also satisfied public demand for a high standard of craftsmanship.

Finally, by the time of the Civil War photographic processes had multiplied, and some had achieved a high degree of reproductive accuracy. For a relatively small fee, a sitter could buy a memory of the moment which would satisfy his nineteenth-century admiration for technique and finish as well as for verisimilitude.

For all of these reasons, it took the American artist a long time to discover that pure etching had unique advantages to offer. The most intimate of the graphic arts, etching was a logical extension of drawing and could satisfy the need for experimentation and spontaneity in the selective creation of an image. Because the artist scratched through waxy ground rather than carving through metal, he could execute a freer, more expressive line. Furthermore, that original image could be multiplied by the artist himself without the intervening technical interpretation of a reproductive engraver. These factors contributed to the development and eventual growth of etching in general and portrait etching in particular; and when the advantages became apparent, a new class of graphic artist, the "painter-etcher," was born.

Though Sylvester Koehler's primary interest was in original works by painter-etchers, his exhibition of 1881 drew attention to two accepted modes of portrait etching: the original freehand print and the highly finished reproductive etching after works in other media. He attributed to freely drawn original prints the highest application of the art, but he also acknowledged consummate reproductive work as the result of skilled technique and analytical ability. This dichotomy was recognized by J. R. W. Hitchcock in his 1886 book on American etching: "On the one side is . . . the elevation of etching from its fallen state of servitude to supremacy among the linear arts. On the other, there are signs of a growing tendency to ignore free-hand painter's etching and be influenced by popular demand

1

Mr. Wignell in the Character of Darby (Thomas Wignell, 1753-1803). Etching, 1789, by William Dunlap from life, 12.5 × 9.2 cm. From William Dunlap, *Darby's Return* (New York, 1789). (*Prints Division, the New York Public Library, Astor, Lenox and Tilden Foundations*)

into a style of elaborate work which differs little from the engraver's etching of our fathers."[2]

The prevailing taste today agrees with Koehler, that freely drawn original etching is a finer art of suggestion and selection; and we have come to view the reproductive print of the period as an exercise in labored detail and mechanical precision. Both approaches to portraiture remained viable through the end of the century and were often practiced concurrently by the same artists. Gradually the trend toward original portrait etching, which more fully utilized the medium for its inherent characteristics, found favor with the twentieth-century moderns.

In the 1881 exhibition Koehler included some of the isolated examples of pure etching in America that predated the revival. The standing figure of the actor Thomas Wignell executed by William Dunlap after his own drawing is thought to be the earliest etched portrait.[3] Dunlap, the well-known chronicler of the arts in this country, wrote the words to a comic song, "Darby's Return," which was performed and published in 1789 in

2 J. Ripley W. Hitchcock, *Etching in America* (New York, 1886), p. 4.

3 Frank Weitenkampf, in his chapter on etching, suggests that Joseph Wright's 1790 profile portrait of Washington is probably the first etching executed by a painter. He was not aware that Dunlap's portrait of Wignell, which he also mentions, was first published in 1789. Frank Weitenkampf, *American Graphic Art* (New York, 1912), pp. 1–2.

2
Washington Allston, 1779-1843.
Etching, 1843, by David Claypoole
Johnston after Shobal Vail Clevenger,
16.2 × 13 cm. From the *New York
Mirror*, Oct. 14, 1843. (*National
Portrait Gallery, Smithsonian
Institution*)

New York. Having learned the theory and practice of etching from the silversmith and mechanical engraver Peter R. Maverick in 1787–88, Dunlap executed a freehand, simplified, linear portrait of *Mr. Wignell in the Character of Darby* (fig. 1) for the sheet-music cover.

Thomas Wignell was a much-praised English comedian who first appeared in this country in 1785. Depicted as a short, athletic figure with stooping shoulders and bowed legs, he was well qualified physically for the low comedy he portrayed. Dunlap, who also painted portraits, used the graphic media in an experimental fashion. His representation of Wignell could be construed as just a caricature, though it is doubtful that this was his intent. Nevertheless, he did place the emphasis on character, and not on likeness or facial expression, which in this profile view was hardly visible.

Over the next four or five decades, neither etching nor etched portraiture interested the artistic community. A portrait of the artist Washington Allston (fig. 2) drawn and etched in 1843 by David Claypoole Johnston was another isolated example of the early use of the technique which Koehler included in his 1881 exhibition. Johnston, a painter and recognized practitioner of the art of etching and engraving, learned metal-plate engraving in 1815 and showed a talent for caricature and social satire. He became a leading Boston printmaker during the period preceding the Civil War. Beginning in 1828, he etched more than three hundred vignetted caricatures on aspects of American culture in his time, patterned after those of the English satirist George Cruikshank. Johnston also made prints to illustrate books and magazines that, while aimed at seriousness, were subtly overlaid with an element of humor.

Johnston's portrait of Washington Allston, based on a bust by S. V. Clevenger at the Boston Athenaeum, was published in a popular magazine, the *New York Mirror*.[4] A fragile line drawing with simple parallel shading, it does not take advantage of the linear and tonal effects that could have been achieved through a more complex use of the medium. So great is the emphasis on facial likeness that the remainder of the image has an almost childlike naiveté. As a depiction of the artist at work, it is the precursor of many such portraits, indicating a growing reverence for the artist as a romantic subject.

Koehler included a few other pre-1850 etchings in his exhibition. *Henry Clay* by William Hendrik Franquinet and *George Washington* by William Wilson were two, but these were uninspired, tentative works by neophyte etchers who showed no awareness of the style and technique that were slowly developing in Europe.

The etching revival had begun in France in the 1850s and in England in the 1860s. American artists studying in Europe were certainly exposed to its growing popularity; and in 1866 French publisher Alfred Cadart arrived in New York to exhibit European work, instruct in the technique, and organize the first etching society in America, a branch of the French Society of Etchers. His work was followed by the publication in 1868 of Philip Hamerton's treatise on etching, which broadened knowledge of the basic technique. Neither event, however, had a major impact on the artistic community. In fact, at the Philadelphia Centennial of 1876 only a few etchings were exhibited, and those were divided between the "drawings" and "engravings" sections.[5] The formation of the city etching societies, however, starting with the New York Etching Club in 1877, marked the real beginning of the revival in America. In 1880 alone, etching societies were founded in Boston, Philadelphia, and Cincinnati. Sylvester Koehler played a major role at this time, with his publication of the *American Art Review* (1880–81), his translation of Maxine Lalanne's

4   David Tatham, "D. C. Johnston's Satiric Views of Art in Boston, 1825–1850," *Art and Commerce: American Prints of the Nineteenth Century* (Boston, 1978), p. 23.

5   *Official Catalogue of the International Exhibition of 1875* (Philadelphia, 1876), pp. 54, 59.

treatise on the technique (1880), and his influential exhibition at the Museum of Fine Arts in Boston (1881). Following Koehler, the etching clubs began to have regular exhibitions, giving the general public an exposure to works by the old masters, contemporary Europeans, and their own local artists.

The etching revival had inspired new appreciation of the work of Rembrandt and Van Dyck, and exhibitions and collections of their prints provided some prototypes for etched portraiture. In Boston a selection of portraits by both artists was included in the European section of the 1881 exhibition. In Koehler's introduction to the catalogue, he praised Rembrandt's *Burgomeister Six* as "the most celebrated drypoint thus far produced" and noted that "very rich effects, as velvety as mezzotint may be produced"[6] by the drypoint line. Executed in a chiaroscuro manner, this print exemplified Rembrandt's dramatic use of the medium, the freedom and richness of his technique, and his ability to reflect character and capture a mood. Koehler undoubtedly recognized the dynamic quality of life in Rembrandt's portraiture that contrasted strongly with the static reproductive images despite their impressive surface finish.

Shown alongside the old masters in the American exhibitions were works by contemporary European artists. These nineteenth-century etchers were concerned primarily with landscape—to which the freehand sketched line lent itself so perfectly—but some portraits can be documented in the exhibitions. The majority of European etched portraits were tightly constructed, reproductive in character, and set in a fully worked, dark background, as exemplified in Paul Adolphe Rajon's *Charles Darwin,* shown in the 1882 exhibition of the Philadelphia Society of Etchers. However, American artists also might have noticed in the same show Felix Braquemond's *Alphonse Legros* and Leopold Flameng's *Seymour Haden,* both of which showed a more individualized treatment of the subject.[7]

American engraver-etchers of the 1870s, however, were not yet aware of the spontaneity and linear freedom that could be obtained through pure etching. Their experimental attempts at portraiture in the new medium during this period are exemplified in the work of Stephen A.

6 Koehler, *Exhibition,* p. 9.

7 *Catalogue of the First Annual Exhibition of the Philadelphia Society of Etchers Held at the Pennsylvania Academy of the Fine Arts, Dec. 27, 1882–Feb. 3, 1883* (Philadelphia, 1882).

238

3

Mrs. Charles Francis Adams, 1808-1889. Etching (second state), 1879, by Stephen Schoff after William Morris Hunt, 19.3 × 15.1 cm. (*National Portrait Gallery, Smithsonian Institution*)

Schoff, who began his career in line engraving in Boston under Oliver Pelton. After two years in Europe in the 1840s, he returned to specialize in bank-note work. His large portrait of Ralph Waldo Emerson (1879), after a crayon by Samuel Rowse, is a line engraving of particular interest for its freedom and openness. Although reproductive, it was sympathetic to the character of Emerson and went beyond a mechanical treatment of the subject to express a feeling for the subtleties of form and light. Among the engraved portraits of the period, it was outstanding.

Schoff was not always able to convey these same qualities in his early etched portraits, where engraving and drypoint are combined with etching in a formal, mechanical manner. The economy of line and the soft, melting edge of the facial contours in the Emerson print are not evident in his portrait of Mrs. Charles Francis Adams (fig. 3), after a painting by William Morris Hunt, shown in the 1881 exhibition. Engraving the first state of the print, Schoff then used a transparent ground to etch tonal lines in the forehead, the hand, and the right side of the neck. In the compilation of techniques and the overworked lines, much of the effect of the Emerson engraving was sacrificed. Like his etching of Mrs. Harrison Gray Otis (1879), after Gilbert Stuart, Schoff's print of Mrs. Adams is typical of the historical subject matter, finish, and formality demanded of reproductive portrait etchings in the 1870s. In its detailed description of form and its careful buildup of tone and line, it betrays Schoff's long training as a line engraver. He was too absorbed in trying to reproduce the special effects of painting to do free, expressive work with the etching needle.

Some reproductive etching did show sensitivity and interpretation. The Philadelphia painter Anna Lea Merritt, who developed a specialty of

4
Sir Gilbert Scott, b. 1811. Etching,
1879, by Anna Lea Merritt after
George Richmond, 18.4 × 12.4 cm.
(*Museum of Fine Arts, Boston*)

etched portraits, copied in an imaginative manner from drawings, photographs, and paintings. Born in Philadelphia, she settled in London, marrying the artist and author Henry Merritt. After his death in 1877, she published two volumes of his writings under the title *Art Criticism and Romance* (London, 1879) and learned to etch in order to provide the frontispiece portrait. Koehler called the result "one of the few rare instances in which true conjugal love can be traced as a motive power in art."[8]

In the first volume of the *American Art Review* (1880), Koehler included Merritt's etching of the English architect Sir Gilbert Scott (fig. 4), which he felt showed great improvement over her book illustrations. Merritt told Koehler that the artist George Richmond, who had done the original chalk drawing for the portrait, criticized the etching because "it did not reproduce the style of his drawing which was bold and sketchy."[9] Instead, it was an individualized treatment of the subject with Merritt's own interpretation. Koehler greatly admired it: "The marvelous combination of delicacy and strength in the modeling of the head is such that this plate may justly claim rank among the best of modern etched portraits."[10] He included the etching in his 1881 exhibition and in an 1887

8   Sylvester R. Koehler, *American Art Review* 1 (1880): 230.

9   Anna Lea Merritt to S. R. Koehler, Oct. 27, 1879, Sylvester R. Koehler Papers, Archives of American Art, Smithsonian Institution (hereafter AAA).

10   Koehler, *American Art Review* 1 (1880): 230.

Boston exhibition of women etchers in which Merritt was the main portrait artist.

In her 1883 article on "American Etchers" critic Mariana Van Rensselaer also admired Merritt's work and thought of her as an "original" artist: "Her plates are chiefly portraits, done from painted or photographic originals, often from her own pictures, but though quite elaborate in workmanship, are not exactly to be called 'reproductive' etchings. Whenever she finds her theme, she treats it in a somewhat interpretive way."[11] Van Rensselaer reproduced Merritt's portrait of the naturalist Louis Agassiz (1879) in her article. Copied from a photograph which Agassiz had given to the artist in 1861 when she was his student,[12] the etching exemplified her distinctive style and approach. She liked to work from photographs or from her own life sketches in crayon. "Etching from life directly," she explained to Koehler, "except in a very small size would be too tedious to the sitter."[13]

The engraver Stephen Ferris, who with his brother-in-law, Thomas Moran, had learned the process of etching as early as 1860 from the engraver John Sartain,[14] was also fascinated by portraiture. Ferris was born in New York in 1834 and moved to Philadelphia, where he studied at the Pennsylvania Academy of the Fine Arts under Christian Schussele and Samuel B. Waugh. He later became an instructor at the Philadelphia School of Design for Women and was known mainly as a portrait painter. A prolific portrait etcher as well, he was one of the founders of the Philadelphia Society of Etchers in 1880, and his work was shown in the 1881 exhibition and in most of the New York Etching Club exhibitions which began in 1882. He executed reproductive and original portraits concurrently to meet both the growing demands of collectors and his own personal aesthetic.

Particularly influenced by Spanish painter-etcher Mariano Fortuny,

11   Mariana Van Rensselaer, "American Etchers," *Century Magazine,* Feb. 1883, p. 22.

12   Merritt to Koehler, September 23, 1879, Sylvester R. Koehler Papers, AAA.

13   Merritt to Koehler, Dec. 3, 1879, Sylvester R. Koehler Papers, AAA.

14   Henry Russell Wray, *A Review of Etching in the United States* (Philadelphia, 1893), p. 53.

5
Mrs. Philip Nicklin, 1765-1845.
Etching, 1879, by Stephen James
Ferris after Gilbert Stuart, 18.5 ×
14.2 cm. From *American Art Review*
1, pt. 2(1880). (*National Portrait
Gallery, Smithsonian Institution*)

Ferris collected photogravures of his work and copied his etchings. The only two American etched portraits in the Philadelphia Centennial Exhibition were Ferris's two 1875 prints (one a glass etching) of this Spanish master.[15] Although the handling is stiff and unsophisticated, particularly in the rubbery quality of the arm in the profile portrait, the highly simplified, vignetted composition of these images became the model for his later work.

Ferris executed reproductive etchings all his life. Featured in Koehler's *American Art Review* (1880) and in the Boston exhibition of 1881 was the portrait of Mrs. Philip Nicklin (née Juliana Chew) (fig. 5), dated 1879,

15 *Official Catalogue of the International Exhibition of 1876* (Philadelphia, 1876), p. 59; Joseph Pennell, *Pen Drawing and Pen Draughtsmen* (1889; rept. New York, 1977), p. 197. According to Pennell, "Ferris was one of the first artists to practice etching on glass as it was miscalled at the time." While Ferris used the technique for a portrait of Fortuny in 1875, it had been employed earlier by Emanuel Leutze for the nonspecific portrait of a "Puritan" included in *Autograph Etching by American Artists,* published by John Ehninger in 1859. Having learned of the process from a German newspaper article in 1857, Ehninger instructed his artists to draw with a needle on a collodion-coated glass plate which was then placed over a sensitized paper and exposed to the sun. The resultant impression was a facsimile of the drawing executed in what might be called the *cliché verre* technique. According to Pennell, Ferris used a similar process.

6
Stephen James Ferris, 1835-1915.
Etching, 1880, self-portrait, 12.4 ×
9.2 cm. (*Library of Congress*)

after a painting by Gilbert Stuart. It illustrated an article on historical portraiture by Charles Henry Hart, who commented that the etching was a "beautiful portrait...etched from the original, with much nicety and feeling." His only criticism was the lack of modeling in the face and the lack of Stuart's "dainty use of delicate tints," which, he acknowledged, was difficult to achieve in black and white.[16] Like many others, Hart expected in the reproduction not only a likeness but the very texture and quality of the painted surface. Stephen Ferris, according to Koehler, "believes in finish, and strives to obtain depth of tone and suggestion of color by close and careful working."[17] Before his etching was published Ferris was in constant contact with Koehler and attempted to follow his suggestion to rework the plate of Mrs. Nicklin for more modeling and character by rounding the chin and darkening the shadows on the cheek. He sent his plates to Koehler to be printed in Boston by Estes and Lauriat, who conveyed Koehler's concern for warmth of tone in ink and paper.[18]

In about 1880, Ferris began a series of private pieces—likenesses of

16   Charles Henry Hart, "The Stuart Exhibition at the Museum of Fine Arts Boston," *American Art Review* 1, pt. 2 (1880): 487.

17   Koehler, *American Art Review* 1 (1880): 104.

18   As Ferris did not print his own work, the drier, blacker impression at the Boston Museum of Fine Arts was probably printed in Philadelphia by a Mr. Newnam, Ferris's favorite printer (Stephen J. Ferris to S. R. Koehler, April 2, 1880, Sylvester R. Koehler Papers, AAA).

his family and friends—that were etched from life. Discarding the dark background of the reproductive images, he used a vignetted composition similar to his portraits of Fortuny. It was in this style that he etched from life the portrait of Charles Henry Hart (1880), then a director of the Pennsylvania Academy of the Fine Arts, who may have been responsible for organizing there the first exhibition of the Philadelphia Society of Etchers in 1882. Ferris etched a self-portrait, *The Etcher* (fig. 6), in the same style for this exhibition. Showing an honest attempt at likeness and a straightforward description of texture and form, these images nevertheless lacked the spontaneity of successful life portraits. Combining etching and drypoint with stipple and roulette work, remnants of the engravers' trade, Ferris failed to achieve the freedom and dynamic quality of the etched line.

Some impressions of Ferris's 1881 portrait of his wife, Elizabeth Moran Ferris, were printed on satin, which, according to a treatise published in Philadelphia in 1884, could be used to achieve a sumptuous surface shine.[19] The resulting emphasis on highly finished surface effect indicated that Ferris's attitude toward his private life portraits differed little from his approach to reproductive work. The format and general effect of the portrait of his wife so closely resembles his reproductive etching of Christopher Columbus (1886) after Velázquez that one might say it is only a hairstyle away.

Ferris never fully reached the sketchlike freedom of line or warmth of tone advocated by Koehler. However, in his desire for experimentation, his use of a simplified compositional style, and his portraiture taken from life, he became a bridge between reproductive, historical portraiture and the expressive, individualized sketch.

By the mid-1880s, etching had become fashionable for both collectors and artists. Koehler was still its spokesman; and, appropriately, in 1885 Walter Shirlaw etched a portrait of him lecturing to some New York art students (fig. 7).[20] Executed with sketchlike ebullience, this likeness is an interesting contrast to the contemporary portrait, *S. R. Koehler,* by W. H. W. Bicknell (fig. 8), which relies on Rembrandtian chiaroscuro qualities

19 Carl Lutzon Jutsum, *La Collection Choisée* (Philadelphia, 1884).

20 Clifford S. Ackley, "Sylvester Rosa Koehler and the American Etching Revival," *Art and Commerce: American Prints of the Nineteenth Century* (Boston, 1978), p. 150, n. 5. (The note on the Koehler portrait in the Library of Congress Collection says that it was sketched before "Gotham" art students.)

244

7

Sylvester Rosa Koehler, 1837-1900.
Etching, 1885, by Walter Shirlaw,
12.5 × 8.7 cm. (*Library of Congress*)

8

Sylvester Rosa Koehler, 1837-1900.
Etching, date unknown, by William
Harry Warren Bicknell, 10 × 8.1
cm. (*Library of Congress*)

and pose without the necessary subtlety and selectivity. While both types of portraits were being done during this period, it is the expressive, open, vignetted style and economy of line that was more successful in capturing both character and appearance.

Seminal to the development of this individualized, expressive portrait style was the work of James McNeill Whistler, whose views on the qualities that distinguished fine etching were advocated by Koehler. Both preferred small scale; both favored the richness achieved through tonal or "artificial" wiping (Koehler's term for retroussage); and both recognized "suggestiveness—the art of saying much with little"[21] as the highest achievement in the medium.

Although some Americans, such as Samuel P. Avery, collected Whistler's prints during the 1870s, the first published appreciation of his work was an article by W. C. Brownell in the August 1879 issue of *Scribner's Monthly*. The accompanying illustrations were reproductive wood engravings of two drypoint portraits from the Avery collection, a profile entitled *Riault, the Engraver* and a full-face view of Jo Heffernan, Whistler's mistress during the 1860s. The author referred to the latter portrait, which he entitled "Joe," as Joseph Whistler, the artist's brother.[22] This is a curious comment, as the portrait is hardly androgynous, but it does point up the fact that Americans were barely familiar with the life and works of Whistler. The same illustration, also mistitled, appeared in Mariana Van Rensselaer's article on "American Etchers." Crediting Whistler with a superiority among modern etchers, she praised his figure and portrait etchings as "the finest that have come from any living hand."[23]

Koehler was one of the first to exhibit Whistler's etchings, including in his 1881 exhibition the series of prints known as the "Thames Set" (1859, printed 1871). Whistler's work was shown with increasing frequency throughout the 1880s;[24] and in 1893 a representative survey of his

21 Sylvester R. Koehler, *Etching* (New York, 1885), p. 162.

22 William C. Brownell, "Whistler in Painting and Etching," *Scribner's Monthly* 18 (Aug. 1879): 490; Joseph Pennell, *Etchers and Etching* (New York, 1919), p. 6.

23 Van Rensselaer, p. 16. This article was reprinted in 1886 by Frederick Keppel, who became Whistler's dealer in New York in the mid-1870s.

24 One unspecified etching was included in the Salmagundi Sketch Club's *Third Annual Exhibition of Black and White Art* (New York, 1880). In 1882 seventy-one

etchings was given a special, conspicuous place of display in the arts building of the popular World's Columbian Exposition in Chicago.[25]

The influence of this exposure was felt in portrait as well as landscape etching. Several of Whistler's earliest portraits were shown in the Philadelphia Society of Etchers exhibition in 1882, which featured, according to Koehler's catalogue introduction, "painters' etchings"—prints that were "executed by the artists who conceived them without the intervention of the engraver...in fact, original works of art." Whistler's *Becquet ("The Fiddler")* (1859), the only portrait considered part of the "Thames Set," was included, as well as *La Mère Gerard* and *Annie* from the "French Set" (1855–58). These revealed his interest in the realist current that was championed by the Barbizon painter-etchers Charles Emile Jacque and Jean François Millet. *La Mère Gerard* is a depiction of a poor flower seller outside the gate of the Luxembourg Gardens. The portrait of his niece, Annie Haden, was etched from life during a visit Whistler made to the home of his half sister, Mrs. Seymour Haden, in London.

From 1858 to 1863 Whistler made more than eighty etchings, one-third of which were portraits that were remarkably freer than the "French Set." Another etching of his niece, entitled *Annie Haden* (fig. 9), reflected Whistler's changing view of subject and style. The earlier *Annie* is a realistic portrayal of a child in tight, linear technique which is predominantly etched, using drypoint only for the finishing touches. *Annie Haden* is a picturesque figure, described by a broad sweep of drypoint tint that is both monumental and volumetric in its crisp angularity of form. On an early impression of this etching Whistler wrote, "one of my very best," and later he commented that if he had to make a decision as to which plate was his best, he could rest his reputation on *Annie Haden.*[26]

---

etchings were exhibited in Washington, D.C., at the V. G. Fisher Art Galleries. The New York Etching Club included Whistler's works in exhibitions in 1882, 1889, and 1891; however, no portraits are listed. In 1883 fifty etchings and drypoints were exhibited at Wunderlich Gallery in New York and, in 1888, the Ohio Valley Centennial Exposition in Cincinnati had a graphic arts section (organized by Koehler) which featured the etchings of Whistler, Merritt, Ferris, and Blum.

25   The Chicago exhibition included the following portraits: *Early Portrait of Whistler; Becquet; Arthur Haden; Self-Portrait; Fanny Leyland; Weary; Annie Haden; Mr. Mann Axenfeld; Riault, the Engraver;* and *Jo.*

26   Edward G. Kennedy, *The Etched Work of Whistler* (New York, 1910), p. 24.

9

Annie Haden, b. 1848. Etching, 1859-69, by James McNeill Whistler,
34.8 × 21.4 cm. (*Freer Gallery of Art, Washington, D.C.*)

In general, Whistler's portraits were private pieces that recorded friends and family. Subject as subject alone did not greatly concern him. He wielded the etcher's needle with peculiar authority and an adroit hand, and he used the human face and body as a vehicle to convey sentiment and character. The portraits of two of his friends, *Drouet* (1859), the sculptor, and *Astruc, a Literary Man* (1859–60), were sketched from life in Paris. Whistler's freedom in the handling of the rich drypoint line is remarkable for its bravura and selectivity. Drawn with a powerful sense of form and a shrewd instinct for character, his faces of this period have a distinctly human significance and presence.

The etched portraits of the early 1870s were Whistler's last major portrait group. Depicting members of the family of his patron, the shipbuilder Frederick Leyland, they closely parallel his major oil portraits of the period. In both media, the figure was especially prominent. The likenesses of the daughters, Fanny Leyland (1873) and Florence Leyland (1873), reflect a change in Whistler's style. Stressing suggestion rather than close depiction, he used a delicate, feathery, broken line and more rounded curves to convey a sensuous and impressionistic quality.

Whistler's influence in portraiture was first seen in America in the work of Robert Blum. In 1876 Blum, who was born in Cincinnati and had studied art with Frank Duveneck, visited the Philadelphia Centennial, where he saw Japanese and European art as well as American work. Returning to Philadelphia in 1877, he found a friend in Stephen Ferris, who shared his interest in the work of Mariano Fortuny. Ferris's collection of reproductions and photogravures after this European master influenced Blum's early etchings. In the spring of 1877 Blum made his initial experiments in this medium: "My first attempt accompanied with the usual damage to clothes was an exciting failure. With the same acid, I bit my second plate 'A Difficult Place.' "[27]

In 1878 Blum moved to New York to work as an illustrator for A. W. Drake, art editor at *Scribner's Monthly*. In the following year, the magazine published Brownell's article on Whistler, which Blum surely saw. He actually was aware of Whistler as early as 1876, when he received a letter

27   J. R. W. Hitchcock, *Representative Etchings* (New York, 1887), p. 22. Koehler chose *A Difficult Place* for his 1881 exhibition. Another of Blum's plates, *A Modern Etcher*, depicting his friend William Merritt Chase at work in his studio, was illustrated in Van Rensselaer's article in 1883. It was not a true etching, however, but a drawing transferred photographically to a zinc plate before being etched.

10
Jenny Gerson. Drypoint, 1882, by
Robert Frederick Blum, 13 × 13 cm.
(*Prints Division, the New York Public
Library, Astor, Lenox and Tilden
Foundations*)

from the artist Kenyon Cox containing a sketch by Whistler and instruc-
tions for preparing an etching ground.[28] In 1880 Blum visited the artist in
Venice with Drake and stayed to study with him for two months.

After returning home, Blum began a series of portraits in which he
employed an expressive drypoint line. His delicate profile of Jennie Gerson
(fig. 10), sister-in-law of William Merritt Chase, is executed in a style
reminiscent of the romantic flickering line of Whistler's portraits of the
Leyland family of the early 1870s and is typical of Blum's directness and
sensitivity. In 1883 a writer in the *Studio* noted that "Robert Blum has
lately devoted much attention and time to work with the drypoint. His
profile sketch head of himself is a strong artistic piece of work."[29] In this
fascinating self-portrait (fig. 11), the freedom and linear force generated
by bold, long strokes, the warmth of drypoint line, and the brilliancy
obtained through judicious printing are reminiscent of Whistler's style and
technique in those portraits executed between 1859 and the mid-1860s.
Blum captured likeness and character through subtle use of contrasting
depth of line. Using the head alone, he silhouetted the profile contour

28 Kenyon Cox to Robert Blum, June 10, 1876, Archives of the Avery Library,
    Columbia University, New York. I would like to thank Bruce Weber, Curator of
    the Norton Gallery, Palm Beach, Florida, who has generously allowed me to quote
    material from his Ph.D. dissertation, "Robert Frederick Blum (1857–1903), and
    his Milieu" (in progress, New York University). According to Weber, Koehler was
    planning an article on Blum's etchings for the *American Art Review,* but it was never
    published during the life of the periodical.

29 " 'Notes' from Other Papers," *Studio* 1, no. 20 (May 1883): 210.

11
Robert Frederick Blum, 1857-1903. Drypoint, 1883, self-portrait, 20 ×
14.6 cm. (*Prints Division, the New York Public Library, Astor, Lenox and
Tilden Foundations*)

dramatically against dense shading in a light and open background. While the portrait has the look of great spontaneity, this impression is the last of six or seven states. Its carefully developed spareness and selectivity distinguished Blum as an incisive portrait-etcher.

By the 1890s etching had ceased to be the vital medium for graphic expression that the 1880s had promised. Continued commercial dominance of reproductive etching and involvement of so many amateurs in the field drowned the efforts of painter-etchers in a flood of mediocre work. Even the American print dealers were not promoting American etchings. They preferred to exhibit the work of European etchers (including Whistler) in the attempt to satisfy a continuing consumer aesthetic that looked to Europe as the arbiter of culture and taste.

Predictably, many creative artists turned away from etching, and those that were interested in portraiture experimented with photography. By 1890, even the yearly portfolios of the New York Etching Club were illustrated with photographic portraits of the artists whose etchings were featured.

Thus, the appearance of the major body of original etched portraits by the hand of the painter J. Alden Weir represents a unique statement in the 1890s, and one that reflects the specific influence of Whistler. Weir was exposed to Whistler's influence at an early stage in his career when in 1873, at the age of twenty, he traveled to Paris for the traditional course of study under Jean-Léon Gérôme at the Ecole des Beaux-Arts. While he was sketching at the Louvre, he met Whistler and formed a lasting friendship, visiting him in London in 1877 and 1881. Like Whistler, Weir respected the European artistic tradition, but early in his career he broke with the conservatism of the past. As portraitists, both were less interested in verisimilitude than in an attempt to convey the soul and substance of the sitter through a suggestive approach to describing form. In Weir's works, we see a development toward expressive portraiture, in which the inherent qualities of etching and drypoint are used with optimum dexterity and illusion and yet are subservient to the artistic idea.

Weir learned to etch in 1875 in Paris.[30] He was familiar with graphic art from his father's own etchings, engravings, and print collection; but it was not until he met Whistler, Frank Duveneck, John Twachtman, and other contemporaries in Europe that his interest in etching developed. In

30 Robert H. Getscher, *The Stamp of Whistler* (Oberlin, Ohio, 1977), p. 160.

1881 Weir and his brother John joined Twachtman and his wife on a sketching tour of Holland. It was not uncommon for Twachtman to carry copperplates and needles with him on their walks and etch *en plein air.*[31]

On his return to this country, Weir joined the New York Etching Club in 1882, but it was not until five years later that he began active experimentation in etching and eventually purchased a printing press. Weir considered etching a recreation compared to the more serious business of painting, and as a result his intimate portraits of family and friends have particular freedom and spontaneity. Like Whistler's portraits, they are small in format, worked directly on the plate from life, and generally shaded with parallel lines, reserving the use of cross-hatching for background and black areas. This method gives an open, luminous quality to the likenesses, which is increased by large areas of white space.

Although most of his portraits were etched in 1890 and 1891, one of his earliest was *Lucas Vosterman* (1888). A copy of a Van Dyck print in his own collection, it was an experimental learning exercise. But it still showed Van Dyck's influence in the play of light over the head, and it prefigured Weir's own concern with light and shadow in later work. The influence of Van Dyck's three-quarter format continued to be apparent in Weir's portraits from life of his brothers Dr. Robert Weir (1891) and John F. Weir (1890). In these he developed a surety of draftsmanship and a strong sense of volume combined with a sensitivity to the artistic potential of the drypoint line. Like Whistler, Weir found drypoint a congenial medium, and his carefully developed plates—both his brothers' portraits are worked through six states—maintained a feeling of spontaneity. His portrait of his friend the bibliophile Robert Hoe (fig. 12), however, is an interesting contrast to the linear bravura in the etchings of his brothers. Executed at a time when he was also experimenting with engraving, the delicate drypoint line is more controlled in its delineation of the head and profile despite the autographic scribbles used to suggest the plushness of the coat.

Weir's portraits of children convey a tenderness of mood and a combination of gravity and innocence that is reminiscent of Whistler. The drypoint entitled *On the Porch* (1889) recalls the standing figure of Whistler's *Annie.* His drypoint portrait of *Gyp and the Gipsy* (1890) (fig. 13)

31 Janet Flint, *J. Alden Weir; An American Printmaker, 1852–1919* (Provo, Utah, 1972), p. 5.

253

12
Robert Hoe, 1839-1909. Drypoint,
1891, by Julian Alden Weir, 20 ×
17.3 cm. (*National Portrait Gallery,
Smithsonian Institution*)

13
Gyp and the Gipsy. Drypoint, 1890,
by Julian Alden Weir, 19.8 × 15 cm.
(*National Museum of American Art,
Smithsonian Institution*)

14
Ignatz Marcel Gaugengigl,
1855-1932. Etching, circa 1910, self-
portrait, 29.3 × 20.5 cm. (*Library of
Congress*)

is comparable to Whistler's etching of *Bibi Valentine* (1859): both images are pulled forward in the picture plane, indicating an awareness of Japanese art; both are drawn with sharp, crisp lines; and both have a haunting look of wide-eyed solemnity.

When Weir aimed at completeness of effect, it was tone he had in mind, and not detail of form. In a study of his wife entitled *By Candlelight,* the emphasis is on tonality and the play of light, which is achieved through the richness of the drypoint line and a careful wiping of the plate. A study of mood and sentiment, it is again reminiscent of Whistler.

From 1891 to 1893 Weir's portraits were shown in the annual New York Etching Club exhibitions and in 1893 in the Columbian Exposition in Chicago, where both he and Whistler took prizes for etching. Though 1893 marked the end of Weir's etching career, due to his failing eyesight, his prints were widely exhibited through the first two decades of the twentieth century. The richness and delicacy of his drypoint line and the directness of his portraits occasionally are echoed in the work of his contemporaries and of younger etchers.

Exhibitions of the etchings of certain European artists, particularly Paul Helleu and Anders Zorn, had an effect on both printmakers and the buying public in the late nineteenth century. The *Self-Portrait* by Ignaz Marcel Gaugengigl (fig. 14), for example, is reminiscent of the slashing,

15
Cadwallader Washburn, 1866-1965.
Etching, circa 1930, self-portrait, 18
× 13.7 cm. (*Library of Congress*)

parallel strokes of Zorn's technique. The German-born Gaugengigl had
been taught to etch by Koehler, who showed a few of his studies of heads in
the 1881 exhibition. Most of Gaugengigl's etchings, however, were reproductions of his eighteenth-century-style paintings, and his personal expressive self-portrait[32] was a rare exception.

The etched portrait continued to appeal to some artists. Ernest
Haskell, Otto Schneider, William Auerbach Levy, Ann Goldthwaite,
Cadwallader Washburn (fig. 15), Walter Tittle, and Arthur Heintzelman
all made specialties of the etched likeness, and much of their work has an
honesty, vigor, and freshness of vision that set it apart from the dark,
reproductive portraits that were still accepted at the turn of the century.
Most of these artists, nevertheless, are little known today. For, underlying
the growth of original portrait etching, there had been a search for an
individualized expression that conveyed character and mood as well as
likeness; and in the twentieth century that search turned to innovative
portraits executed by the photo-secessionists who acknowledged Alfred
Stieglitz as their spokesman and Whistler as their god. These artists
developed in photography the same qualities of suggestion and selection
that Sylvester Koehler had described in his essay on etching in 1881.

32 A photograph of I. M. Gaugengigl is reproduced in Carnegie Institute, *Sixteenth
Annual Exhibition* (Pittsburgh, 1912), illus. no. 115. This seems to be the source of
the etching, although there is also a related self-portrait in oils (1909) in the Isabella
Stewart Gardner Museum.

Introspection and Imagination

Portraiture in Twentieth-Century Prints

ALAN FERN

As the preceding essays have made clear, nineteenth-century American printmaking is a field still unfamiliar to most of us; there is much yet to be learned about the work of the artists discussed in those chapters. It is a different story when we enter the twentieth century. The printmakers and their works are altogether more familiar, there is an abundance of portraiture in the graphic arts, and today there is an unprecedented level of activity in printmaking of every kind.

But, more than this, both the character of printmaking and the nature of portraiture have changed during the past eighty or ninety years. To bring this exploration of the place of the portrait in American printmaking to a close, it may not be out of place to take a brief look at the nature of these changes.

First of all, the advent of photoengraving in the 1880s began to relieve the printmaker of his monopoly on the manufacture of printed reproductions. No longer was the printmaker first and foremost an interpreter of paintings and photographs (usually made by others), and no longer did he need to be as much a businessman as a craftsman, searching for profitable publishing ventures to repay himself for the tedious work of translating images into printable form. Instead, following in the footsteps of Whistler, Degas, Bonnard, or Munch, the American printmaker in the twentieth century could see himself as an independent artist, using the graphic media for expressive purposes.

Portraiture was changing as well, and also through the intervention of photography. In the nineteenth century, though the power of photo-graphic portraiture was widely recognized, painted or sculpted likenesses were still the only ones accepted for grave and formal purposes. When the photograph of the bride, the bank president, and the cabinet officer became acceptable, the artist was liberated to make portraits by choice, as he might make landscapes by choice. Since printmakers were now artists, too, and no longer simply manufacturers of printing plates, this new attitude is reflected in twentieth-century American prints.

These two areas of change should not be exaggerated. Naturally, there were expressive printmakers in the nineteenth century, and there continued to be reproductive craftsmen in the twentieth. Nor was there an abrupt, or even a complete, abandonment of commissioned, formal artists' portraiture in the twentieth century. But the trends were there, and attitudes were changing; therefore it is instructive to consider some of the results against the background of portraiture in nineteenth-century American printmaking.

As the twentieth century opened, the work of certain American printmakers was practically indistinguishable from that of their European colleagues. Mary Cassatt, for instance, in her extraordinary color prints shared with Degas a delight in the recently revealed qualities of the Japanese print, along with a fascination with the intimacy and informality of people seen in their familiar surroundings. Later on, Milton Avery was in tune with the spare linearity of Matisse in his drypoints that evoke the appearance and character of his family and friends.

Other artists showed less concern for European antecedents and seemed more occupied with achieving an individual style. Rockwell Kent's dramatic, sculptural lithograph of the typographic designer T. M. Cleland (fig. 1) sets a character before us, theatrically lighted, in a bold, simple composition that owes nothing to contemporary European art. Peggy Bacon observed her fellow creatures with a wicked eye, etching her friends and neighbors in a trenchant caricature style all her own. John Sloan, William Glackens, Reginald Marsh, and their New York colleagues may have started with an understanding of the bravura etching of their northern European contemporaries, but they quickly evolved un-mistakable personal styles unrelated to European printmaking.

These printmakers saw the portrait as a means to express something about a personality, a mood, or an interplay of characters. Ben Shahn,

1

Thomas Maitland Cleland,
1880-1964. Lithograph, 1929, by
Rockwell Kent, 24.6 × 17.8 cm.
(*Library of Congress*)

placing his people in their ordinary urban surroundings, describes human
and economic conditions as well. Shahn also used the photograph as a
"sketch pad" for his work and for a time made photographs for the
documentation project of the Farm Security Administration. From that
project came one of the major portraits of twentieth-century American
graphic art, Dorothea Lange's *Migrant Mother* (fig. 2). This enduring
symbol of the great depression of the 1930s suggests that photographers,
like printmakers, were coming to be conscious of themselves as visual
artists and were exploring the expressive possibilities of portraiture just as
other graphic artists were. Alfred Stieglitz is well known for his missionary
role in this transformation of twentieth-century photography, and the
remarkable series of portraits he made of Georgia O'Keeffe represents his
greatest achievement as portraitist. For Stieglitz, formal relationships
were more significant than the recording of facial features; a pair of hands
or the curve of a shoulder could evoke a personality as movingly as a study of
a face.

Technically, as well as expressively, photography is akin to print-

2
Migrant Mother. Farm Security Administration photograph, 1936, by Dorothea Lange. (*Library of Congress*)

making. Just as nineteenth-century printmakers were fond of publishing their prints in series and in albums, so there are scores of photographic albums (those of the Civil War are the most familiar, perhaps) and published photographic series issued on uniform mounts, with characteristic printed borders. The etcher or lithographer works directly on the plate or stone; the photographer is involved with the creation of a negative. These printing masters are not legible in themselves, as a painting is, but exist in order to make possible the production of multiple originals.

This quality of multiplication makes one wonder why print media would be chosen for portraiture today, if the intention is primarily expres-

3
Happy Days (George Overbury
["Pop"] Hart, 1868-1933). Etching,
drypoint and roulette, 1925, self-
portrait, 26.6 × 22.6 cm. (*Library of
Congress, J. and E. R. Pennell Fund*)

sive rather than commercial. An artist might expect to sell a hundred
impressions of the image of a President or a hero, but he could hardly have
the same expectation for a picture of a hungry clothing worker, an artist's
wife, or a self-portrait—unless these were sought after as works of art, not
as likenesses of someone. With printmakers working in portraiture today,
the choice of medium relates to the expressive and technical qualities of
relief, intaglio, and planographic processes, and not simply the ability to
make multiple impressions. There is a quality of line, tone, and texture
available to the printmaker not possible in other media.

Recognizing these possibilities, a considerable number of American
printmakers in our century have made remarkable self-portraits. This can
be a matter of deep introspection, or it may represent the artist's public
face. "Pop" Hart's exuberant etching of himself (fig. 3) toasting the viewer
with a foaming beer glass, Milton Avery's pensive drypoint, or Mabel
Dwight's lithograph depicting herself at serious work on a lithographic
stone—all reveal different aspects of artists' explorations of their own
features and moods while exploiting the qualities of printmaking with
great effectiveness.

261

4
Antonio Frasconi, 1919-   . Woodcut,
1952, self-portrait, 57 × 20 cm.
(*Library of Congress, J. and E. R. Pennell
Fund*)

A number of artists of our time have shown themselves at work, as did
Mabel Dwight. There is a fine woodcut (fig. 4) of Antonio Frasconi
standing at his press. Rudolph Ruzicka created a charming color wood
engraving in which his hands hold a block on which his self-portrait is
being cut.

5

Mao Tse-tung, 1893–1976. Serigraph, 1972, by Andy Warhol, 91.5 × 91.5 cm.
(*Leo Castelli Gallery*)

In other self-portraits there is a more probing quality, harking back to Rembrandt's unequaled series of analytical self-portraits in the seventeenth century. Leonard Baskin, Mauricio Lasansky, and Jim Dine are among the major artists who have turned again and again to self-portraiture in their printmaking, leaving a record of their different moods, circumstances, and ages.

Other artists, while attracted to the self-portrait as an idea, seem to wish to avoid self-scrutiny. When Andy Warhol repeats a photographic image across the surface of a serigraphic print (fig. 5), he successfully avoids penetrating this surface either visually or psychologically. Robert Rauschenberg's life-size X-ray lithograph penetrates the skin and viscera, but not the personality of the artist. Even Jim Dine, though he frequently reveals his features in his superbly drawn etchings, in other prints removes himself almost completely, leaving only an object, a landscape, or some other relic in the print to suggest his involvement with it. In one of his

6

Souvenir (Jasper Johns, 1930-   ). Lithograph, 1970, self-portrait, 60 ×
44.4 cm. (*Philadelphia Museum of Art, given by the artist*)

best-known self-portraits, Dine's bathrobe serves as an "attribute" of the
artist, bearing the imprint of his body but not revealing his features to the
viewer. In a 1970 lithograph (fig. 6) for the Philadelphia Museum, Jasper
Johns surrounds himself with the tools of his trade but reduces his own
image to a tiny place in the corner. He takes the notion of imprint even
further than Dine when he puts his handprints on a lithographic stone,
using soap for one imprint and oil for another (both identified with

264

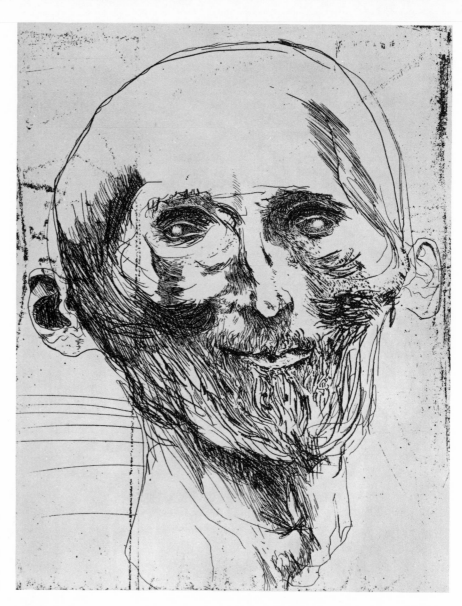

7

Jean-Louis-André Théodore Géricault, 1791-1824. Etching, 1969, by Leonard Baskin, 42.6 × 35 cm. (*Library of Congress*)

handwritten notes), but leaves no other traces of himself on the print. Robert Indiana, in his 1969 *Self-Portrait,* gives us a series of words having autobiographical significance, but he does not show his face.

The portrait is commonly regarded as an authentic record of the appearance of the sitter. When artists depart from the appearance of the face, as so many have done in the twentieth century, one at least expects the references to the sitter to be based on some genuine affinity or some specific quality of relationship. When Leonard Baskin creates one of his portraits of an artist (fig. 7), he carries us into a new realm. He is not at pains to evoke the nose or ear of the artist but to suggest what he must have been like without being too hampered by the facts of the case. We are not invited to ask "Is this a good likeness?" but instead we must reflect on the quality of determination in Eakins, fevered imagination in Fuseli, madness in Géricault, and so on. Baskin tries to hit the emotional center of the artists he depicts and thereby tells us as much about himself as about the

IF IT HAD NOT BEEN FOR THESE THING, I MIGHT HAVE LIVE OUT MY LIFE TALKING AT STREET CORNERS TO SCORNING MEN. I MIGHT HAVE DIE, UNMARKED, UNKNOWN A FAILURE. NOW WE ARE NOT A FAILURE. THIS IS OUR CAREER AND OUR TRIUMPH. NEVER IN OUR FULL LIFE COULD WE HOPE TO DO SUCH WORK FOR TOLERANCE, FOR JOOSTICE, FOR MAN'S ONDERSTANDING OF MAN AS NOW WE DO BY ACCIDENT. OUR WORDS - OUR LIVES - OUR PAINS NOTHING! THE TAKING OF OUR LIVESLIVES OF A GOOD SHOEMAKER AND A POOR FISH PEDDLER-ALL! THAT LAST MOMENT BELONGS TO US- THAT AGONY IS OUR TRIUMPH.

8

Sacco and Vanzetti (Nicola Sacco, 1891-1927, and Bartolomeo Vanzetti, 1888-1927). Serigraph, 1958, by Ben Shahn, 65 × 44.5 cm. (*Library of Congress, J. and E. R. Pennell Fund*)

subject. This is perhaps related to such other notable "icons" of twentieth-century American printmaking as Ben Shahn's *Sacco and Vanzetti* (fig. 8), in which the figures portrayed accumulate meaning from our own knowledge of their lives and from the emotional involvement of the maker of the print.

To give a complete picture of the printmakers' approach to portraits in the twentieth century, the poster should also be considered, as should the many forms of multilayer and three-dimensional work that are now blurring the edges between sculpture and the graphic arts. Space does not permit this, nor does it allow more than a passing mention of graphic artists' increasing preoccupation with the book. Edward Ruscha, Claes Oldenburg, and many others have been exploring the possibilities of the self-produced book, often devoted to an extended portrait or self-portrait in both words and multiple images.

Today artists have returned unapologetically to the figure, after a decade or two during which it seemed that all critical attention was being paid to nonobjective art. This shift has been significant in printmaking, of course, and helps to explain the growing importance of artists such as Peter Milton. In his "Jolly Corner" series, for example, Milton deals with the portrait in a most extraordinary way. Henry James (fig. 9)—whose stories inspired the prints—is witness to the events in several of the plates. The James portrait is far from imaginary, based as it is on authentic painted and photographic sources. Though it appears photographic, the image here is drawn on mylar and then transferred to the plate. The transfer process preserves every nuance of the sense of photographic light and shade to which Milton constantly refers in his prints.

The photographic portrait itself remains important today. Diane Arbus, for example, left a body of haunting images, often of odd or disturbing people confronted directly. In looking at her work, there is such a strong sense of concentration and such a curious perspective (perhaps the result of the focal length of the lens she used) that even ordinary things begin to look strange. One has a similar reaction to the work of Chuck Close (fig. 10), in which the scale and composition have such force that normal relationships of size and of objects are altered.

Close also refers in his etchings to photographic effects, and it is likely that his works are derived from photographs; but, unlike Milton, he consciously destroys the sense of photography through his drawing. He replaces the photograph's imperceptible modulation from light to dark with a screen of carefully rendered etched lines. The viewer is always aware of the origin of the image in the camera; yet the hand of the artist is never effaced.

This brings us to last year or the year before. If a critic had been asked fifteen or twenty years ago—in the heyday of Franz Kline, Willem De Kooning, and Frank Stella—to imagine where American printmaking was going, he might not have predicted Jim Dine or Chuck Close. Neither can one know how the twentieth century is going to end. So, perhaps inconclusiveness is the right note on which to end this brief survey, leaving the

The Jolly Corner III: 7 (Henry James, 1843-1916). Etching, 1971, by Peter
Milton, 37.6 × 24.9 cm. (*Franz Bader Gallery*)

Chuck Close, 1940-   . Etching, 1977, self-portrait, 90.4 × 113.1 cm. (*Library of Congress, J. and E. R. Pennell Fund*)

door open for more work to be created and more critical thinking to be done.

In our time we have seen the coming together of photography and printmaking, and the alteration of both to their mutual enrichment. We have seen how often twentieth-century American printmakers have used the portrait as the jumping-off place for the imagination, and how frequently a personage is the starting point for a basically visual or emotional construct. In our century, conveying outward appearances has usually been less important than conveying something about the structure of art, the essence of imagination, or the world surrounding artist or sitter.

Whether we look at portraits or self-portraits, whether we consider literal, excellent likenesses or oblique allusions to a person, we always come back to the artist. This recognition was the underlying philosophy of the "independent" artists whom we now see as the most powerful guides out of the nineteenth century. Every work of art carries the personality of the artist—or, as Samuel Butler wrote in *The Way of All Flesh:* "Every man's work, whether it be literature or music or pictures or architecture or anything else, is always a portrait of himself."

Photograph Credits

PHOTOGRAPH CREDITS

Frick Art Reference Library	Miles: fig. 14
Eugene Mantie	Miles: figs. 1, 3, 4; Marshall: figs. 2, 3, 4, 5, 7, 8, 9, 12, 13, 14; Reaves; figs. 1, 2, 4, 5, 7, 17; Martinez: figs. 5, 8, 14, 16; Stapp: figs. 2, 3, 7, 8, 11, 12, 14; Rubenstein: figs. 2, 3, 5, 12
Richard Merrill	Miles: fig. 16
Mark Sexton	Stapp: fig. 16
Robert Vogel, National Museum of American History	Miles: fig. 17
Rolland White	Marshall: figs. 1, 6, 10, 11, 15, 16, 17; Reaves: figs. 3, 8, 9, 10, 11, 12, 13, 14, 15, 16; Martinez: figs. 1, 2, 3, 4, 6, 7, 10, 11, 12, 13, 17
Edward Whiteman	Miles: fig. 15

Index

272

274